Football Talk

Other titles by Peter Seddon

A Football Compendium (British Library)
Steve Bloomer: The Story of Football's First Superstar
(Breedon Books)
Law's Strangest Cases (Robson Books)
Tennis's Strangest Matches (Robson Books)

Football Talk

The Language & Folklore of the World's Greatest Game

Peter Seddon

ROBSON BOOKS

First published in Great Britain in 2004 by Robson Books,
The Chrysalis Building, Bramley Road, London W10 6SP

An imprint of Chrysalis Books Group

British Library Cataloguing in Publication Data
A catalogue record for this title is available from the British Library.

ISBN 1 86105 683 4

Typeset by SX Composing DTP, Rayleigh, Essex
Printed by Creative Print & Design (Wales), Ebbw Vale

Contents

Acknowledgements

My gratitude extends to all those who have ever written or talked about football. Without the 'language of football' they created, there would be no book. In particular, John Goulstone, Nick Hornby, Alex Leith, Morris Marples, David Pickering, Dave Russell, Phil Shaw and Percy Young encouraged me to look at the game more deeply. Likewise Bill Bryson, David Crystal and John Moore on the language front.

Thanks closer to home to Julie Ibbitson, Ian Methven, Rebecca Marshall, Alick Seddon and Steve Swanwick for chipping in with valuable assistance. Kate Ibbitson's support was, as ever, fundamental, as was Richard Marshall's careful reading of the draft. Sincere thanks to Jeremy Robson, Jennifer Lansbury, Clive Hebard, copy-editor Steve Gove and the team at Chrysalis Books Group for embracing a mere idea so enthusiastically and seeing it through to publication.

1

Football – By Far the Greatest Word the World Has Ever Seen?

'Football and cookery are the two most important subjects in the country.'

Delia Smith, TV chef, after becoming
a Norwich City director, 1997

'FOOTBALL: (Soccer). See Association Football.' That stark entry in the most recent edition of *Encyclopaedia Britannica* says so little yet encapsulates so much. For those who cherish the game, or simply quite like it, the word football, even in the nakedness imposed upon it by the pages of a reference book, conjures up a myriad of emotions. Boundless joy, abject pain, waves of nostalgia, bitter regret, gnawing hope, anger, passion, heart-stopping excitement, and the most wretched bleak despair it's possible to know this side of genuine tragedy. That's why we like it.

Britannica's disquieting 'see elsewhere' tone also suggests that there's an 'all things to all men' aspect to 'football'. Those not entirely captivated by the game's charms, for example, tend to refer to it by that odious little word in parenthesis which I can't bring myself to write again just yet. Surely they are missing something. Football may be just one word in a world of millions (there are 615,000 English words alone listed in the *Oxford English Dictionary*), but it's one that has come to transcend international boundaries like no other, spawning a huge lexicon all of its own.

3

The great English dictionary-maker, Dr Samuel Johnson, would be astonished if he were alive today. Not just because he'd be a few years short of his 300th birthday, but to witness how much football, modestly included as one of the 43,000 words in his *Dictionary of the English Language*, has changed in its inherent meaning since his two-volume tome was published in 1755.

Johnson's work included *a football*, the spherical object which actually christened the world's greatest game, but football as an activity is missing. Not because the good doctor was ignorant of it (the British had actually played football in both mass, and smaller controlled forms since at least the third century), but simply because it wasn't the uniform, organised game that the formation of the Football Association in 1863 would later make it. All Johnsonian England knew football existed, but it was just too informal, perhaps too 'common' in both senses, to warrant a place.

As such, football is one of the most 'changed' words in the English language. The humble noun that rolled noiselessly from Johnson's house in a quiet square off Fleet Street, has since been the subject of billions more words churned from the once-clattering presses of that thoroughfare. Now football is written about far beyond the capital, and discussed wherever men gather. It was Johnson who said, 'When two Englishmen meet, their first talk is of the weather.' Were he writing now, the elements could surely be substituted by 'football'.

It's fair to assume that Johnson would have looked quizzically upon certain events reported around the world in June 2003. Indeed, even some of us with a passion for the game had to ask serious questions. It's a total myth to assume love is blind in the world of football supportership. In fact the truest football lovers are often the most critical of 'the game' in its all-embracing sense. It's all about protecting something you value. Think of the money, greed, hooliganism, agents, and merchandising rights. It's quite possible to cherish something, but also to intensely dislike certain aspects of it. The culprit was a 28-year-old 'ordinary working-class Essex boy' born in Leytonstone. On 17 June 2003, he was sold by Manchester United, an English football club with a worldwide fan base of 50 million, to the Spanish side Real Madrid. He was about to embark on a promotional tour of the Far East with his celebrity wife when the news broke.

The momentous words 'Beckham's gone to Real' first reached me on a tennis court as I was about to serve. Note that 'David' wasn't necessary, such is the surname's celebrity. Only 'The Queen's been assassinated' or 'England have won the Ashes' could have been delivered with the same sense of drama and faintly morbid triumphalism. I served a double. The fee was £25 million, the salary a reputed £90,000 a week. The potential package, including image rights and sponsorship deals, was a cool £50 million per annum. Hordes of squealing schoolgirls awaited his arrival at Tokyo airport, eager down to the last pigtail and pair of white socks to peer into a camera and tell the world 'I lov Day-veed Bear-cam.' In the blink of an eye, the Spanish club's shirts, 'made in China' with an Englishman's name on the back, were selling to Japanese kids, watched on TV by people in Africa, South America and India.

Madrid's marketing boys were quick to point out that the signing would probably be worth £35 million 'in shirt sales alone' and would 'enable us to brand Real in the lucrative Far Eastern market'. Next day, at the other end of the spectrum, even as Posh and Becks were flashing their smiles to promote jewellery, handbags, motor oil, chocolate and Vodafone, nine men 'of a certain age' (there's always one who doesn't turn up) and various interesting shapes, gathered on a school play-ground in Derby for their weekly five-a-side, each of us paying £2 for the privilege.

This all suggests that the term 'global phenomenon' for a humble game isn't too strong. The latest survey from FIFA, football's world governing body, confirms there are 30 million registered players worldwide. Millions more, young and 'old', play casually in school playgrounds, parks, streets, shanty towns, jungle clearings, in gardens and on beaches. FIFA has 203 member countries, appreciably more than have bothered to sign up to the United Nations. Almost one in three of the world's population watched at least part of the 2002 World Cup Final on television. And in most countries the game is widely recognised by its English appellation 'football', even when the native word for the game, as with Italy's *calcio*, is entirely different.

If you suspect I'm building a case to make the outrageous claim that football is the most widely recognised word in the world, you'd be right. We can start by kicking *Coca-Cola*, *Adidas* and *McDonalds* firmly into touch, always a satisfying experience in itself. Brand names are disqualified. So too *Madonna, Superman, Kylie, Frank Sinatra, Laurel and Hardy, Elvis, Sherlock Holmes, God* and even *Beckham* itself. *America, USA* and *OK* are non-starters. Proper names and abbreviations never count in word games.

But everybody recognises *football*. It's not necessary to like the game to have heard of it. No English-speaker, not even the most rabid football-hater, could claim to be unacquainted with the word itself.

But what of the wider world? Does football really get a nod of recognition in China, Albania or Ecuador? That would depend on how well English itself is understood. Worldwide, 400 million people speak English as their mother tongue and another 350 million use it as a regular second language. A further 100 million use it fluently as a foreign language, and most of the rest of the world so desperately want to learn it that they'll gladly pay for lessons or chat to any British tourist in sight. Mandarin Chinese may be the most widely spoken language in the world, but when the BBC first broadcast its English-teaching television series *Follow Me* in China, almost 100 million people tuned in. There are currently more people learning English in China than there are people living in the whole of the United States. It seems fair to suggest that the English name of the world's leading participation and spectator sport has entered the vocabulary of quite a few of our fellow men.

It helps, too, that the British, the 'inventors' of modern football, also spread the word itself, which was quickly appropriated by other languages either in identical or easily recognised form. The British businessmen, soldiers, sailors, and missionaries who took football out to the world in the late nineteenth and early twentieth century, certainly weren't slow to tell the locals 'the name of the game'. So in German, Dutch, Swedish, French,

Spanish, Norwegian, Hungarian, Danish, and Portuguese, the talk is, respectively, of *fussball*, *voetbal*, *fotboll*, *football*, *fùtbol*, *fotball*, *futboll*, *fodbold* and *futebol*.

Nor is football's linguistic influence overseas merely confined to its first name. Wherever football is played, words derived from English are heard. The ubiquitous *'Penalty!'*, *'Corner!'* and *'Offside!'* are the English language's most exclamatory exports. The Spaniards still call their managers *el mister*, a respectful vestige of the form of address used by their players in the early nineteenth century, when Spanish sides ambitious for success turned to English coaches to teach them the game. In similar vein, the Austrian football tactician Willy Meisl wrote in 1955 that 'when Southampton beat the Viennese City XI 6–0, their goalkeeper Jack Robinson tackled low shots by flying through the air with great ease. To this day that type of save is called a "Robinsonade" in Austria and Central Europe.' In dark corners of smoky bars, where old men gather, it probably still is. Yet the match in question was in 1899. There was a time in the 1960s and 1970s, too, when it was impossible to be taken to the right destination by taxi on the Continent without first uttering the ritual incantation 'Bob-ee Charl-ton'.

Even in countries whose language differs dramatically from our own, English-speaking visitors can feel strangely at home. In Japan, otherwise unfathomable commentaries are surreally relieved by a comforting spattering of thinly disguised adopted English. Listen for the confident *kipa* plucking the *boru* from the air just as the *refuri* blows for *hafu taimu*. What a tribute to the English football lexicon. It's a shame the Japanese blot their copybook by calling the game itself *sakka*, but they make up for it in other ways. Tell them you like Beckham and you'll soon find a *garufurendu*. Or stick with the boys, for a *biru* or *jin tonniku* after the *gemu*.

Football-related written English, too, tends to appear in the most unexpected places: 'RED BOYS RULE' on a bridge in Moscow, or 'WELCOME TO HELL' at Galatasaray's charming Ali Sami Yen stadium in Istanbul. Homage to football English is sometimes more respectful. Prior to departing for Wales's game against Azerbaijan in Baku in November 2002, a *Daily Telegraph* reporter described the venue as 'one of the most remote and inhospitable imaginable' only to be astonished on arrival to find an English-style pub called the Lancaster Gate near the ground, its sign complete with the Football Association's three lions crest, and its interior a shrine to British football.

I'm tempted to say 'I rest my case.' Who could even attempt to deny that *football* is the world's best-known word? But there are dark counter-forces at work. In Bill Bryson's masterful study of the English language, *Mother Tongue*, he lists the English terms that *The Economist* magazine's editorial team considered to have become the most universally used and recognised. They were: *airport, passport, hotel, telephone, bar, soda, golf, tennis, stop, OK, weekend, jeans, know-how, sex appeal* and *no problem*. Fair comment by and large, and congratulations to golf and tennis for making the squad, but how does *know-how* get in there ahead of *football*?

It's tempting to conclude there was a US bias to the research team. Their own American football, after all, has nothing like worldwide recognition, and they're potentially blind to the real football. So, not even a place on the bench. Even Bryson's book itself stretched to 269 pages without once mentioning football or anything to do with it. But of course he's American too, and despite his love affair with our country, it's odds-on he's immune to the charms of association football. Which in any case he'd call by the name I still can't bring myself to repeat.

It seems there may be a hidden agenda at work. Football has been routinely marginalised in works aimed at an intelligent readership. Either it's deliberately ignored as being a 'common game' for the 'common people', which in erudite circles often means 'far too common for you and me, dah-ling', or writers are simply blinkered. Intellectual snobbery, sublime indifference or crass ignorance? None is very laudable. It seems football is still the dirtiest F-word of all to some.

Time and again in my preliminary work for *Football Talk*, I encountered this attitude. Working to restore some balance was what pushed me on. Take *Encyclopaedia Britannica*'s 'see else-where' trail, which leads first to the *Micropaedia*. 'Association Football' gets 47 lines, 27 fewer than the preceding entry for

'Association Croquet'. 'Asceticism', which is 'the practice of the denial of physical or psychological desires in order to attain a spiritual ideal', gets a whacking 400 lines. So that's what the rest of the world does while we inadequates are idling away our time at the match. Likewise, is it really on for 'The Football Association' to be dealt with in 160 words, a quarter of the number lavished on 'Gonorrhoea' and a mere sixth of the grand total for 'Jellyfish'?

The *Macropaedia* entry is little more encouraging. Football gets four and a half pages to American football's eight. Let your eyes wander, and you'll soon know that '*polyphenoloxidase* causes fruit to brown', because the entry for 'Food Processing' bizarrely stretches to 69 pages. Nor are our sporting heroes any better treated. There are 32 worthies named Moore in *Britannica*. They include the American boxer Archie Moore who became world light-heavyweight champion in 1952, the sculptor Henry Moore, and the Irish novelist Brian Moore, all arguably in on merit. But then things go awry. I'm not sure I want to know that the American zoologist Carl Moore was 'noted for his research on animal reproductive organs and internal secretions'. I'd much sooner be told that 'Robert F Moore was the first man to lift the Jules Rimet Trophy for England in 1966 and died tragically young of cancer', but he's nowhere to be found. And it gets no better. George Best is left out but Charles Best is in: one a supreme exponent of the world's leading sport, the other 'an American scientist famous as the first to obtain a pancreatic extract of insulin in a form that controlled diabetes in dogs'. If it wasn't so annoying it might be funny.

And I could go on. In fact I think I will, because there's no doubt that our national game is shoddily treated by that large body of literature known as 'word books'.

Dictionaries are more guilty than most. The *Oxford English Dictionary* (*OED*) cites the word *nutmeg* in 121 different guises, with 35 more 'new entries' ready for its next edition, but fails to include football's celebrated 'ball through the legs' one at all. *The Collins English Dictionary 21st Century Edition*, billed as 'the most comprehensive, wide-ranging and up to date coverage of today's English, with an additional 18,500 encyclopaedic entries', doesn't include David Beckham. But on *his* page, you will find our German friends Boris Becker and the 'world-famous' chemist Ernst Beckmann. Perversely there *is* a footballer, but not one of 'ours' – it's Franz Beckenbauer, closely followed by another popular icon, the Labour politician Margaret Beckett. Similarly, *Collins Dictionary* enjoyed much media hype in December 2001 for including 'a *Delia*', meaning 'a dish cooked or prepared in the style of Delia Smith', because 'it has entered everyday English'. But where is 'a *Beckham*', routinely used since August 1996 for 'an outrageous attempt on goal by a player inside his own half'? Like the Wimbledon keeper Neil Sullivan, absolutely nowhere. And no major dictionary is any different. Is the lexicography industry dominated by German-loving foodies? Something very odd indeed seems to be going on.

The game is also routinely sidelined by historians. Football doesn't appear in the index of Simon Schama's epic 1,240 page *A History of Britain*. But railways, broadcasting and cricket are quite rightly routinely credited in history books for their contribution to the development of our 'great British nation'. I've lost count of the indexes I've scoured in vain for 'football'.

Rest easy. The rant is now over. But it needed to be said. Of course snubbing football, whether by pointed omission or more covert means, is nothing new. Men of letters and politicians have been criticising it for centuries. Reigning monarchs or local authorities regularly tried to ban it right up to the mid-nineteenth century, the dawn of the 'civilised' modern game itself. The chronicler of a violent contest in the late fifteenth century hardly sits on the fence: 'A game, I say, abominable enough, and in my judgement more common, undignified and worthless than any other kind'. And had the seventeenth-century law laid down by the Court Leet Records for the Manor of Manchester been assiduously applied, Manchester United could never have existed:

October 12th 1608: Whereas there hath beene great disorder in our towne, wee of this jurye doe order that no manner of persons hereafter shall playe or use the footeball within the said toune of Manchester.

Three centuries later, Rudyard Kipling was labelling players 'muddied oafs at the goals' and A A Milne, creator of that gentle soul Winnie the Pooh, was launching a frenzied double attack on the game and its rulers in the December 1908 issue of *Punch*. The same year, in *Scouting for Boys*, Lord Baden-Powell had a pop at supporters:

> Football is a vicious game when it draws mere onlookers at a few paid performers, thousands of boys and young men, pale, narrow chested, hunched up, miserable specimens, smoking endless cigarettes, betting, learning to be hysterical as they groan or cheer in panic unison with their neighbours.

It's us he's talking about. That 'them and us' agenda in society's relationship with football, and all that surrounds it, still prevails. But it's a testimony to the irresistible draw and innate character of 'the people's game' that it not only emerged as a survivor, but flourished worldwide.

Yet its language is still securely 'ring-fenced'. Football talk may be everywhere in the pub, office, school and media, but in a sense it's also nowhere. In technical terms, it's what's known as a restricted language, one used only by a 'knowing minority'. It's a sobering fact that the '1 in 3 watched the 2002 World Cup Final' statistic also means that '2 in 3' didn't. And that David Beckham's remarkable 356,000 internet hits are eclipsed by the 976,000 for William Shakespeare and the 1.22 million for the 'honest drudge' himself, Samuel Johnson. Although 'football' itself gets 21.5 million, the fact remains that if our libraries are being combed by alien life to discover what makes earthlings tick, they'll settle on 'Food Processing'. The most omnipotent leader in world history was the man who launched tinned food in the United States in 1822. Take a bow, Ezra Daggett.

The British pub would be a better research ground. After a round of good honest footie chat, no half-intelligent alien could fail to conclude that the whole paraphernalia surrounding the game, what's termed 'football culture and folklore', is far too huge to be ignored. And without language, that couldn't exist. Imagine a game with anonymous players, no team names or match reports, no nicknames, commentary, fanzines, magazines, programmes or bar-room analysis. I'm not sure I'd renew my season ticket.

There's also much to be learnt about football by checking out its language, a sort of inside-out deconstruction of what makes the game work. The novelist David Nobbs once created a character named Reginald Iolanthe Perrin, who made a great success of selling square hoops via a chain of shops called 'Grot'. Nobbs, clearly a man well worth listening to, pursues a similar theme in his novel *Going Gently* via a flamboyant artist character named Arturo Rand, who decides to paint all his pictures upside down and is naturally feted by the art world as a genius. When a sceptic asks him what the point is, Arturo has a ready answer: 'We look at things in a preconceived way. We bring to our study of things a whole range of assumptions, a whole language of satisfied expectations which prevent us from seeing anything as it really is. To see anything as it really is, we have to start to look at it as it really isn't, in order to reassemble it as it really is.'

Suitably absurd, but therein lies a truth. So it's with a degree of Arturian logic that I now embark on *Football Talk*. In the same topsy-turvy spirit, whether you are a passionate us, a 'nothing but a bag of wind' them, or an undecided in-between, by all means select the chapters in whatever order you please. Just be mindful of the momentous words spoken by the Coventry City manager Bobby Gould in 1992: 'Football is all about football.'

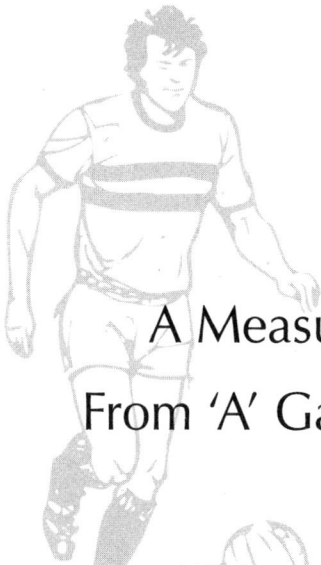

2

A Measured Build-Up –
From 'A' Game to 'The' Game

A round ball and an oblong goal
Suggest the shape of the Yin and Yang.
The ball is like the full moon,
And the two teams stand opposed.
Captains are appointed and take their places.

In the game make no allowance for relationship,
And let there be no partiality.
Determination and coolness are essential,
And there must be no irritation for failure.
Such is this game. Let its principles apply to life.

Translation from Li Yu, Chinese philosopher describing
tsu-chu, first century AD

It's an old chestnut that 'football is a funny old game', but it is also 'a funny old word'. Superficially, it looks transparent enough. Foot + ball surely says it all: a joyful marriage of Old English *fot* and Old Norse *bollr*. A joint gift from the Anglo-Saxons and Vikings. The best thing they ever gave us. End of chapter. Arguably end of book. But there's more to it than that.

What makes *football* an unusual word is not only its power to evoke such extreme emotions, but that it survived against powerful odds. Becoming a world dictionary superstar doesn't happen overnight. To emerge top of the pile football has had to fight off challenges from a multitude of other words, including many sneaky foreign ones, which in their time named ball games that are the ancestors of modern association football.

Had just one of those ancient relatives been developed with the vigour later reserved for British football when it came of age in the nineteenth century, the name of the world's greatest game might have been something entirely different. Like *tsu-chu*. Vivid written accounts describe the Chinese playing this sophisticated ball-kicking game with rules, tactics, costumes and even supporters' banners, certainly in the third century BC, and possibly as far back as 2500 BC. But the Orientals missed their one golden chance. The modern Chinese word for football is still the derivative *zúqiú* (kickball), but it might have become a global word had the original game not been successfully banned by the Emperor Zhu Yuanzhang in 1389. Running out of steam early never was a good trait in football.

Other exotica of the 'what might have been' brigade include *kemari*, a sort of ritualised keepie-uppie popular in Japan between the seventh and fourteenth centuries, the Ancient Greek *episkyros*, the football-rugby hybrid *harpastum* played by the Romans for at least 800 years from the fourth century BC, *palone* from Germany, *la soule*, *choule* and *l'éteuf* ('the stuffed one') from medieval France, and a host of others. Centuries ago, Alaskan and Canadian eskimos were playing *aqsaqtuk*, with goals up to ten miles apart and a ball stuffed with grass, moss and caribou hair. And when the Pilgrim Fathers landed in North America from Plymouth in 1620, they encountered the indigenous people playing 500-a-side games on the East Coast beaches. It's as well the game and the name didn't survive. The 'endless hours of excitement' promised on the cheery and unnecessarily large box of Waddington's Table *Pasuckuakohowog* (= 'they gather to play ball with the foot') just wouldn't have seemed right.

Pilimatun in Chile went the same way. So too the *tchoekah*, beloved of the natives of Patagonia. Central America's *tlatchli* meekly followed suit. Even Italy's rousing 27-a-side thirteenth-century Florentine game, *calcio* ('I kick'), failed to impose itself sufficiently, leaving the field open for the raw and ancient British pastime to come through strongly at the finish. It was the only strain sufficiently popular to survive its detractors, staying the course long enough to benefit from the makeover that football's first administrators so meticulously applied to it to create its modern appearance. When Victorian gents with ordered minds, a strong sense of tradition, and a love of good honest play, had the foresight to form the Football Association in 1863, they gave us the highly organised 'new' game of association football now known to the world simply as 'football'. It had taken at least two millennia to get there.

Make no mistake, football is an ancient game, centuries older than the word itself – although even that is no youngster. The *OED* traces its first usage to 26 May 1424, when the Scottish parliament began writing its statutes in English (actually a strangulated brand known as Scots English), rather than the French favoured after the Norman Conquest of 1066. So the hand-written decree slapping a ban on the disruptive and idle pastime of ball-kicking is a historic one, James I of Scotland taking the credit. Freshly returned to his homeland after nineteen years in custody south of the border, he'd been scared so witless by English football of the big-sided cross-country or street variety (what historians term mob, folk or mass football) that he ordered his first parliament, convening in Perth, to get heavy:

> It is statut and the king forbiddes that na man play at the fute-ball under the payne of fiftie schillings to be raysit to the lorde of the lande alss oft as he be tayntyt, or to the shref of the land or his ministeris gif the lordis will not puniss sic trespassouris.

But this royal proclamation was no more successful in stopping football than any other, no matter what language they used. Edward II tried in French in 1314, likewise Richard II in 1388. Invoking Latin (*ludus pilae* = 'the game of ball') made no difference. Nor did appealing to national pride. In 1477 Edward IV forbade football so that 'every strong and able-bodied person shall practise with his bow, for the reason that the national defence depends much on bowmen'. Just as futile as 'banning' under-age drinking now. Even when the mass versions were gradually quelled (today's Ashbourne Shrovetide

Football in Derbyshire is a rare authentic survivor), smaller-sided contests or casual kickabouts prevailed countrywide.

World-wise, the first known appearance of 'football' in 'English proper' dates to 1486, in a glossary of sporting terms from *The Book of St Albans*. This was also its debut in print, William Caxton having printed the first book in English in 1473. It was an unremarkable first outing, this time referring to the ball itself, rather than the game, but it subtly implied that British football already had a long history:

It is calde in Latyn *pila pedalis*, a *fotebal*.

At a time when the English language was beginning to take on its modern form, that was a sort of 'stocktaking' which renamed an ancient game in line with new linguistic trends.

All of which begs the obvious question: if Britons had been playing 'football' since ancient times, why does the word only appear in the fifteenth century? If the Chinese were chronicling their game in the third century BC, why weren't we? It has everything to do with language and nothing to do with sport. The Chinese had a sophisticated written language even then, one readily decipherable today. Britain didn't. We have a very messy linguistic history, and the great language which is English came late to the world. 'Football' couldn't have existed in Britain 2,300 years ago for the simple reason that English itself didn't exist. And of the language that was spoken then, right up to the Norman Conquest, so little has survived in writing that the chances of finding anything describing 'football' are extremely slim.

Yet I'd certainly wager that the Gaelic-speaking Celts, native to Britain from around 500 BC, did play a form of football, probably as part of pagan ritual, at exactly the same time as the Chinese were footling around with *tsu-chu* at the imperial court. But nothing survives to tell us so. Only when some diligent archaeologist triumphantly holds aloft a freshly excavated leather ball from the pre-Christian era, will we know for sure that ancient Britons were in at the kick-off.

Similarly, the Romans who occupied Britain from AD 43 to AD 410 wrote little of 'sport'. That's a pity, because we can decode ancient Latin readily. The writings of the Greek comic dramatist Antiphanes (388–311 BC) confirm that the Romans played *harpastum* in Rome ('Seizing the ball, the player delights to pass it to a team-mate while dodging another'), and it seems likely they did so here, thus influencing the development of British football in the process. Some antiquaries even claimed they invented it. In *Old Church Lore* (1891), William Andrews asserted: 'Football was introduced into England by the Romans and is our oldest sport.' Folk tales say Julius Caesar was 'a fine player', and had an irreverent kickabout with a dead Briton's skull during his second attempted invasion in 54 BC. But it's all too woolly. Not a single casual jotting survives.

The Anglo-Saxons, whose raids on our islands began in AD 449, were even worse. Despite the 'Angli' (aka 'Angles') christening our country and developing the language of *Englisc* (Old English) which evolved, with huge influxes from Norse, Latin and French, into modern English, they were pretty reluctant to write things down. Old English was first written using runic symbols, but only about thirty examples have survived in Britain, mostly on monuments, jewellery or weapons. The earliest, from AD 450 to 480, turned up in Suffolk. It would be marvellous if the inscription translated as 'How well he struck the ball goalward with his trusty left foot', but annoyingly it says 'This she-wolf is a reward to my kinsman'. Only the most rabid football historian could construe that as a post-match presentation. Similarly the famous eighth-century inscription on the Ruthwell Cross, near Dumfries: 'IC WÆS MIϷ BLODAE BISTEMID' means 'I was with blood bedewed', but probably not as a result of a late tackle.

Britain's literary age only started to develop after the Christian Roman missionary St Augustine arrived in Kent in AD 597. Much was written down, mainly in Latin, but sixth-century chroniclers were a little too preoccupied with religious matters to report on the latest local derby (the term comes from the town of Derby, where the now defunct annual Shrovetide game between rival parishes was the most celebrated of its kind). That more scholarly approach did lead to fuller and earthier Anglo-Saxon texts being written from around AD 700, but any chance of football descriptions surviving was vastly reduced when the Viking raids began in 787. Although they enriched our language with many Norse words, they also routinely set fire to countless Old English manuscripts that might have enriched our knowledge. Alfred the Great routed them at Ethandun in 878, effectively saving the English language, but no early football literature survives.

However meticulously historians have combed surviving texts, no reference to a British game recognisable as football has been found prior to the twelfth century. Perhaps something will turn up. Maybe historians are just football blind. Gilt-edged open goals might have been missed by the stars of academia as they scout the often minuscule texts. Who knows?

As it is, the earliest recognisable reference to football in Britain is a Latin one from 1175 quilled by the monk William Fitzstephen in *Descriptio Nobilissimae Civitatis Londoniae*. Didn't we always know deep down that the game had religious overtones? It was a fine effort. This is the translation of his account of a London Shrove Tuesday:

> In the afternoon, all the youth of the city go to a flat patch of ground for the famous game of ball. The older men come on horseback to watch the competitions of the younger men and they appear to get excited at witnessing such vigorous exercise and by taking part in the pleasure of unrestrained youth.

We know the feeling.

That it took another 250 years for 'football' to appear in English in 1424 is significant, but only linguistically. Old English had suffered a setback when William of Normandy ('The Conqueror') beat Harold II at the Battle of Hastings in 1066. For several hundred years, French became Britain's 'official' written language. And if not French, then Latin was second choice. English only gradually fought back, and it re-emerged as a vastly different tongue. Eighty-five per cent of Old English words are no longer in use today, and nearly half of modern English derives from French or Latin. Once English reasserted itself in the fifteenth century, *football*, being neither Latin nor French, was already a linguistic dinosaur, a coarse survivor even at the time of its first recorded appearance. And it still had battles to fight, not least in the matter of spelling. Before the widespread introduction of printed books, words were spelt regionally however the locals thought they sounded. From the fifteenth to seventeenth centuries, the game appears as *football*, but also as *futball*, *fotebal*, *foote ball*, *foot ball*, *footeballe*, *foethebal*, *ffotebal*, *futebal*, *fuitballe*, *foot-ball* and countless others. Only via repeated printing did a standardisation gradually evolve by the eighteenth century, but even so the odd hyphenated 'foot-ball' still cropped up in newspapers as late as the 1920s.

These inconsistencies actually suited the football played in Britain from the twelfth to mid-nineteenth centuries, because there were as many types of game as there were spellings. It's a mistake to believe that the descriptions applied to football in that era by recent historians – 'Mass football', 'parish v parish', 'thru town and o'er dale', 'rough', 'several hundred a side', 'generally played on Shrove Tuesday or Christmas Day' – represent the only way the game was played. They're all true, but far from giving the complete picture. Only 'big' games were routinely chronicled, but countless smaller-sided games were played.

Another challenge to football's transition from 'a' word to 'the' word was that regions gave their games dialect names, any one of which might have gained ascendancy. *Knappan* was all the rage in Pembrokeshire in the seventeenth and eighteenth centuries. *Hurling to goales* reigned supreme in Cornwall. In Scotland, where they hate to expend breath needlessly, the game was simply *ba'*. One word, though, came closer to taking football's crown than any other. John Ray's *Collection of English Words* (1691) includes: '*camp*, to play at football, this word extends over Essex as well as Norfolk and Suffolk'. In 1710 a similar work by Daniel Hilman asserted that '*camping* is football playing, at which they are very dextrous in Norfolk'. Although we still *camp* in fields (Latin *campus*), without a ball, 'football' ultimately prevailed over 'camping' to emerge top of the pile.

Yet only via a lucky last-minute winner. The christening of the foremost game took place on Monday 26 October 1863 at the Freemason's Tavern, Great Queen Street, Lincoln's Inn Fields, London, when a group of male enthusiasts gathered 'with the object of establishing a definite code of rules for the regulation of the game of football'. They met of necessity. By the mid-nineteenth century, too many windows and fences had been broken, too many innocent citizens scared half to death, and too many fatalities occurred among the players, for 'mass football' to continue. So the game had been progressively miniaturised. The public schools had proved particularly adept at this, tailoring the 'old' game to whatever space their school grounds could accommodate. (That miniaturisation, by the way, is now complete, although with the advent of roofed-in stadia we've now started on encapsulation. Some outsiders, it seems, still treat football as a contagious disease.) The result for the schools was lack of uniformity. Some handled the ball and others didn't. Some played 20-a-side, others 15 or 11. By the 1850s, when one school challenged another, chaos reigned. Consider a modern equivalent. Anyone for 'a game of cards'? But which game? And what rules? Football was no different.

Some establishments ultimately perpetuated their school's title in the name of their preferred game. The oval ball 'handlers' formed the 'Rugby Football Union' in 1871. Their game became known as *rugby*. Had the round ball fraternity adopted a similar approach, today's 'football' would almost certainly be toponymic, that is, a game named after a place. (*Badminton* is another.) The 'London Football Association', a distinct possibility, would have seen 'London' take the crown as the English propensity for abbreviation kicked in. Though we might just as easily have ended up playing 'Barnes', 'Charterhouse', or 'Forest', all leading advocates of the perfectly spherical.

When Ebenezer Cobb Morley of the Barnes club opened proceedings at that meeting in 1863, he proposed simply 'that the clubs represented at this meeting now form themselves into an association to be called "The Football Association"'. This absolute masterstroke, probably accidental, was duly carried. Never has the definite article done a more complete job.

Although some shortened the game's name to *association,* that was unwieldy. In no time at all it became simply *football.* The game grew as the word spread, and the word grew as the game spread. In due course both went global, and with that came an entire new vocabulary. 'A' word had become 'the' word.

The game was afoot.

Under the Influence

3

Into the Field of Battle
– Is It War?

'Football is a battle, a small war, and sometimes
players do stupid things.'

Sven-Goran Eriksson, England manager, 2002

Football's core language was influenced by two key bodies of
men: the Football Association and the press. The lexicon they
created was rapidly taken on board by a public who just as
quickly spread it at home and abroad. Most of it is still with us
now, so it follows that today's football talk is a legacy of
linguistic fashions from the game's formative years. Were
football evolving now, it would draw from the vernacular of
film, television, space and computers. But the Victorians had
none of that. Their world, instead, was shot through with war.
Every journalist knew the language of conflict and no self-
respecting FA man was without military pedigree.

Men in uniform were not a rare sight when football found its
feet. It's not insignificant that a British Army team, Royal Engi-
neers, nicknamed 'The Sappers', played in the first ever FA Cup
Final. Their captain, Major Sir Arthur Francis Marindin, became
President of the FA in 1874. Nor is it coincidence that Third
Lanark joined the Scottish FA in 1873 under their original name
of The Third Lanarkshire Rifle Volunteers. Or that one of the
Football Association's founder members was the War Office FC.

Hardly a day of Victoria's reign passed without some conflict
bearing on British interests being reported in the press. English

25

is replete with the legacy. Little wonder that the language of war shares common ground with that of football.

The link existed even in the game's ancient history. Both the Roman *harpastum* and Greek *episkyros*, ball games with evolutionary links to football, formed part of military training, teaching teamwork, discipline, tactics and strategy, common to both battleground and football ground. Chinese *tsu-chu* was first chronicled not as a recreation but in a military handbook.

In Britain men were shooting arrows at the opposition or a target in the field many centuries before they did the same in earnest with a ball. This led some anthropologists to theorise that football is ritualised war: a stylised territorial battle, complete with casualties, which can only be resolved by the victory and defeat that produces winners and losers.

The analogy is open to debate but what is beyond dispute is the crossover in vocabulary. Look at any football report: *attack, defence, flanks, reserves, captain, advance, retreat, scout, marksman, battler, raider, manoeuvre*. All military terms long before football adopted them.

Victorian journalists revelled in imagery. The goal was the *enemy citadel*, regularly besieged and sometimes breached if the *last line of defence*, the *sentinel* (goalkeeper), was finally *forced to surrender* in the face of the *relentless onslaught*. Teams were *annihilated* or *massacred*. A heavy loss was a *rout*. Goals, like defenceless villages, were *plundered*. The Blackburn *ranks* finally succeeded in *lowering the Preston colours* after *mounting raid after raid* against their *depleted forces*. Despite a brave *rearguard action* and staunch *last-ditch* defending, the Prestonians finally *fell*. Two of their *gallant braves* were *stretcher cases*. Another was given his *marching orders* for *gross insubordination*. All the players *deserved a medal*.

Positions, formations and technique incorporate similar imagery. The *midfield general* goes *man to man*, a forward *leads the front line*, the *back line holds firm*. A keeper recklessly *mounts a forward charge*, only to be stranded in *no-man's land*. A *young gun* or *raw recruit*, a recent *capture* just signed up to the *squad*, fires in a *volley*. A threatening *shot* was a *cannonball, bullet, howitzer* or *bazooka*; now it may be a *rocket, missile* or *exocet*, which might *ricochet* off an unfortunate defender who has otherwise *patrolled his area* effectively to keep the *foe* at bay.

Although the Victorians started this bizarre mode of reportage, today's commentators and journalists show no inclination to discard the imagery of war, although the flowery excesses of yesteryear have given way to more directness.

Contests against 'enemy' nations present unique opportunities. When England beat Argentina in Japan during the 2002 World Cup via a Beckham penalty the *Sun* rabidly invoked both the spirit of the 1982 Falklands war and previous 'unfortunate' football reverses: 'UP YOURS SENORS. BECKS' ARGIE REVENGE' took the front-page spot as 'the goal gave us our first win over the cheats and divers of Argentina since 1966'. Pages of 'patriotic' prose hailed Beckham as 'Captain Courageous' and the England team as 'Bulldogs' who 'marched to victory with all guns blazing'. As in war, the monarch's blessing duly followed: 'The Queen is delighted,' said an aide. 'I'm sure she'll be pleased for David Beckham.' The *Sun* confirmed that England's heroes were 'saluted throughout the land', and no one was left in any doubt that every man had 'done his duty'.

So the pudding is over-egged, but that's a mere fraction of the crossover. Even apparently modern terms derive from ancient battleground jargon.

Consider the holy grail of today's game, the Champions League. From the thirteenth century, a knight or other nominee sent on to a duelling field to fight a 'trial by battle' on his master's behalf came to be called a *champion*, derived from *campus*, Latin for 'field'. It also gave us the recreational activity *camping*, which as we have seen was once the East Anglian name for 'football'. Also *campaign*, via the French *campagne* for countryside, literally 'a march through the land'. A football team's 'League campaign' is just that. Victory might well be celebrated with 'champagne'.

All of which field-related trivia should serve to remind you, next time you're moved to chant 'Champions!', what it's all about. Homage to 'mercenaries who earn their living fighting battles on fields on behalf of others, their ultimate paymasters' – that's professional football.

Other medieval battling terms infiltrate the game. Knockout competitions are still *tournaments*. Fans, like fair maidens favouring their chosen knight, can still sport *favours*. Strikers are *poleaxed* in the box. Referees *run the gauntlet* of irate supporters. And *skirmish*, the fourteenth-century term for 'an irregular engagement between small bodies of fighters', was corrupted to give football its goalmouth *scrimmage* and rugby its *scrummage* or *scrum*.

Archers breaking their bow-strings in battle once replaced them by a spare, usually of inferior quality. Now it's managers fielding weakened sides who resort to the *second string*. Also attributed to archery, but keenly disputed, is scoring from *point blank range*. Used since the sixteenth century, the story goes that to be sure of hitting the centre of an archery target, in France originally a white mark (*point blanc*), bowmen needed to shoot from very close in. Archers also chose 'a mark' to aim at to allow for the effect of a wind. That's said to have given us the euphemism for a shot off target, one *wide of the mark*.

Football's naval crossovers are more limited. One is *fluke*, first adopted in sport by billiards for 'an unforeseen success'. From the sixteenth century a *fluke* was 'the flattened end of a ship's anchor', notoriously difficult for a ship's captain to 'ground' in a stormy sea; hence 'landing a fluke' was a complete stroke of luck. The captain, incidentally, was the skipper, from the fourteenth-century Dutch *schip* for 'ship', football's most enduring seafaring link.

Our fighting forces also played a broader role in developing football language and the game itself by spreading it abroad. Soldiers and sailors helped introduce the game around the world, particularly in India, China, Chile and the rest of South America. Many men heading for the front in the First World War packed footballs in their belongings. The Christmas Day 'kickabout truce' between the British and Germans in 1914 is a staple of football folklore and a legend of the war.

A number of evocative soundbites survive from the war years. The 1915 Cup Final at Old Trafford, the last before the end of the First World War, attended by many men in uniform, will forever be 'The Khaki Cup Final'. Sheffield United beat Chelsea 3–0, but more memorable was Lord Derby's address to the crowd:

> You have played with one another and against one another for the Cup. It is now the duty of everyone to join with each other and play a sterner game for England.

That set the tone as football imagery was used as both a recruitment tool and morale booster. Following criticism that football had continued after the outbreak of war, Football League competition ceased after 1915 but friendlies continued throughout the conflict. Recruitment posters shamelessly targeted the football fraternity:

> Do you want to be a Chelsea Die-Hard? Join the 17th Battalion Middlesex Regiment and follow the lead given by your favourite football players.

In truth professional footballers had been slow to come forward, but by Christmas 1914 over 100,000 fans had taken the bait and the 17th Middlesex became known as 'The Footballers' Battalion'.

Some regiments and war heroes became part of football folklore. Second Lieutenant Donald Bell, a former Bradford Park Avenue defender, became the only Football League player ever to win a Victoria Cross, awarded posthumously for his bravery on the Somme in 1916. Derby County's Lance Corporal George Brooks of the 24th York and Lancaster Regiment was killed just before 11 a.m. on 11 November 1918, only seconds before the Armistice took effect, possibly the very last man to die before the official ceasefire.

On 1 July 1916 the 8th Battalion of the East Surrey Regiment went 'over the top', kicking footballs ahead of them as a symbolic diversion as they advanced through 'No Man's Land' to attack German positions on the Somme. Many men fell under heavy German fire, among them Captain W P Nevill who provided the four balls. The assault was a success, the regiment winning fifteen decorations for the day's work, commemorated in verse by 'Touchstone':

On through the hail of slaughter,
Where gallant comrades fall,
Where blood is poured like water,
They drive the trickling ball.
The fear of death before them,
Is but an empty name,
True to the land that bore them,
The Surreys played the game.

When the Second World War began in September 1939 the authorities again capitalised on football's capacity as morale booster and fund-raiser. This time conscription ensured that most professional players took to uniform, but flexible leave or home-based duties enabled many to keep playing. Although an Air Raid Precautions regulation banning the assembly of crowds initially brought the professional game to an abrupt halt, it quickly resumed on a regionally organised basis.

Seventy-five professional footballers died on war service but the game survived stronger than ever. World leaders have since recognised that football can be used politically as a healer. Locals versus troops seems to have become the unofficial endgame in so-called wars of liberation. In April 2003, days after Baghdad was liberated, even as looters stole everything in sight, Kuwait was extending invitations to the English and American football authorities to play 'aid games' against them.

But as Simon Kuper observed in his award-winning *Football Against The Enemy* (1994), the game can also create conflict:

Football is much more than just the most popular game in the world. It can start or stop wars, it can fuel revolutions or it can keep dictators in power.

He travelled to 22 countries to prove it beyond doubt.

Seven years later, the terrorist attack on New York's twin towers on 11 September 2001 brought the language of football and war closer together than ever before. Pending the 2002 World Cup the *Daily Mail* employed the age-old alliance, but no longer metaphorically:

Anti-aircraft missiles will be deployed inside the Seoul football stadium when France kicks off the World Cup on Friday. The operation will also include fighter jets and helicopters patrolling the skies, a direct reaction to September 11. Military forces across South Korea are on high alert with submarines and warships off the coast to thwart a maritime attack. All flights within a six mile radius of stadiums hosting games have been banned from two hours before kick-off until an hour afterwards.

That's one step closer to a head-on collision between two of the media's most frequently used words, 'football' and 'terrorism'. Experts have already suggested that globally televised games such as the World Cup Final are potentially the best targets of all.

For 140 years military jargon enriched football language, adding more quaintness than vitriol, but the joke is beginning to wear thin. We have moved full circle. Now we ask not only 'Is football war?' but 'Is war football?'

In spring 2003, when American and British forces bombarded Baghdad live on television in the world's first 'real time' war, US troops whooped as they hit targets. Embedded journalists gave shot-by-shot commentary on the state of play. Studio pundits analysed endless action replays. One interviewee in England observed 'It's more like a football match than a war', arguably the most chilling words of the entire war in Iraq. The shrewd judge was one of a breed who know all about playing football and playing at war: a ten-year-old boy.

It seems the two most ubiquitous world pastimes – one a game, the other far from it – are moving in opposite directions that nevertheless bring them inexorably closer. By the time you read this, one of our more crass football commentators will already have blurred the lines further by referring to an own-goal as 'friendly fire' and an early away goal as a 'pre-emptive strike'. And terrorists have openly declared they have football stadia on their agendas.

Major Sir Arthur Francis Marindin, late of the Royal Engineers, would understand today's language, but he'd surely be bemused by the context in which it's used. Even George

Orwell, who in the 1940s cynically described football as 'war minus the shooting', would be surprised at how much closer the two seem to have moved.

Following the 1994 World Cup, the Colombian defender Andres Escobar was shot dead after scoring an own goal against the United States which effectively cost his side a place in the second round. Football and warfare have changed radically since 1863, but should the day arrive when their linguistic relationship departs further from the metaphoric, it may well be the game's darkest.

4

Classic Encounters – The Latin Touch

Ludere Causa Ludendi – 'To Play the Game for the Game's Sake'

Motto of the Scottish club Queen's Park, the only senior club in the UK to retain its amateur status

When the Latin-speaking Roman legions withdrew from Britain in AD 410 it was 367 years since their arrival, but in language terms it was almost as if they'd never been here at all.

Their occupation of Spain and Gaul led to the development of entirely new languages, Spanish and French, and the Latin tongue understandably had such an influence in Italy that it's still possible to construct long passages of modern Italian that are identical to ancient Latin.

But in Britain less than 200 pure Latin words were incorporated into the Old English language which developed following the Anglo-Saxon invasions of AD 449. Coming from what is modern Germany and Denmark, it was these invaders, not the preceding Romans, or indeed the native Celts who had been in Britain since around 500 BC, who truly shaped the English language in its earliest recorded form. That's why English is now classed as a member of the Germanic rather than Romance group of languages, and why *football* not *calcio* is the name of the world's greatest game. But consider the following passage:

33

Victory eluded both sides as the *City versus United fixture* ended *nil-nil* today. The *League Table* now *confirms* the *title* and *Championship Trophy* will go to *Villa*, for whom *Cup medals* also look likely at the end of a *magnificent campaign.*

All the italicised (and there's another one) words have a Latin origin, either directly, via Greek, or through a French intermediary. So somewhere along the way, Latin influence must have crept back in.

In fact 'crept' isn't a strong enough word. After the Roman missionary St Augustine landed in Kent in AD 597 intent on spreading the doctrine of Christianity, the Latin language, the favoured tongue of the ecclesiastical world, was reintroduced with mounting zeal.

Most influential books and important documents published in Britain over the next thousand years came to be written in Latin, or if not that, in French. Such was the influx of these later Latin 'loans' that by the fifteenth century over 2,000 Latin-influenced words had been introduced into the English language.

That the very name of football itself was able to escape a permanent Latin tag (remember it might easily have remained *pila pedalis* or *harpastum*) was partly due to its great antiquity as a native British pastime, but much more to do with the activity's social standing. For 95 per cent of its history until it became the organised 'association game' we know today, it was the 'rude and manly game', largely the province not of Latin-speaking academics but of earthy rustics and common townsfolk.

So when 'football' was christened as such in the fifteenth century it simply wasn't on for men of letters to bestow upon it a 'classy' Latin name. Instead it was the language of the common people which gave the pastime of ball-kicking its basic early vernacular.

As we've seen, *fot* for foot was Anglo-Saxon, while *bollr* for ball was from the Old Norse brought to our language by Viking raiders between the eighth and tenth centuries. So were *bóti*, *skor*, *skyrta* and *grund*, which gave us boot, score, shirt and ground. *Kike* for kick is one of the English language's mystery words, but certainly not Latin; more like a Scandinavian borrowing. In fact most words relating to football as a basic physical activity are rooted in the vulgar language of the masses. Football's linguistic roots, like the origins of our version of the game, are basically North European.

But where Latin did make inroads was in the terminology overlaid on to the game much later, when its structure and rules were formulated by the Football Association in the 1860s and 1870s. Mindful of the privileged educational background of the FA's early administrators, this is no surprise. G M Trevelyan's *English Social History* reminds us that 'for four centuries from 1400–1800 Latin was a second language for every cultured Englishman' and that 'at most of the Public and Grammar schools, boys were required to speak Latin at all times, even out of school hours'. The legacy for the nineteenth century was that Latin-influenced English words became an integral and preferred part of everyday educated speech.

In that light, consider again the commonly used words in the football passage at the start of this chapter. *Victory* (*victoria*), *City* (*civitas*), *United* (*unire* = 'join together'), *fixture* (*fixus* = 'firmly held'), *cup* (*cupa* = 'tub/vat'), *medal* (*metallum* = 'metal'), *title* (*titulum* = 'inscription') and *Villa* ('country house') are all simple derivations from Latin.

Championship and *campaign* from Latin *campus* ('field') are more indirectly derived, and *trophy* comes via Latin's *trophaeum* from the Greek *tropaion* meaning 'to defeat', used originally to refer to the captured colours or standards of enemy armies. *League* relates to the Latin verb *legare* ('to bind together', also responsible for 'ligament' injuries). *Table* is from *tabula*, Latin for the 'plank' or 'tablet' on which lists were traditionally written.

This added veneer of classically influenced language suited the intentions of football's earliest high-hats perfectly, imbuing a game generally regarded as 'vulgar' with high-sounding touches of class which helped to make it more palatable to educated tastes. Even the game's prefix name, 'association', came from the Latin *associare* for 'join together in a group'. As such the much-reviled *soccer*, if its 'accepted' origin is to be believed, is also a classical term. Then, as now, football was undergoing gentrification.

Despite these fine antiquarian touches, the organised game didn't receive universal acceptance straight away. The respective merits and morality of 'professional' and 'amateur' players were hotly debated once professionalism was legalised in England in 1885. That schism itself was shot through with echoes of classical language.

Anyone who did Latin at school will remember *amo, amas, amat* if nothing else. *Amat* ('he loves') gave us *amateur*, one who plays purely for the love of the game. The dastardly fellows who played for money, meanwhile, were dubbed *professors* and then *professionals*, but not, as is sometimes said, because they were 'clever' with a ball. Both words come from the fourteenth-century verb 'to profess' (Latin *professus* = 'declared aloud') used originally to denote a 'public declaration'. An academic professor was originally someone who gave public lectures promoting or 'admitting' his beliefs or theories, and his footballing counterpart was a man similarly prepared to openly declare, in a climate of hostility to his breed, that he did indeed ply his trade for filthy lucre.

Late nineteenth-century football literature is replete with many more words of Latin origin. *Referee* is from *referre*, Latin for 'carry back' or 'refer to', which also explains the apparent curiosity of being asked to give the name of 'two referees' when applying for a job. The 'man in black', 'knight of the whistle', 'arbiter', 'whistleblower', 'an outright homer', and other names less charitable still, have since been bestowed on 'the man in the middle', but he has always remained someone whom players and crowds refer to for an opinion.

Some Latin terms have survived largely unchanged, including two of the most frequently used words in the game. The first interposes itself in every single fixture ever played. That's *versus*, which doesn't actually mean 'against' but 'pointing towards' or 'facing'. The second appears as a result of a substantial percentage of games. *Nil* was a nineteenth-century invention, a contraction of *nihil*, itself an abbreviation of the Latin *nihilum* meaning 'a small thing' or 'trifle', which is also why teams get 'annihilated'. *Area* is a pure Latin word meaning 'plot of ground'. And don't we all love a brilliant *solo* run, from the Italian via Latin for 'alone'. Nor is the Roman presence confined to words. First *XI* instead of 'eleven' is still surprisingly well used.

Such was the educated Victorian's familiarity with Latin that the all-rounder Charles Burgess Fry was able to incorporate full phrases without translation in an 1897 coaching manual. One wonders how today's forwards might react to his advice: 'It is sound policy to shoot whenever there is a chance of scoring, and certainly in this case *bis dat qui cito dat*.' A touch of Anglo-Saxon might well emerge from the likes of Robbie Fowler, but Fry's advice was sound – 'he delivers twice as much who does so quickly'. Basically 'make it count son, shoot early'.

Provincial newspapers also sprinkled their florid prose in like manner. Defeat was often accompanied by the stoical reminder to fans, *'nil desperandum'* ('don't despair'), and a hack from the *Burton Mail* was so keen to allude to Jupiter as the 'bringer of rain' that he described an abandoned match thus: 'The precipitation which had several times threatened to curtail proceedings finally triumphed as *Jupiter Pluvius* forced the arbiter to call time prematurely.' Pure Stuart Hall.

While the modern footballer might well eschew this Latin stuff, it's much closer to the heart of many a highly paid player than he might realise – unless he's had a close look at the club badge recently. Latin *mottoes* (Italian *motto* = 'I say') were incorporated by many clubs into their *crests* (*crista* = 'plume') at their foundation dates and survive today.

Mottoes, defined as 'a short expression of a guiding principle', were first used as rallying cries in combat, becoming fashionable among the retinues of tournament knights in the fourteenth century. Many towns incorporated them into their arms and some football clubs adopted these directly, which is why today they aren't always entirely appropriate or sufficiently manly. Leeds United's *Pro Rege et Lege* ('For King and Law') is one such example, although the law bit might come home to roost. Bournemouth's rather effeminate *Pulchritudo et Salubritas* ('For Health and Beauty') is another. Should they wish to change, a number of genuine mottoes remain up for grabs. *Ad Metam* ('To the Goal') would suit an attacking side. Those shutting up shop might prefer *Defendendo Vinco* ('I Conquer by Defending'). Others already taken up were tailor-made for the sporting context, like Arsenal's *Victoria Concordia Crescit* ('Victory Through Harmony') and Rochdale's *Credo Signo* ('Believe in the Badge'). Around forty Premiership and Football League clubs still use Latin mottoes on their shirts or club stationery. Here's today's test:

Blackburn Rovers: *Arte Et Labore* . . .By Skill and Hard Work

Bristol City: *Virtute Et Industria* . .Through Valour and Effort

Bury: *Vincit Omnia Industria* . . . . .Effort Conquers All

Carlisle United: *Unita Fortior* . . . . . . .Strength In Numbers

Crewe Alexandra: *Iuvare Non Impedire* . . . .Help Not Hinder

Mansfield Town: *Sicut Quercus Virescit Industria*
. . . . .Industry Flourishes Like an Oak

Oldham Athletic: *Sapere Aude* . . . . .Dare To Be Wise

Swansea City: *Floreat Swansea* . . . . .Blossom Swansea!

Tottenham Hotspur: *Audere Est Facere* . . .To Dare Is To Do

Tranmere: *Ubi Fides Ibi Lux Et Robur*
. . . . .Through Faith Comes Strength and Light

Watford: *Audentior* . . . . .More Brave

There is something of a 'Latin can be fun' campaign going on today, and cod-Latin phrases are apt to emerge. The magazine *FourFourTwo* pursued an irreverent line in suggesting alternative mottoes for a number of clubs. Nottingham Forest were blessed with *Semper Sursum Deorsum* ('Always Up and Down'), Chelsea with *Id In Novem Linguis Iterate* ('Repeat That In Nine Languages') and Arsenal with *Unus Nihil Armamentario*, which needs no translation. *Urbs Villae Cacet* ('City Shit on the Villa') was suggested for Birmingham City and *Nihil Nisi Le Tissi* for Southampton – 'Nothing Without Le Tissier' (if not for the talented but laid-back Guernsey boy, the club might several times have lost its place in the Premiership during the 1990s). Manchester City were strongly urged to adopt *Faeces Sunt Et Se Esse Cognoscunt* ('You're Shit and You Know You Are'). This was only topped for crudity by the suggestion that Sunderland, hapless recipients of endless 'going down' chants in 2002–03, should ditch *Consectatio Excellentiae* ('The Pursuit of Excellence') and replace it with the age-old favourite, *Cunnilingus Et Fellatio.*

Even when football tries desperately to be progressive in its use of language, it can unwittingly fall back on ancient tongues. 'Football ground' is now increasingly usurped by the 'modernist' *stadium*, which in fact was an ancient Greek and Roman measurement equivalent to one circuit of their athletics tracks, hence by metaphorical extension their use of the word for the sporting venue itself. A similar process applied to the now much in vogue *arena*, Latin for the 'sand' spread on to the combat area in an amphitheatre to soak up the contestants' blood. When the Premier League was launched in 1992, the powers that be probably didn't think of the medieval ecclesiastical term *primus* (first) for 'the earliest of the canonical hours', but it's that which gives us the biggest buzz-word in football today.

There is one sense, though, in which the classical languages have failed football entirely. We have marvellous *-phobia* (Greek = 'dread') words for all manner of irrational fears and psychological troubles, yet how odd that our dictionaries include *medectophobia* (fear of displaying the contour of one's penis through clothes) and *coprostasophobia* (fear of constipation), but nothing whatsoever to comfort the timid boy scared witless by the prospect of having to join in with the rough boys at a school football session. Fear of attending matches, missing gilt-edged chances, soiling your shorts in front of 60,000 people, getting hit by the ball where it hurts most, awarding penalties to the away side at Old Trafford, none of them are covered.

The absence of football-related fear-words is partly due to a snobbishness on the part of word-makers, but also because 'football' itself isn't a very good prefix. *Footballphobia* just doesn't work. Some writers refer to *soccerphobes*, but that goes against the grain. *Pilapediphobia* would probably do the job for those who aren't too keen on our national pastime.

And why should someone with a mania for the game always have to be described as a 'football nut', whereas anyone with an excessive interest in crossing bridges is grandly accorded *gephyromaniac* status and someone displaying an undue desire to perform surgery can brag to his friends that he's suffering from *ergasiomania*? How fair is it that a man with an unhealthy interest in young children is neatly packaged as a *paedophile* but one with a healthy interest in football is just a plain old 'football-lover'?

The English language desperately needs a range of new words for all things football-related. Adidas recently achieved a measure of advertising success with 'footballitis', but *calcio* might well do the prefix job with a bit more style. I am a 'calciophile'. Someone who goes in search of half-inch quadrant beading at B&Q on a Saturday afternoon is a 'calciophobe'. Gianfranco Zola's magical mastery of the ball was 'calciomancy'.

When we say football needs 'the Latin touch' we usually mean 'more silky skills', but arguably today's troubled game needs first to remind itself of much more ancient principles. The best known Latin motto in football is Everton's '*Nil Satis Nisi Optimum*', literally 'Nothing Will Satisfy Except the Optimum', colloquially 'Only the Best Will Do'. Yet a leading Everton fans' website recently said this:

> The problem at Goodison is the progressive takeover of 'Nil Satis Nisi Optimum' by 'Ah well that'll do'. It's a fault all over football in a game which has shown itself unable to slough off a culture built up over a century of incompetence in the boardroom. Shambolic ticket sales procedures, poor service and dire conditions inside the grounds. Most clubs can't even deliver a hot half-time pie and a cup of Bovril before the restart.

That isn't just a rant. It's spot on. Football's glossy exterior hides a rotten core that its Victorian forefathers would have been ashamed of. In May 2003, at considerable pain to himself, David Beckham seemed mindful of turning back the clock when he mounted a one-man 'Bring back Latin' campaign by splashing out £150 on two new tattoos. His right arm now reads *'Perfectio In Spiritu'* ('Spiritual Perfection'), and his left says *'Ut Amem Et Foveam'* ('So that I love and cherish'). Now Latin is officially cool (the *Sun* said so), maybe it's high time for all the clubs and their players to follow Beckham's lead by taking a much closer look at their badges. Fans certainly want more for their money, as many supporters take up their own cod-Latin rallying cry: *'Calcio Supportus Demandit'*.

Stripped For Action

5

Nothing But a Bag of Wind?
– Balls

And Eton may play with a pill if they please,
And Harrow may stick to their Cheshire cheese,
And Rugby their outgrown egg, but here
Is the perfect game of the perfect sphere.

Brighton College football song, 1857

The only truly indispensable item required for playing football is the football itself. So it's fitting that 'football' the game is named after the object. 'A football' existed before 'football'. Few other sports share that characteristic. A 'cricket ball' came after 'cricket' itself. Golf, hockey, tennis, rugby and badminton all fail the test. Basketball looks a candidate, but again the game named the ball. Darts, bowls, cards and dominoes make it in plural, but mere sedentary games don't count.

Many scholars have attempted to trace the origin of man's favourite 'toy'. That it's a compound of *foot* and *ball* rightly suggests there were plain ordinary balls before there were footballs. Theologians given to extremes of logic dreamily assert that God's creation of the earth makes him the inventor of the ball. They forget that our planet is flattened at both poles. If God were a ball tycoon, his product would have been routinely vetoed by the most supreme power of all – it would not be FIFA approved.

Anthropologists just as dreamily plump for prehistoric man. Wasn't he familiar with pebbles, nuts, fruits, berries, and the odd dead relative's skull? Obviously he saw these roll. He found their movement intriguing. So when Ig first cast a rounded stone or nicely turned lump of dung at Ug, he invented the ball. They even claim evidence, suggesting that hand-crafted Stone Age balls excavated from a Maltese temple were used in some sort of bowling game. Not so: the latest considered opinion says they were either weapons or primitive ball-bearings used in some rudimentary mechanical device. The stark reality is that no anthropologist has yet discovered prehistoric carvings or paintings depicting the leisure use of 'a ball'.

That leaves the archaeologists, who do have both physical and artistic proof but from much later. The oldest surviving play balls in the world are ancient Egyptian. Made of stitched linen panels stuffed with cut reeds, they're held by the British Museum. And frescoes from the tomb of Beni Hasan show Egyptian maidens playing 'ball' circa 2000 BC. Further representations from Ancient Greek and Roman artworks, along with written descriptions, are proof positive that structured ball games were also played in Europe at least 2,500 years ago.

Not that these foreign-made items were called 'footballs', nor did their names pass into common English, but they have influenced a number of current words. One intriguing legacy is from the Roman *follis*, the nearest ancient equivalent to a modern-day football. This was an air-filled animal bladder encased in cured skins, a form that gave the ball the novel element of bounce and 'give' that stuffed balls largely lacked. Via the figurative meaning 'windbag', it gave us the thirteenth-century abbreviation *fol*, now *fool*, for anyone full of huff and puff but little besides. Romans used the *follis* in Britain during their occupation, and the word might well have usurped 'football' had the Britons been more receptive to the retention of Roman import words after the occupation. A narrow escape for our national game, it seems. Its detractors would doubtless have made great capital of its 'foolish' roots.

Ancient Greek balls also left a mark. From *sphaira* we retain *sphere* and all things *spherical*. Savouring the big-match 'atmosphere' is all about inhaling a heady 'ball of vapour'.

Latin's *pila*, the most common word for 'ball' in written accounts of British pastimes up to the fifteenth century, has made a deep and lasting impression. It gave us *pill* (for tablet), and its sporting context is retained in public school slang where a football has long been 'the pill' to boys familiar with Latin. The fastest ball game in the world is *pelota*. Welsh for football is *pel droed*, literally 'ball foot'. And who hasn't been hit plum in the *pills* by a goalbound shot? Also from the basement department, *pila* gave us the irritating 'little bubbles' that are *piles*.

It was but a simple step from *pila* to add the Latin *pedalis*, and from there to its English translation debut in 1486, a 'fotebal'.

Etymologists explain the 'new' word thus. *Foot* is a descendant of the Indo-European *pod* and *ped*, which led via Latin *pes* to numerous foot-related words (*pedal, pedestrian, pedestal, pedometer, quadruped*, and the archaic word for football, *pedipulation*). *Ped* evolved into Old English *fot* via corrupted pronunciation from Germanic, and this was later standardised to *foot*.

Ball is more mysterious. Its Old Norse root, *bollr*, is itself of obscure origin. Symbolic links to Old English *bula* for 'bull' have been suggested, since balls were leather encased ox-bladders. Some word-detectives have mused that *bollr* has figurative links to the impressive testicular attributes of the bull. No one truly knows.

What should seem beyond debate is that *foot* and *ball* became linked because the ball was kicked 'with the foot', but the obvious inconsistency is that most ancient forms of 'football' saw the ball equally, if not more so, conveyed with the hands.

To explain this paradox, some etymologists have offered an imaginative suggestion. Emanating as it did from a medieval age accustomed to leisure pursuits on horseback (jousting, hunting etc.), a football wasn't 'a ball to be kicked with the foot' but rather 'a ball to be used in the pursuit of leisure *on foot*'. Like a *foot-soldier*, who isn't 'a soldier to be kicked' but simply one 'on foot' rather than horseback.

Such semantic arguments have definite head-exploding potential so let's just say that by the fifteenth century, the fascinating round thing already known to generations of Britons had acquired the name 'a football'. And since then, the word has played a significant role in both the lexicon of the game and the English language itself.

The most intriguing element of its usage is a perverse one. In truth, when referring to the item itself we hardly use the word at all. To players a football is simply 'the ball' or 'it', familiarities born from the urgency inherent during a game. Hence 'hit it' (or the strangulated "i' 'i'" in the southeast). Likewise commentators, spectators and managers. The latter occasionally bemoan 'our inability to keep the football', but that's self-consciously ironic.

Avoidance of the f-word is nothing new, but early reporters were more imaginative. The Victorians loved synonyms, hence *orb*, *globe*, *sphere* and *projectile* were all well used, but favourites by far were the *bladder* and the *leather*. The eccentric Irish international Archie Goodall invariably called football 'chasing the *pluff*'. Today's hacks are more direct, although these archaisms still surface occasionally as a nod to nostalgia.

By contrast it's worth noting what happens overseas. Take the ball's masters. In *Futebol: The Brazilian Way of Life*, Alex Bellos elucidates the love affair between Brazilians and their *spheres* by citing no fewer than 37 synonyms for 'the football' in Portuguese. These include *menina* ('baby'), *gorduchinha* ('little podgy one') and the female names *Maricota*, *Leonor* and *Margarita*. The abiding message is one of tenderness. To South Americans the ball is undeniably feminine. Pelé 'kissed her' when he scored his thousandth goal. Real Madrid's Argentinian-born legend, Alfredo di Stefano, placed a bronze sculpture of a football in front of his house when he retired. The plaque translated as 'Thanks old girl'.

Compare British football. 'Margaret' isn't on the list. When Beckham 'does the business with Victoria' it doesn't imply he's had a good game. I've used nine synonyms so far, of which 'it' is as intimate as they get. Jimmy Greaves's rare favourite, the *onion* ('stick the onion in the old onion bag'), makes ten. Two more, a *footie* and its variant spelling *footy*, are almost affectionate, as are the now almost obsolete schoolboy favourites, *casey* for case-ball (literally an 'encased ball'), and *lacey* for laced ball.

But beyond that, it only gets abusive. The game's detractors favour the much-overused *bag of wind* or *pig's bladder*. That's sixteen. I can add six more regulars from my Sunday League days.

In order of popularity (with apologies to the easily offended) these were the *fucker*, the *bastard*, the *bugger*, the *sod*, the *bleeder* and the *thing*. Hence such loving phrases as 'hit the fucker', 'belt the bleeder' and many affectionate combinations thereof. That's England 22 Brazil 37. What does it all tell us about our very British relationship to the ball? Is it an object of love or something to bully? Perhaps a rogue male which threatens our manhood? Or are we the wife-beaters of the football world? On one hand, English is replete with evidence supporting the much-abused victim theory. In his *Comedy of Errors* (1590), Shakespeare used a football metaphorically to formulate an abused character's complaint:

> Am I so round with you as you with me
> That like a football you do spurn me thus?
> You spurn me hence, and he will spurn me hither;
> If I last in this service you must case me in leather.

And consider this recent newspaper report of a violent assault:

> The victim was kicked about the head with the sort of venom usually reserved for a football.

On the other hand, the 1960s Rangers and Scotland player Jim Baxter, he of the silky *ball skills*, spoke of the ball as an object of desire. But even then only with a view to self-gratification:

> I've always believed in treating the ball like a woman. Give it a cuddle, caress it a wee bit, take your time, and you'll get the required response.

Devotees of *The Fast Show* will discern the sexist tone of 'Swiss Toni' in Baxter's rhetoric. Man–ball relationships are evidently complex affairs.

It may well be an age thing. For children there's undoubtedly a love affair going on. The archetypal schoolboy in fiction, 'Just William', regularly pressed his nose against a toy-shop window to gaze longingly at a 'prize football'. In my own childhood,

there was no better present than a chocolate-brown Size 5
'Frido'. Bursting one on the roses was a tragedy, losing the life-
giving adaptor almost as bad. Even today's streetwise youngsters
seem drawn to pick up a 'real ball', to hold it, press it and
examine it. And who could be more despised than the sulky brat
who *takes his ball home*? George Best once summed it all up:

> When I was a kid the only thing I shared my bed with
> was a football. I used to take a ball to bed with me. I
> know it sounds daft but I used to love the feel of it. I
> used to hold it, look at it, and think, 'One day you'll do
> everything I tell you'.

Professional psychologists would have a field day with that one.
Significantly Best introduces one of the foremost themes
associated with the football, that of *control*.

Juveniles are content to play with the ball, treat it as a friend,
give it free rein. Adults seek to become its master. Football
writers, anthropologists, folk historians and sociologists have all
tried to explain this 'domination fixation' by analysing football's early history in terms of man's inner relationship with the
ball, imbuing both 'it' and the game with a deeper and more
mystical significance than mere sport. Some of the ideas may
seem far-fetched, but careful perusal of centuries-old accounts
of mass games suggests there's almost certainly more to
football's ancient history than meets the casual eye.

The most common theory is that the ball was originally
symbolic of the sun. Ancient Aztec and Egyptian cultures both
used balls in sacred ceremonies as early as 1500 BC. A thousand
years later Celtic tradition mirrored this in Europe. To pursue the
ball, toss it high, toy with it and ultimately possess it, was a
demonstration of man's control over the giver of life. To do so
over field and dale ensured a bountiful crop. Such traditions
prevailed for centuries. This sixteenth-century verse advised East
Anglian farmers to allow *camping* (in its early sense) in their fields:

> In meadow or pasture to grow the more fine,
> Let campers be camping in any of thine.

Folk historians pursue similar themes, noting that the Christian festival day Shrove Tuesday, for centuries the main football day of the year, coincided with the vernal equinox of the pre-Christian era, an important time for pagan rituals intended to enhance productivity and fertility in the summer months ahead.

A more earthy theory notes the fact that the ball was made of animal entrails, which in many cultures long held supernatural significance. In that sense, the leather-clad blown bladder of a thousand years ago was imbued with the qualities of the beast itself. Only by control and possession of the ball could the attributes of strength and virility be harnessed.

Some academics have seized on that to present reasonably convincing arguments that medieval mass football already had ancient roots which effectively made it a ritualised hunt. The ball was the quarry which had to be captured in the face of the opposition and then paraded as a trophy, the symbol of the victors' supremacy over both 'the beast' and their rival town or village. That spirit prevails today in surviving Shrovetide football games, where the winning side retain the ball as a trophy and revel in its possession. Even first-class footballers still 'claim the match ball' after a hat-trick.

The anthropologist Desmond Morris popularised this 'pseudo-hunt' view of football's genesis in *The Soccer Tribe*, but argued that the imagery didn't carry through into the modern game. His point was that today the ball is dispatched into the so-called 'opposition' goal rather than returned 'home'. In that sense, he says, the ball has become a symbolic weapon rather than a beast, and the goal at which it's aimed has become the target or quarry in its place.

That seems an over-elaboration. If ancient symbolic meaning must be extrapolated into the modern game, surely the ball is still the quarry and the goal the trap into which it has to be collectively hounded against the will of the opposition. Fortuitously, the game's language lends some credence to the 'ball as quarry' analogy. Midfielders *hunt the ball down*, and it's *trapped, brought down, killed* or otherwise forced into submission with a view to being *driven into the net*.

Football may have more in common with bull-fighting than we generally acknowledge. In early medieval England, bull-baiting or 'running' was regularly practised in many towns. When it was banned, hounding the ball instead of the bull remained as a good alternative. Now, just as the *aficionados* claim to love and respect *el toro* despite their shameful treatment of it, so the modern British footballer loves the ball but seeks to *bury the bastard* into the bargain. A grown-man and his ball. It's a love–hate thing.

Whether you empathise with such interpretations or not (by now you'll either be nodding sagely or saying 'what a load of crap'), there's certainly something in the quality of the football which is elusive and magical. At its most passive, when it's a *dead ball*, it's devoid of both life and personality. But once set in motion, it's made to do things it ought not be able to, appearing at times even to have a mind of its own: 'The ball *refused to go in*' or 'it just *wouldn't run for us*' are every manager's favourites. 'Twas ever thus – a Victorian reporter bemoaned the ball's brazen recalcitrance by observing that 'it evinced a decided repugnance to the space between the posts'.

That such a free spirit should have to be mastered entirely by use of the feet is what truly makes football a magical game. The French writer Jean Giraudoux understood this:

> The ball is that thing which most easily escapes from the laws of life. It has the quality of some force which has not been fully tamed, but the team imparts to it the motor of eleven shrewd minds and imaginations. And if the hands have been barred from the game it is because their intrusion would make the ball no longer a ball, the player no longer a player. The hands are cheats, and the ball will not permit cheating but only techniques which are sublime.

Fellow philosopher Albert Camus, a proficient goalkeeper in Algeria in the 1930s and therefore a legitimate 'cheat', also acknowledged how difficult the ball was to master:

I quickly learned that the ball never came to you where you expected it. This helped me in life, where people are not always wholly straightforward.

With the ball's 'will o' the wisp' personality in mind, consider the following three matter-of-fact snippets from the world of *keepy-uppy*. In the 1990 Prague marathon, the Czech Jan Skorkovsky ran the entire 26 miles juggling the ball with his feet without letting it drop once. In July 1994 the Brazilian Ricardinho Neves kept a football in the air without it touching the ground for a total of 19 hours 5 minutes and 31 seconds. And in December 1997 the Brazilian Milene Domingues set a women's world record of 55,187 touches in 9 hours 6 minutes. This so impressed Ronaldo, aside from the fact she was a stunning blonde, that he married her.

With apologies to the great scientific minds in question I can honestly say I find each of these feats more incredible than anything achieved by Leonardo da Vinci, Albert Einstein and Stephen Hawking combined. Flying to Mars is a doddle by comparison. I'm sorry, but there it is. If you disagree, the man to convince you is the new kid on the block, the Korean Hee Yong Woo, so good he was employed by Pelé to perform at his birthday party. Brazil's Ronaldinho was so impressed with Mr Woo's trickery, he asked for his autograph.

Woo makes ball control look easy. Be assured it isn't. That's why players who master it are described in terms that suggest supernatural powers. Stanley Matthews, 'The Wizard of Dribble'. Hughie 'Magic Feet' Gallacher. And consider the commentators' metaphor, 'he's got a left foot like a magic wand'. They really do say it. Note that it's always the left, the *sinister* one, never the right, the *dextrous* one.

By way of atonement to science, I'm bound to point out that without scientific advances such consummate ball skills, and indeed the very being of the modern game, could never have developed. Pig, ox and sheep bladders were irregularly shaped and prone to easy bursting. So balls used in any size of game, mob or otherwise, right up to the mid nineteenth century, were never controllable in the modern sense, even when cased with leather. And the alternative, stuffed balls (hair, cork, bran, moss, wood shavings and seed heads were favourites), neither bounced nor were kind on the feet, hence the tendency to play handling games with them. Solid rubber balls, meanwhile, used for centuries by the Guaranie Indians of the Bolivian Amazon, were a closely guarded secret.

In fact it took an American, Charles Goodyear of tyre fame, to change everything. Only when he discovered how to vulcanise raw rubber in 1839 by heating it with sulphur to make it resilient, did the technology for manufacturing strong, regularly shaped rubber bladders or 'inner tubes' for footballs begin to develop. It wasn't by pure chance that the kicking and dribbling versions of football developed apace in the mid nineteenth century. The game's historians have too often overlooked the role of ball technology in the 'invention' of association football.

By the late nineteenth century, football manufacture had become a veritable boom industry. Today forty million footballs are sold worldwide each year. With that came an entire vocabulary.

Nowadays, synthetic materials and waterproof coatings have changed the nature of the ball. So, although the once ubiquitous heavy ball is no more, other vestiges of superseded technology remain as linguistic curiosities.

Commentators who say 'he had time to take the lace out of it' hark back at least fifty years. The laceless 'valve ball' was invented in the 1930s by three forgotten Argentines from Cordoba – Tossolini, Valbonesi and Polo – but it wasn't until the 1960s that it was perfected and widely used in Britain. Once the unsightly gash which had for so long made the ball not quite 'entire' had healed, players were at last spared the threat of laceration or serious eye damage from a flailing loose end.

Today's balls fly further, spin faster and move in the air more readily than at any time in the game's history, but all at the sole behest of the players, more in control than ever before. As the saying goes, 'It's a *whole new ball game*'.

Much to the confusion of the game's detractors, what a glorious capacity for befuddlement has arisen, for example,

from the acquired term *ball* for 'a pass'. What must they make
of the *long ball*, *short ball* and *square ball*? Or *good balls*, *bad balls*,
superb balls, *atrocious balls*, cheeky little *tickled balls* and *early
balls*. But where's the *second ball* the coaches always bang on
about? Players complain about *hard balls*, but still whinge if you
give them a soft one. Others exhort colleagues to play the *easy
ball* while the manager shouts '*our ball*' or '*corner ball*' and the
voice in the crowd yells '*Shit ball!*' one minute and '*Shit-hot
ball!*' the next. As for every player's nightmare, the *hospital ball*,
I won't even try to explain.

Those who denounce football as 'only a game', and the
much-abused ball in particular as 'nothing but a bag of wind',
need putting right. In the immediate aftermath of the 1989
Hillsborough disaster, the British writer Bernard Levin
described football in the *New York Times* as 'twenty-two grown
men chasing a piece of leather round a field'. That was a
disgraceful betrayal of the game at the time it most needed
support. Like a New York journalist describing the twin towers
in *The Times* as 'just some big iron girders and a lot of glass'
after 11 September. Someone should have put Levin in his
place. But where to start? The traditional riposte, quoting from
J B Priestley's 1929 novel *The Good Companions*, has become
too hackneyed by far:

> To say that men paid their shillings to watch twenty-two
> hirelings kick a ball is merely to say that a violin is wood and
> catgut, that *Hamlet* is so much paper and ink. For a shilling
> the Bruddersford United AFC offered you Conflict
> and Art.

Michael Parkinson uses it so often, it's lost its clout. There's a
much better weapon. Words aren't the answer.

An old Scottish proverb says, 'He who cannot make sport,
should mar none'. It makes a particularly valid point. Ask
yourself what Bernard Levin's keepy-uppy record was. Could
he spray forty-yard passes to either wing at will? Did he have a
good first touch? In my experience one of football's universally
accurate tenets is that those who denounce the game most

vehemently are never any good at it. The ball is their master, and humbled by it, they resent it. So never waste breath arguing with the 'bag of wind' fraternity. Just toss them the magic orb and ask them to do something with it. As we believers say: '*Let the ball do the talking.*'

6
All Day I Dream About . . .
– Boots

'Three things draw crowds of wide-eyed, curious onlookers in school playgrounds: a fight, a pool of vomit,
and someone showing off their new football boots.'

Ian McArthur, professor of bootology, 1995

WARNING: While reading this book, resist the temptation to dig out your football boots past or present. You'll
only want to touch, smell, or possibly even kiss them. The
memories connected to your boots are magical. So cherish
them, exalt them, even mount them on a marble plinth,
but above all be grateful.

Thus did Ian McArthur and Dave Kemp, the world's foremost
football boot enthusiasts, begin their homage in their
cryptically titled *Elegance Borne of Brutality* (1995). The title is
a translation from 'On Football Boots', a poem in French by
Henri de Montherlant entirely dedicated to the most essential
items in a footballer's kit-bag:

Still sticky with good oil, still crusted with chunks of earth,
Strong, smoking smell of seaweed, elegance borne of
brutality.

If you thought there was no such thing as 'the language of
football boots', think again.

Boot itself, a fourteenth-century latecomer to English, is one of modern football's misnomers. Deriving either from the Old Norse *bóti* or Old French *bote*, both from sources unknown, its dictionary definition has always been 'a covering for the foot and lower part of the leg, usually in leather'. That's spot-on for the high-ankled Victorian originals, but we ought strictly to be calling them 'football shoes' or even 'football slippers' today. Not a hope. Football boots are far too precious to be tampered with.

And words are important in what is a hugely lucrative market. We all know the drill. Does the boot sound attractive? What special features has it got? Generations of punters hovering on the brink of self-delusion have asked themselves the question: 'Will those gismos really make me a better player, just like the adverts and star endorsements say they will?' Of course they will. Jimmy Greaves of Tottenham Hotspur and England guarantees it. Roy Keane swears by them. Mr H C Parry of Redcar says they 'have improved my left-footed kicking beyond measure'.

It's been said we all remember our first registration number. I don't. But I remember my first boots – St Crispin Wings, 1963 model. Probably the only model they ever made, but as a naïve seven-year-old I was hopelessly seduced. They sounded vaguely exotic. I was a winger. No one else in the class had them. In truth that was because they were deeply unfashionable. My mother ought really to have vetoed the whole sorry act, but the 'extra ankle protection' flash on the box hit all the right maternal buttons. My first boot deal was done. And so was I.

While other boys swanked in Adidas and Puma and asked me who St Crispin played for, I searched in vain through my bubblegum cards. A French side perhaps? Years later I discovered he was the patron saint of cobblers.

Today's choice is unnerving. Adidas, Lotto, Nike, Reebok, Umbro, Puma, Diadora, Mitre, Asics, Bukta, Mizuno – it goes on, each a range 'superior to the rest'.

But what of etymology? *Adidas* claims supremacy; it's a global word that even gives *Coca-Cola* a run for its money. Popular myth has it that the name was coined as an acronym for 'All Day I Dream About Shoes'. Nothing so clever. It's a contraction of the first and last names of the German entrepreneur Adolph 'Adi' Dassler, who founded the firm on 18 August 1949. Naming Adidas wasn't his only piece of lexical trickery. He was actually christened Adolf not Adolph, but changed the spelling on launch day to avert a public relations nightmare: 'Step into a pair of Adolf's boots and conquer the world' – he'd never have captured the post-war British market with a slogan like that. As it is, British football should be eternally grateful for Adi's success. It's surely a delicious irony that Geoff Hurst scored his 1966 World Cup Final hat-trick not in a mythical pair of 'Hursty Hot-Shots' but in a very real pair of Adidas, craftsman-made in Germany. A goal for each stripe.

Other manufacturers' names that could mystify are readily explained. *Nike* is the Greek goddess of victory. The American company were once Blue Ribbon Sports, but changed after the triumphant deity bizarrely featured in a dream of one of their employees. But for Jeff Johnson's nocturnal imaginings, they'd have been *Dimension 6*, the choice of one of the firm's founders.

Reebok is the Dutch name for a small, sharp-horned, nippy South African antelope, aka *Antilope capreolus*. The English equivalent is *roebuck*, the male roe deer, proving unequivocally that a pair of Reeboks is two deer. Don't these marketing boys think anything through? *Umbro* meanwhile are not, as their name might suggest, a shady company. It's a contraction of Humphrey Brothers.

This name game is as old as the Football League itself. Although the earliest players turned out in ordinary work boots, specialist footwear was widely available by the time of the first League match in 1888. Some years earlier, Mercer & Co. of Bolton boasted – no pun intended – that they were 'sole manufacturers' of the 'Premier' boot personally endorsed by Blackburn Rovers' Hugh McIntyre: 'The boots are splendidly made and look good enough to play football themselves without any assistance.' What was the fee, Hugh? Little is new in football.

Then, as now, product differentiation was key. Would sir care to try the Benetfink *Defender*? Or would the *Popular* be better? Would *studs* be preferable to *bars* or *cleats*? Could anyone have resisted the 'Patent Indestructible Toe' offered by

Joseph Leeson of Leicester? Stevens & Co. tried manfully to lure people away with the seductive promise of 'russet Paris calf instep-strap, wedge heel and special stiff shanks'.

Not all such campaigns were successful. Banana skins scuppered even the best long-term marketing plans. West Ham's Syd Puddefoot glowingly endorsed W Abbott & Sons' prime product in the twenties, but you won't find 'Abbo's' on today's shelves. Nor did 'Concrete Football Boots', registered in 1911, survive for many seasons. Rumours that David Seaman wore a pair for games against Brazil and Macedonia in 2002 have been officially discounted, as indeed were the boots by many a disgruntled shopkeeper.

Slogans, too, can be equally 'of the moment'. 'Improve Your Play the Hungarian Way with Artex Boots' was brilliantly catchy, but only during the 1950s when Ferenc Puskas and his men were humbling England at the game we invented. Once cake-icing ceilings became fashionable the game was up.

Nor were players entirely blooper-proof. Everton sides of the early 1900s, supplied with boots by former star Frank Sugg, were quite comfortable, declaring 'Nothing plays better than a pair of Frank's'. But there was no similar endorsement when 'Fanny Walden's Kupwinnas' were launched in the 1920s.

Dictionaries generally omit brand names but that's not to say bootspeak doesn't have a place in English language history. It's odds-on that more men in pre-war Britain had heard of the long-term brand leader 'The Mansfield-Hotspur' and its famous *Nulli Secundus* ('Second to None') Latin motto than could have named their MP. But as brands come and go, so the once-magic words slide into sad obsolescence, resurrected only in the interests of nostalgia. The proudest words a boy could say to his mates in the early seventies were, 'I've got a pair of George Best "Stylo Matchmakers".' And quite right too – they had 'revolutionary side-laces' no less, 'eradicating embarrassing miskicks and mis-placed passes at a stroke'. Best's agent-manager Ken Stanley understood wordpower: 'If George had endorsed stair-rods they'd sell millions,' he remarked on his way to the bank.

Yet in the blink of an eye 'Stylo Matchmakers' became words uttered only by boys of the feeblest kind, as the FA's officially endorsed Power Points briefly ascended the throne. These came with a coaching booklet and a set of numbered stickers to apply to the boots: 'Number 6. To place the ball accurately with the instep strike here.' Chris Waddle once confessed to having followed the regime zealously as a youngster. Regrettably, during the 1990 World Cup 'penalties' debacle against the Germans he forgot the numbers in the heat of the moment, choosing '4' (long, high clearance) instead of '6'.

Homage, too, must be paid to coloured boots. Or should I say 'boots of colour'? *Green, red, yellow, gold, silver, blue* and *pink* have all done good service in their time but none are so memorable as *white boots*. These two completely inoffensive words, once married, quickly came to be uttered within earshot of the poseurs who wore them in the sort of condemnatory tone now reserved for serial killers: 'Like the Human Fireball Himself, Explode in the Fabulous Alan Ball White Soccer Boots by Hummel'. It's with an appropriate level of shame that I confess to having succumbed to the copywriter's charm. My game failed to explode, but it did go off. Maybe the ad-men had a cruel sense of humour. Worse still, boys who'd been my closest chums mercilessly mocked me in unusually shrill tones and called me 'Ginger'. I binned the boots, narrowly averting suicide.

The football lexicon is littered with a myriad of other boot-related words and phrases. Hand someone a pair of boots and I guarantee the first thing they'll do is turn them over. The famous *screw-in stud* entered the dictionary only in 1940 and is still with us. Not so the *swivelling stud foreplate*, the innovatory 1970s aid to *turning on a sixpence* (still in currency despite the coin's demise) which was modelled (but never played in) by Spurs' Steve Perryman. Excruciating ligament injuries far outstripped sales.

The humble stud can even prove injurious to wordsmiths. The *rubber stud*, developed to help players keep their feet in icy conditions, once famously tripped up the hapless commentator who informed his listeners: 'I'm told that in the interests of avoiding nasty accidents most of the players will be wearing rubbers tonight.'

The gaffes don't stop there. Soon after Gary Lineker gushed that 'I always wear Protec insoles to protect my bones, joints and muscles. They're great', 'The Queen Mother of Football' suffered the most famous big toe injury of all time.

One wonders where the glamorisation of the once-humble football boot could possibly end. Reebok appeared to have plumbed the heights with their 1995 ad campaign for their Instapump Removable Stud model:

Featuring a specially designed external chamber which when inflated with the hand-held inflater provides a snug fit, the Instapump weighs 8.5oz, features kangaroo leather vamp, cemented sock liner and an R.S. plate with 6 aluminium-tipped pyramid studs.

Yet even as I write, today's manufacturers are topping them. Ironically the current fad is for *blades*, not studs, which the Victorians ditched as passé over a century ago.

Beyond the ephemeral, boots have also given the English permanently recognised words and phrases. *Boot* the noun became *boot* the verb centuries ago, but the archaic exhortation *'boot it'* is still a regular instruction aimed at dallying defenders today. Being one of those accidentally onomatopoeic words, children especially favour it. That is, like the contrived *bang*, *splash*, *thud* and *plop*, it sounds like what it represents. BOOT. Starting hard, progressing long and round, finishing with a soft distant landing. The classic upfield clearance.

A retiring footballer is said to *hang up his boots*, now a general euphemism used for the end of any long-standing activity, especially one relinquished reluctantly. Similarly adapted to everyday life is the fiercely vitriolic 'He's not fit to *lace his boots*', said of one person's status or ability relative to another. And when a favourite player leaves the club, supporters fret not over who will 'fill his shorts' but whether someone will turn up capable of *stepping into his boots*.

And *fill your boots*, sometimes heard as *stuff your boots*, also has archaic links to football. It means to take full advantage of a situation, usually in an opportune and not always moral fashion. Prior to the legalisation of professionalism in 1885, all players purported to be unpaid amateurs, but club officials keen to secure the best talent were not averse to making clandestine illegal payments. In one favoured mode of transaction, a player would make the mock-shock discovery of 'appearance money' discreetly placed inside his boots before or after the game.

On-pitch action has also made its contribution. A player said to have *got his shooting boots on* finds himself in a particularly rich vein of form.

Even comic fiction has made a lasting impression. The most celebrated footwear in history, 'Billy's Boots', first appeared in a comic called *The Scorcher* in 1970. Billy Dane could never get a game for his school until he put on the ancient leaky, smelly pair of boots once belonging to football hero Dead-Shot Keen, who probably ended up like his boots. With the 'magic boots' Billy was transformed and scored all the time.

It's become a sort of code word for unexpected success. A friend of mine always says 'Billy's Boots' when he thinks he's on a promise.

Such magical potential runs through boot history. Stories of players wearing *lucky boots* until they fall to bits are legion, while former Birmingham City manager Ron Saunders once painted the soles of his team's boots bright red to ward off a curse thought to afflict their ground. African sides, known for their use of witch doctors (*muti-men* or *sangomas*) have even been known to urinate on their precious footwear for similar effect.

In more savoury vein, the humorous writer P G Wodehouse devoted an entire short story to the subject of football boots. 'The Goalkeeper and Plutocrat' (1912) centres around an obsessive collector desperate to get his hands on the boots worn by the early England legend Steve Bloomer. Five years earlier, cricketer-footballer and all round 'clever dick' C B Fry enhanced his reputation for eccentricity by regaling *Daily Express* readers with 'An open letter to a pair of football boots':

Dear old pals, I want to speak to you seriously man to man, because you're not mere dead hide are you? Ah! booties, booties, you little beauties, what a lot you mean to us, yet how hardly we treat you.

Six hundred words later Fry signs off: 'How tightly you will
clasp us, how firmly you will grip our pliant toes. Good-night
booties.' Boot fetishism at its most worrying.

This has to stop. But it won't. The internet auction site eBay
is awash with player-signed discards. Several universities already
offer a degree course in 'football boot technology'. Somewhere
out there at one of our finest educational establishments, there is
surely a bright young student preparing to deliver the ultimate
thesis: *Elegance Borne of Brutality – The Football Boot in English
Language, Myth, Folklore and Literature.* I'd put my shirt on it.
But not my boots.

7

Stuff Not to Forget
– The Kit Business

'Blues, blues, always lose.'
'Green, green, can't be seen.'
'Yellows, yellows, scaredy fellows.'
'Reds, reds, wet their beds.'

Traditional playground chants, 20th century

If you feel undressed without a replica shirt, or have offspring threatening to call Social Services unless you buy them the third-change strip, you'll be looking for someone to blame for your depleted bank balance. Etymologically it's the Dutch. Workmen in medieval Holland kept their tools in a wooden tub called a *kitte*, which English absorbed as *kit* in the fourteenth century, hence *toolkit*. It later came to mean any assemblage of 'bits' forming a meaningful whole. Thus *footie kit*.

Practically though, blame the Italians. *Costume* (Italian = 'custom, what is customary') was first written of in fourteenth-century Florence, *calcio* players being described as wearing 'red and green liveries'. Britain probably wasn't far behind, although the first concrete record is from a 1720 poem describing 'six men of Lusks and six of Sourds' playing near Dublin, both sides wearing all white but distinguishing themselves by *caps* (Latin *caput* = 'head') 'bedecked with red and blue ribbons'. Three centuries later, red and blue still predominate in British football.

Today's strip-obsessed extremes were reached by slow evolution. Initially public schools merely upheld that early nod

65

to headgear tradition. In 1851 W D Arnold wrote that 'for football, all the Rugby School boys wore house caps of different colours'. Footballers might still be wearing caps but for the players of Sheffield FC who invented *heading* in the 1860s. Onlookers regarded it as an eccentric and humorous trick and it was forbidden in the first FA Cup Final (1872), only becoming 'acceptable' in the mid 1870s and finally putting paid to the cap on practical grounds. Now only goalkeepers, not being habitual headers, sport caps. Likewise the tradition prevails in cricket and a universal link survives symbolically when a player is *capped* for an international appearance.

Once caps were discarded, coloured shirts became fashionable, again pioneered by public schools. Engravings show Winchester boys wearing long white trousers (*ducks*) with coloured shirts as early as 1840. Harrow boys wore long whites with matching shirts, still current in cricket. Only the more urgent need for footballers to distinguish opponents from team-mates ensured that colours were to make a lasting impact, credit for their spread going to the author of the 'useful hints' section of *Routledge's Handbook of Football* (1867):

> For excellent fellows at football the prettiest costume is a coloured velvet cap with tassel, a tight striped jersey and white flannel trousers. It is a good plan, if it can be previously so arranged, to have one side with striped jerseys of one colour, say red, and the other with another, say blue. This prevents confusion and wild attempts to run after and wrest the ball from your neighbour.

A stroke of genius! Note again that red and blue prevail.

Early clubs enthusiastically embraced the idea, spawning a huge industry in the last quarter of the nineteenth century. Although kit today has essentially changed little since, linguistic labels certainly have. In 1872 the constitution of the Lancashire village club, Turton FC, stated that 'the Uniform of the Club shall be Blue Knickerbockers, White Stockings and White Jerseys'. *Uniform* (literally 'one form') lapsed into disuse after barely a decade, but *knickerbockers*, *stockings* and *jersey* survived long after the terms were technically obsolete. Knickerbockers, knee-length trousers fastened at the bottom, were named after Diedrich Knickerbocker, a Dutch-sounding pseudonym used by the American author Washington Irving in *Knickerbocker's History of New York* (1809). The book's illustrations depicted the city's early Dutch settlers (New York was originally New Amsterdam) wearing the characteristic garments, so by association the name passed into English.

Although footballers quickly dispensed with the fastenings so that knickerbockers effectively became shorts, the abbreviation *knickers* lived on in football regulations for decades – much to the amusement of schoolboys, aware from the 1880s that it also meant 'women's underpants'. Yet even in programmes from the 1950s, 'knickers' remained standard. Boys found it equally chucklesome that these should be twinned with *stockings*, a term applied to female hose early in the twentieth century. Football, ever slow to react, only adopted wide usage of the double entendre-free *sock* from the 1960s. The 2002–03 edition of *Rothmans Football Yearbook* still used *stockings* throughout. Nor did it help that *suspenders* was still being used for *garters* well into the 1920s, despite also having acquired a feminine meaning. Such are the dangers of linguistic overlap.

Mercifully there's no sexual deviance (unless you're David Mellor, Helen Chamberlain or the wives of Everton's 1995 FA Cup-winning team, all of whom have enjoyed well-documented good times with a football shirt theme) associated with the word *jersey*. It's a *toponym*, a word deriving from a place name, like *rugby*, *badminton* and *jodhpurs*. Channel Islanders favoured their 'knitted buttonless tops', as did footballers from the 1860s. Yet despite lightweight fabrics having long superseded woollies, *jersey* survives even now. Goalkeepers stuck to knitwear right into the 1960s and we still refer to *the goalkeeper's jersey*. Curiously, another of the Channel Islands also gives its name to an item of sporting garb. In Australian Rules football, a player selected for his state *wins his guernsey*.

Keepers also wear *jumpers*, but not for figurative reasons. It's from Arabic *jubbah*, a type of 'loose outer garment'. A *sweater*, on the other hand, was christened figuratively, a nineteenth-century term for a garment to make one perspire.

One other oddity survives. As thousands of football clubs formed in the late nineteenth century, sartorial approach began to be associated with ability. A well turned out team so often proved to be a talented one that even today we describe an effective side as a *good outfit*. Likewise impecunious ones, dredging up kit from the *rag-bag*, are labelled accordingly.

The earliest football uniforms were certainly more robust and tailored than those from the era of baggy shorts and flapping shirts which was to follow. Football wear developed this more flowing style when the game became more competitive and ease of movement surpassed bodily protection in importance.

From the first decade of the twentieth century, new-fangled elasticated-top *shorts* and lighter *shirts* (an abbreviation of *shirting*) made their entrance. It was, though, a struggle. Ludicrous though it seems now, the first shorts caused such a stir that the FA passed a regulation in 1904 that 'knickerbockers shall be long enough to cover the knees'. Several clubs were fined for breaching the rule before the shameless patella flashers were legitimised in 1905 by a subtle amendment that read 'required to reach the knees'. And this in an era when men of station were not averse to picking up a little of what they fancied within sauntering distance of FA headquarters. Never had the double standards of an era been so laughably demonstrated. Only in the 1907–08 season was the law scrapped completely to allow shorts of any length.

But surely *long shorts* is a contradiction in terms? And *short shorts* a cast-iron tautology? In fact *shorts* is merely a contraction of *shortened trousers*. Its Germanic root *skurtaz* (= 'cut', also related to *score*), literally means 'cut-down'. *Shirt* (via Old Norse *skyrta*) comes from the same root, as does *skirt*, both being garments shortened to less than a full length. It's why getting 'short' with someone is figuratively to get *shirty*. The Japanese, by the way, cunningly employ an Anglo-American hybrid to make an unambiguous case for 'cut-down trousers' – they call them *shoto pantsu*.

That's not quite it for the language of kit. There's also such a thing as the 'language of colour'. Although colours developed of necessity, there was also a huge dollop of show, what the Victorians called *swank*. Looking both good and 'different' really mattered. But for those motivations, teams might have adhered to the rudimentary colours favoured by the gentlemen founders of the earliest clubs, who at first made do with everyday clothes. The easiest way to contrive a matching scheme was simply to use what every wardrobe was guaranteed to contain, namely black trousers and a white shirt. If your team still plays in football's most traditional garb, you have sundry lawyers, bankers, clerks and schoolmasters to thank.

Only when competitive games began did differentiation become a real issue, hence the introduction of hoops and stripes, but particularly the single-colour shirt which could be picked out at a glance. The most visible colour in the spectrum is red. In heraldry it signifies magnanimity and fortitude. It spells danger and says beware. It was perfect. Nottingham Forest, initially known as 'The Garibaldi Reds', began the trend in 1865. Bolton Wanderers' first shirts were red. Even Everton wore it during the 1890s. It's the second most popular colour in British football, but appears to be the most successful. In the 104 League seasons up to 2003–04, the Championship-winning club has played in red or red and white on a remarkable 53 occasions. Since the Premiership was founded in 1992 only one side, Blackburn Rovers in 1995, has won it in a first choice strip other than red.

Blackburn's distinctive halved shirts, an authentic Victorian survival, incorporate the most popular colour in British football. Over a quarter of all English and Scottish clubs wear blue. While colour experts say it signifies hope, peace, loyalty, calm, faith and harmony, in truth many clubs chose it simply as a convenient 'opposite' to red, a slavish adherence to 'Routledge's Dictum'.

On the face of it, every club could have opted for red, with a change strip of blue. All matches would now be Reds v Blues. 'Up the Reds' and 'Up the Blues' would be universal shouts. Makers of *rosettes* ('little roses') would have an easy time of it. And the game's culture would be deadly dull. So thank goodness for swank. Why else would Bolton Wanderers' 1884 side have played in white shirts with large red spots? Their resemblance to England batsmen retiring from the crease was uncanny, but they cared not, for they were distinctive! Likewise other 'Fancy Dans'. In the 1860s the Hackney side Black Rovers wore black jerseys with a white skull and crossbones on the breast. Chesterfield larged it in white shirts emblazoned with a Union Jack. Clapham Rovers caught the eye in 'cerise and French grey', and Sheffield Mackenzie plumped for 'plaid cap with pink shirt'.

The game's early records are littered with colours seldom seen today except on the match-cards of the Dulux Heritage Range. *Vermilion, cardinal, scarlet* and *ruby* abounded. All basically red but they sounded good, the same reason why South Korea declared their 2002 World Cup colours as *hot red*. Sides who play in boring black also put a spin on things. It's now officially *midnight*. Also recorded early were *tan, chocolate, azure, amber, ultramarine, magenta, salmon* and *old gold*, but not every club cared for subtlety. In 1915–16, Blackpool fittingly played in garish 'deckchair stripes' of red, yellow and blue. Their famous *tangerine* (from the small orange grown in Tangier) wasn't unveiled until 1924.

Both psychology and practicality influenced colour selection. Arsenal may have clinched the 1989 League Championship at Liverpool wearing their yellow change strip, and Spurs resembled lemon curd in beating QPR in the 1982 FA Cup Final, but yellow – despite associations with sunny Brazil – has never been popular in British football. In Western Europe it's long been the colour of cowardice.

All-white is also uncommon in Britain, being traditionally associated with fear. It's also heat-reflecting, so favoured by those in sunnier climes, most famously Real Madrid. Not that it hasn't had its moments. To emulate the Spaniards Don Revie consciously chose it for Leeds United in 1963, which is probably why it's now so reviled. In any case it smacks of having forgotten your 'proper' kit, and it shows the dirt.

Other little-used colours are purple and green. Purple material, traditionally expensive to manufacture due to the scarcity of suitable dyeing agents, came to be associated with the emperors of Rome, royalty and the wealthy. So despite symbolising power, 'the people's game' hasn't widely embraced it, although swaggering Real ('Royal') naturally use it as a trim. Nor have many British clubs (Plymouth Argyle and Hibernian are notable exceptions) adopted green as their predominant colour, because it clashes with our pitches and is also said to be unlucky. Celtic successfully diluted the risk in electing to play in green and white hoops, but only to acknowledge, like Hibs, an Irish element in their roots. Burnley, with no such axe to grind, ditched their bright green in 1911 purely to change their fortunes, copying Aston Villa's famous *claret and blue* instead. In Africa, by contrast, green is popular, many of their pitches being devoid of grass.

The dearth of outfield green also explains why our goalkeepers adopted it as their traditional colour. Regulations originally permitted keepers to wear green, scarlet, blue or white, but the nation's custodians proved sufficiently bright to realise that green involved the fewest colour clashes. Keepers wearing yellow for internationals weren't making a fashion statement, but merely following the 1921 International Board directive.

That leaves just one major decision. Plain, stripes or hoops? Both stripes and hoops were popular until the Victorian fashion police interfered. Stripes, they said, made a sportsman look taller and leaner than he really is. Hoops bestowed a modicum of girth even on a lanky streak. So rugby clubs stuck with hoops (try naming one that plays in stripes) while most football clubs settled on stripes. Language recognises this. We instinctively know a *rugby shirt* and a *football shirt* apart.

If you doubt the veracity of the fashion psychology, consider the evidence. In 1986, after eight happy years at Liverpool, the human barrel known as Sammy Lee transferred to Queen's Park Rangers. He only lasted a season, fleeing in a traumatised state to Osasuna in Spain. Who did he sign for on his return? Southampton. Paul Gascoigne played for Newcastle United and joined Rangers rather than Celtic. Jan Molby gave Reading a wide berth. And was Matt Le Tissier's loyalty to Southampton an affair of the heart, or were the shirts the clincher? *Quod erat demonstrandum*, as we don't often say in football.

Fans also have issues with stylistic change, away kits bearing the brunt: 'From a distance it just looked pink' was a Brighton fan's take on a wiggly-lined red and white concoction. A Norwich City diehard described one of their own experiments as 'covered in canary cack'. Allegiance to tradition is sometimes demonstrated in extreme ways. Bradford City have always played in the distinctive combination of claret and amber (posh fans call it *burgundy and saffron*), which is the livery colour of Bradford Council. In 1999, one of the Valley Parade faithful achieved a long-cherished ambition to honour the club's constancy, finally succeeding after three years' experimentation in breeding a primula in their colours.

Since the fans took to wearing replica tops in the last few decades, the humble football shirt, once worn strictly by those on the field, has certainly acquired iconic status. The shirt has become the embodiment of both player and club, a state of affairs now reflected in language. Revered players have their shirts *retired*, and those articulating commitment no longer play *for the honour of the club*, but instead talk of playing *for the shirt*.

Yet on balance, the anti feeling associated with shirtdom far outweighs the worship. The majority of spectators still attend matches in civvies. That unease dates precisely to the day in 1976 when Kettering Town further embellished football's linguistic history by becoming the first English club to carry advertising on their shirts. Trying to make 'Kettering Tyres' look sexy was controversial, but it opened the floodgates and changed football's visual landscape for all time.

The now ubiquitous practice of shirt sponsorship may ultimately drive a coach and horses through the most traditional bastions of football language should sponsors, whose names have already been given to grounds, begin to erode the sanctity of club names. Coventry City once seriously considered changing their name to Coventry Talbot after signing a deal with the car company. The FA deterred them, but at non-league level, Vauxhall Motors and Ford United are already a reality. Fans who value tradition fear that Manchester Umbro v Liverpool Carlsberg may not be far away.

It's comforting to imagine that items of kit embracing 'other equipment' are safe from such indignity. Who in their right mind, for example, would want to sponsor a team's *jock straps*? Well actually a computer company, who did exactly that for Aldershot in 1991. Their name escapes me – so much for covert advertising. Lest you are wondering, the *abdominal protector* made so famous by Litesome (how many players actually wore them though?) has nothing to do with Scotsmen per se. *Jock* is just one of many male substitute names (John Thomas, Dick, Percy etc.) used as slang for the male member. As such, *jock strap* is quite risqué in polite company. Like *berk* (rhyming slang = Berkeley Hunt), few who use it realise its origin. Far better to stick to *athletic supporter*, which also doubles as bad pun fodder to aim at fans of Charlton, Oldham and Wigan.

Many other items of 'equipment' appear in football's written archive. Umbrella, glasses, leotard, hairband, French knickers, toothpick, headband, eye-protectors, 'Phantom' mask, beads, 'Lone Ranger' mask, shin-pads, cycle shorts, false teeth, track suit, ballet tights, gloves, electronic tag, chewing gum, sock tags and bra all feature in celebrated on-pitch 'incidents' from football's history. Only the wig, for practical reasons, seems to remain unrecorded. Unless you know different.

Such are the little extras that players through the ages have passed off as part of their 'stuff', or call it what you will. The schoolboy favourite is *clobber*, of unknown origin, probably from Yiddish *klbr* for 'ragged clothes', or Gaelic *clabar* for 'dirt'. Oxbridge types prefer *togs*, again origin unknown, but thought to relate to Latin's *tegere* (to cover), from which also comes *toga*. Not forgetting *gear*, which despite its sixties flavour is fourteenth century. It has exactly the same sense as a gear of a car or machinery, namely 'that which puts something in a state of readiness to function'. And of course *tackle*, from the Middle Low German *takel*, literally 'that which is taken', hence also used for the act of robbing someone of the ball or *taking him out* in the process.

And now it's *strip*. Having only been fashionable since the 1970s it smacks of modernism, but like much in the game it has ancient roots. It's often wrongly assumed to come from 'getting stripped', but etymologists believe it to be a corruption of *stripe*, an old drapery trade term for a narrow piece of cloth just wide enough for a garment to be fashioned from. So, by association, the name for an outfit itself.

Today's strips may seem far removed from a wooden barrel used by a Dutchman to keep his tools in, but for all its modernity, kit is one of the essentials of the game that it's been difficult to alter radically. In that sense, a change is long overdue. But where can it go? Long shorts and retro shirts are already back in and on the way out again. What else is there? In 2002 a spokesman for Umbro let slip the words 'possibly some sort of all in one, like the swimmers wear'. As I write, Cameroon are already parading a fetching one-piece in the 2004 African Nations Cup. Fabric technologists are already developing a 'chameleon' material with its own 'memory' which can display changing messages and images.

So who knows? Could PVC be the new flannel? Will navy-blue serge make a comeback? What price we go full circle? A hundred years from now when we're playing in self-heating spray-on skin paint, some excitable *fashionista* will hit on a cool new idea and give the range a sexy new name. Probably shirts, shorts and socks.

8

Camping Close and Gay Meadow – Your Ground or Mine?

'Some fans would prefer we went back to Plough Lane and played Third Division football. They aren't true supporters. They'll end up buying a season ticket for Fulham.'

Charles Koppel, Wimbledon chairman, spectacularly failing to understand true supportership in arguing for the club to relocate to Milton Keynes, 2001

Anyone who has been to a football match will know that rush of excitement when first catching sight of the floodlights and stands. Britain's football grounds can be all things to all men. The mention of a famous name can make a youngster's eyes sparkle with eager anticipation or an old man's eyes mist with nostalgia.

Thus ran the introduction to Simon Inglis's *Football Grounds of England and Wales* (1983), the first work of its kind and one which heralded an unlikely boom in publications on the subject of football's homes. But the world's premier football *stadiologist* (Aston Villa fan Inglis deserves the title) understood his market intimately. Here's someone who knows that only being 'the first to see the sea' could possibly compete with being 'first to spot the floodlights'. And don't fret if you've been fooled on a rainy November night by the alluring beacons of a goods yard, or the cunning old Rugby League impostors at Wigan. It happens to us all.

75

There's a good reason why *grounds* exert such a powerful emotional draw. Players are fickle creatures who come and go but a ground offers an enduring link – at least until the much reviled 'relocation', when bonds about to be broken are often strengthened anew. This encourages mildly eccentric behaviour.

Twenty or so times a season for 33 years I visited Derby County's Baseball Ground (the sport really was played there in the 1890s) before the club vacated in 1997. Prior to its demolition I drove by once or twice a year purely 'to see how it was'. And I wasn't alone. Several thousand fans willingly paid £6 for a 'farewell conducted tour' of little but a dilapidated shell. Many purchased a souvenir brick. Some were even moved to tears.

The football geographer John Bale labelled this *topophilia*, the strong 'emotional attachment to a place', something which those in authority betray at their peril. Witness the bitter reaction of loyal Wimbledon fans when the club moved en bloc to Milton Keynes in 2003. The fundamental 'sense of place' was lost at a stroke, and with it the entire ethos of a club.

Life goes on, however, sometimes more vigorously than before. Big names have already fallen. Sunderland's Roker Park, vintage 1898, is now a housing estate, road names such as Goalmouth Close the only reminder that anything monumental ever occurred there. But their Stadium of Light is already a beacon in the community. Bolton Wanderers' Burnden Park, immortalised on canvas by L S Lowry in *Going to the Match*, no longer attracts hordes of matchstalk men angled inexorably towards the shrine of their fortnightly pilgrimage. It now offers thrills of the retail kind, which is why most sensible Boltonians have seamlessly transferred their allegiance to the Reebok Stadium. Football fans are emotional souls, but resilient with it. The grieving done, they move on.

Times are certainly changing. Bolton's ground name illustrates a popular christening trend. Other 'new' stadia acknowledging the sponsor's hand are Leicester City's Walkers Stadium, Wigan Athletic's J J B Stadium and Huddersfield Town's Alfred McAlpine Stadium. Note the increasingly obligatory use of the 'modern' word *stadium*, in fact an antiquity (see Chapter 4, 'Classic Encounters').

Scarborough are often cited as the first club to 'sell their soul', having flogged the naming rights to their Seamer Road ground in 1988 to a frozen food company now famous for oven chips. Should Leicester ever visit the McCain Stadium, press references to 'tasty' goals and 'crunching' tackles are a certainty. But Scarborough weren't the first seduced by commercial considerations. In 1910 'Sloper Park' was favourite for the name of Cardiff City's new ground until Lord Ninian Crichton Stuart, second son of the third Marquis of Bute, stumped up a huge wad of cash. In the blink of an eye he was kicking off the opening fixture. At Ninian Park.

For years the only other eponymous league grounds were Walsall's former home Fellows Park (after Chairman H L Fellows) and Bournemouth's Dean Court, named in honour of its benefactor J E Cooper Dean, but more chairmen's wealth-fired egos have recently boosted the list. Reading moved from leafy Elm Park to the Madejski Stadium, likewise Oxford United from the Manor Ground to the Kassam Stadium.

Admittedly they are still exceptions. Most recent nomenclature reflects a shift away from benefaction to corporate money, most pointedly illustrated when Dean Court was recently renamed the Fitness First Stadium. This has presented clubs with a dilemma as they seek to balance the fans' love of tradition against the demands of the money men. Southampton (formerly known as St Mary's) opted for an each-way bet when they moved from their one-time local beauty spot (the Dell) to a brand new stadium. Its 'popular' name is St Mary's Stadium, but its official letterhead address is the Friends Provident St Mary's Stadium. Likewise Bradford City's charmingly named Valley Parade is also the Bradford and Bingley Stadium. Middlesbrough's Riverside Stadium sounds delightful, less so the BT Cellnet Riverside Stadium. Knowing the names of all the League grounds by heart isn't as straightforward as it was.

Most fans and media continue to use the popular names for dual-identity grounds but in time obsolescence is inevitable. Football's past is littered with long-gone homes that once had a magic ring: Donkey Common (Manchester City), Raikes Hall Gardens (Blackpool), Park Hollow (Notts County) and

Plumstead Common (Arsenal). When the Football League celebrated its centenary in 1988 the 92 League clubs had already moved 179 times between them, 88 per cent of the relocations occurring before 1921.

Considering the obvious allure and sheer scale of stadia, it's astonishing that no one before Inglis regarded the game's physical incarnation as remarkable. The revered architectural historian Nikolaus Pevsner was guilty of one of the worst football snubs when he compiled his mammoth series of guides to *The Buildings Of England* (1951). The dullest church is lovingly described, the unusual fenestration of a town hall drooled over. To Pevsner 'the impressive red sandstone mass of the church, cruciform, embattled and pinnacled, with tall Perp central tower and long Victorian apsidal chancel' is orgasmic. Yet he mentions only two football grounds, Wembley and Hillsborough, and then only in passing. He vividly describes a perambulation of the suburb of Everton, every park, monument and public building noted, yet walks past Goodison Park as if it doesn't exist. Likewise in Highbury, where Arsenal's stunning Art Deco presence isn't worth a single word. This isn't just crass, it's distinctly odd.

Not everyone of high intellect is thus immune, hence this lyrical poem in praise of Goodison by Michael Foot:

> When at thy call my weary feet I turn
> The gates of paradise are opened wide
> At Goodison I know a man may learn
> Rapture more rich than Anfield can provide.

Goodison and Liverpool's Anfield are both named after suburbs, a common if rather dull trait in ground naming. Often the labels are narrower still.

Eighteen league grounds are effectively mere addresses. *Road* (12), *Lane* (4), *Street* and *Crescent* one each. But these urban links don't reign supreme. Although many grounds are now hemmed in by residential or industrial development, their names perpetuate football's more rustic past, when all that was needed to start a club was a local recreation ground, common pasture or friendly farmer's field.

Twenty English league clubs currently play at a *Park*, the most common ground suffix. In Scotland the proportion is higher still. Managers talking of happenings *out on the park* merely reflect an earlier age. The word is thirteenth century, its Germanic base meaning 'enclosed space'. Even today the Gaelic for 'football ground' is *pairc*. Chesterfield's ground most closely reflects the place where many clubs started. Sometimes called Saltergate, its true name is simply the Recreation Ground.

Others are deeply steeped in rural tradition. Notts County's 'enclosure' (the Victorians used that label once they started to enclose grounds securely to capture paying punters) is now surrounded by industry, but the way to the pasture which once lay adjacent to the cattle market was indeed via Meadow Lane. That Burnley should play on a 'grand spot of "Turf" adjacent a "Moor"' made their naming ceremony simpler than most.

Antiquarian maps reveal origins for some grounds that long precede a club's formation. An 1843 tithe map of Swansea shows '*cae vetches*', translated as 'a field for growing vetch'. Now Vetch Field is only matched for its lyrical qualities by Shrewsbury Town's celebrated Gay Meadow, the centuries-old local name for the place where village revelries were once held. It's easy to forget that 'gay' once meant 'happy and carefree', which at one time made Shrewsbury's the only ground conveying emotion. Now one other, though it has belied its name in recent seasons, also wears its heart on its sleeve: Derby's Pride Park, which might have been named 'Chaddesden Sidings' in honour of a nearby railway yard, had the fans not been consulted.

Old maps also confirm that communities enjoyed a designated *ground* (Old Norse *grund* = 'grassy plain') for football long before the game's modern days. Early field names include a Football Field (1668) at Stock Harvard in Essex, a Football Close (1659) at North Leverton in Nottinghamshire, and a Football Garth (1628) at Harewood and Kirkleatham in Yorkshire. Maps of the eastern counties, where football was long known as *camping* (players chose between *savage camp* or the more refined *kicking camp*), are replete with fields labelled Camping Close.

Agricultural history plays a surprisingly significant role in football's development. During the eighteenth century hundreds of thousands of acres of previously open countryside were divided by enclosure into the patchwork quilt pattern which came to be England's trademark. That made the brand of rustic football sometimes labelled 'cross country big-side' difficult to pursue, hastening the containment process that ultimately resulted in pitch markings and enclosed grounds.

When the Football Association was formed, pitch markings weren't specified. Four flags, one at each corner, generally did the job, although some participants had earlier anticipated the need for more definite boundaries. Accounts confirm that 'the Free School boys of Hitchin played with rules, lines and goals in 1819'. At Winchester College the solution was more rudimentary but certainly imaginative. In *Football at Winchester* (1890), James Fort recalled that delineation in the 1850s was effected by 'a tightly-knit line of shivering fags persuaded to stand around the extremities of play'. If only for a boy's health, markings had to come. Between 1870 and 1902 they evolved into what must now be the most universally recognised linear 'shape' in the world, though McDonalds' 'M' is a close second.

Pitch markings gave us a couple of curiosities. Early football codes had no goal kicks or corners when the ball went out of play behind the goal line. Instead the first player from either side to 'touch the ball down' won a free kick. The principle continued in rugby but was dropped in football in 1872, yet still the *touchline* defines the playing area.

Secondly the *bye-line* (now commonly corrupted to *by-line*), the popular name for the goal line on which the goalposts stand. Generations of would-be coaches have insisted that every winger's sole quest in life should be to get there, but could they tell you its origin? *Bye* is a centuries-old dialect word denoting 'the corners and two ends of a field impossible to be turned by a plough'. By association the goals at the end of a field attained the alternative but now obsolete name *byes*, hence football's most enigmatic line. In football's early days, near misses crossing the bye area were sometimes counted as 'points' (termed *rouges*, *behinds* or *byes*) to decide the winner of a match which ended level. The 'behind' still survives in Australian Rules football.

Football's chalked delineations finally separated onlooker and player as never before, permanently influencing popular vernacular. Anyone not joining in an activity is said to be *watching from the sidelines*. More generally, people who feel safe and secure in a situation are said to be *on home ground*, whereas the risky business of displaying ball skills on someone else's swampy mire has given rise to *playing away*, a euphemism for extra-marital dalliance.

Once football had acquired this more formal set-up, it turned to a thirteenth-century word meaning to 'fix in, erect or set out in a fixed place'. The *field* became the *pitch*, leaving *ground* to assume the wider meaning of 'a pitch with added appurtenances' – structures to you and me. The lexicon of grounds would never have extended beyond 'Spectators are requested not to strain the ropes', but for the need to provide first 'better' and then increasingly 'hierarchical' spectators' and officials' accommodation. As such, much groundspeak reflects the story of progressive segregation.

Without that process there would be no *terraces* or *grandstands*, no *boys' pen*, *directors' box*, or *hospitality suite*. No *Shelf*, *Popular Side*, *Cowshed*, *Holte End*, *North Bank*, or any of the hundreds of other preferred vantage points that came to be so evocative for the fans.* No colloquial *away end* or the non-PC *cripples' corner*, no *players' entrance* or *technical area*. Just shivering wretches with damp feet and a close-up view of the back of the neck in front.

There are a few etymological show-offs among them. When clubs first provided players' changing facilities with seats out front for their wealthier patrons, it was labelled the *pavilion*, still current in cricket. The originals were the brightly coloured fluttering tents at Roman amphitheatres and later the jousting field, christened via *papilio*, Latin for 'butterfly'.

Less romantic was that part of the ground 'invented' by the Aberdeen coach Donald Colman in the 1920s when he hit on the novel idea of studying his players' movement at worm's-eye

---

* These were favourite standing haunts at the grounds of Tottenham Hotspur, Derby County (and many others), Tranmere Rovers, Aston Villa and Arsenal.

level. He dug a hole at the side of the pitch and stood in it. Most managers now watch from above ground, but their vantage point remains the *dug-out*.

And what of the humble but mysterious *tannoy*, once the transparently named 'public address system'? It's actually a trade name with catch-all status, like Hoover and Biro. It's a contraction of *tantalum alloy*, a substance used in the system.

Top of the etymology league remains the *kop*, strictly speaking the *Spion Kop*. The original and most famous of the giant terraces was at Liverpool, christened in 1906 by the journalist Ernest Edwards. His inspiration was the real Spion Kop, a hill in Natal, South Africa, which British army officers tried to capture in January 1900 during the Boer War. In Afrikaans it means 'lookout hill'. The bungled operation led to the loss of 322 British lives with 563 wounded, many being Liverpudlians attached to the two Lancashire regiments which led the assault. A fitting memorial to those who perished, but, with the trend towards all-seater stadia, destined to become a mere historical curiosity.

That can't be said for ground names as a whole, which hold a continued fascination. Quizmasters love them. What do White Hart Lane, the Hawthorns and Stoke's former Victoria Ground have in common? They all took their names from pubs near the grounds.

An old favourite was 'Which two League clubs have French-named grounds?' The answer was Wolves, whose *Molineux* is the name of a former landowner and a nearby pub, and Doncaster Rovers, now happily back in the League after an interlude in the Nationwide Conference. I've visited their *Belle Vue* many times. There was a view, but alas not a beautiful one.

Who built the original Craven Cottage, which stood on the site of Fulham's ground before it burnt down in May 1888? Too hard? The answer's in the question: the sixth Baron Craven in 1780.

Which are the only two English League clubs whose grounds' titles include all or part of the club name? They used to be Aston Villa and Port Vale, playing at Villa Park and Vale Park. But Crewe Alexandra recently contrived to make it three. Concerned that Gresty Road made them sound too much like an unglamo-rous club from a northern industrial town who have never won a major trophy, their ground is now officially the Alexandra Stadium! Arsenal were sometimes offered as a hotly disputed answer by those shrewd enough to know that the official name of Highbury is actually The Arsenal Stadium. And those not paying full attention to the question were apt to jump in with Celtic, whose Celtic Park would fit the bill if only it were in England. Since relocating in 2003, Manchester City have become a fourth valid answer. How long before the City of Manchester Stadium becomes the Manchester City Stadium? Uniqueness in the English game is theirs for the taking.

Such is the ever-shifting and duplicitous world of the quiz compiler, not averse to a little skulduggery. An old chestnut used to be 'Which League club plays all its games away from home?' The weak answer was always Grimsby Town because Blundell Park is in neighbouring Cleethorpes. Nottingham Forest's City Ground similarly belies its name because it's in West Bridgford, which County fans delight in confirming is outside the city boundary.

So names may change but the British love affair with their *theatre of dreams* (Bobby Charlton coined the phrase for Old Trafford) is stronger than ever. All tastes are catered for. There's a magazine called *Groundtastic*. If you want the manager's toilet seat from the Baseball Ground it's yours via an online auction. The '92 Club', founded in 1978 for those attending a League game at every ground, lives on.

Yet the *OED* is off the pace. *Groundhopper*, for someone visiting as many grounds as possible, often in a short space of time, hasn't made their list of regularly updated new words. And the language is still evolving. We once thought *Astroturf*, the 'plastic pitch' named after the Houston Astrodome where it was first laid in March 1966, was as far as it could go. Queen's Park Rangers made history on 1 September 1981 when they began playing on its relative, *Omniturf*. Luton, Oldham, Preston and Stirling Albion followed suit. The press roared 'IT'S FANTASTIC ON PLASTIC'. Luton manager Ray Harford turned his nose up at Coventry's grass and punned,

'It'll never replace plastic.' In truth Omniturf was dire. Now it too is a historical curiosity.

Instead, at the 2002 World Cup, odd new phrases crept into the language: 'The pitch is being moved into position'; 'They've decided to close the roof';'Surely they should replace the goal area'.

Might these innovations go the same way as plastic? For wordsmiths that would be a welcome boost, extending the life of *quagmire, glue-pot, badly rutted, waterlogged, just like Blackpool beach* (why always Blackpool?) and other staples of dodgy conditions. Whether we play on the *island, deck, carpet, surface* or *greensward*, we all need excuses when things go pear-shaped.

Whatever the future of football grounds, fan opinion suggests they know what they want. A patch of real grass. An open sky. A sense of belonging. Somewhere to call home. 'Twas ever thus. Ask a Bury fan if he prefers Manchester United's ground to his own. He'll look at you in a puzzled way and say, 'Oh no, Old Trafford's not a patch on Gigg Lane.' And he'll mean it.

Did I Not Say That

9

Poorly Parrots and Lunar Leapers – A Game of Two Expressions?

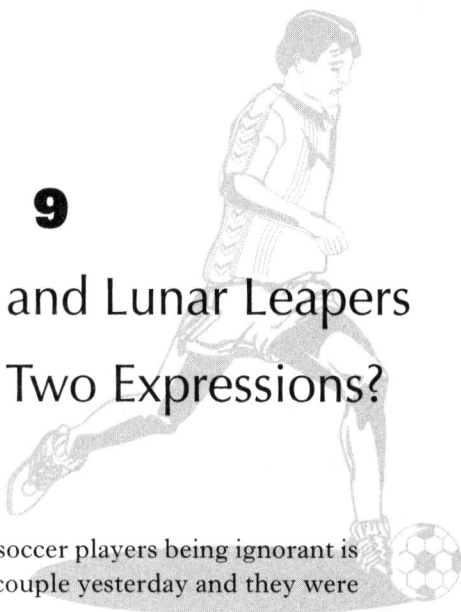

'What they say about soccer players being ignorant is rubbish. I spoke to a couple yesterday and they were quite intelligent.'

Raquel Welch, American actress, after a visit to a Chelsea match, 1973

Had I followed the advice of well-meaning colleagues who suggested a title for this book you'd now be reading *Sick As a Parrot* or *Over the Moon*. Many people, especially the game's detractors, still think these iconic lines define the essence of football itself. Ignorant players, stupid fans, ridiculous game. But they're twenty-five years off the pace. Those tired old catchphrases no longer reflect current football vernacular any more than flat caps and Woodbines represent today's spectators.

Modern players, like parrots taught to talk, now demonstrate verbal skills on cue. Not that they're all Einsteins ('We've equipped [acquitted] ourselves well' is the current phrase), but most can at least feign cleverness once showtime begins.

Many are too clever by far, laughable ineptitude having given way to manipulative and chilling aptitude. Genuine fans find little to chuckle about when Robbie Savage insists that 'categorically there was no contact', despite six different camera angles proving otherwise. Managers are worse still. Arsène Wenger 'did not see the incident'. Alex Ferguson 'saw nothing wrong' in Roy Keane attempting an amputation. Media speak has moved on since the innocent days of poorly parrots and lunar leapers.

So this run through the game's popular expressions is by way of nostalgia. Liverpool's Phil Thompson started all the fun on Wednesday 22 March 1978. Liverpool had just been beaten 1–0 by Nottingham Forest at Old Trafford in the replayed League Cup Final. In the post-match interview Thompson told millions of television viewers, 'I'm as sick as a parrot.'

It was the first high-exposure usage of the phrase and one for which Thompson was mercilessly mocked. Yet had he been a novelist or actor, he might well have been congratulated on his succinct use of imagery. Have you studied many parrots lately? Shoulders hunched, heads bowed, staring dolefully at their own week-old excrement. Brilliantly clothed, yet full of internal suffering. Expected to perform for a gawping public which sees the gilded home, but never the empty husks that litter it. More to the point, have you looked at Liverpool's bench lately? The beaky nose, the shaggy nape. There's more than a passing resemblance. Phil Thompson, master wordsmith, we salute you.

No one knows why he really chose the parrot to articulate his gloom. The writer Aphra Behn used 'melancholy as a sick parrot' as early as 1682. Was Thompson conscious of her work? I think not. Odds are he was merely shortening an old Scouse favourite, 'sick as a parrot with a rubber beak'. Or drawing subconsciously on the then fashionable 'Dead Parrot' sketch from *Monty Python's Flying Circus*.

That's the trouble with trying to rationalise imagery. Words come from nowhere. In 1992 Stuart Pearce saw 'the carrot at the end of the tunnel'. Ten years later Radio Humberside's commentator Dave Gibbins was telling enraptured listeners that 'goalkeeper Gavin Kelly sprang out . . . sprang out . . . like . . . like . . . like an outgrowing radish really'.

The origin of *over the moon* is scarcely clearer, but it was certainly used as early as 7 February 1857. When Lady May Cavendish broke the news of her brother's birth to her younger siblings, she wrote in her diary for that day: 'They were first incredulous and then over the moon', her inspiration probably coming from the eighteenth-century nursery rhyme 'Hey

Diddle Diddle', in which 'the cow jumped over the moon'. But even earlier than that, in 1696, the playwright Sir John Vanbrugh had one of his characters say: 'O Lord, I could leap over the moon.' Alf Ramsey is generally credited with introducing 'moon talk' to football after guiding Ipswich to the First Division title in 1962: 'I feel like jumping over the moon.' Eleven years later, his behaviour moderated by a knighthood, he muddied the waters by stuffily declaring: 'I am not one to jump over the moon, or off a cliff.' In between times, the normally unflappable Bobby Moore got mildly befuddled after England's 1966 World Cup win by declaring himself 'over the world', and Manchester City's manager Malcolm Allison used a variation on the theme pending the club's 1968–69 European Cup campaign: 'My players will take football to the moon.' At that point in its cycle it must have been stuck somewhere over Istanbul, since City crashed out in the first round to Fenerbahce. The most likely explanation for all this lunacy in the 1960s was the race for space which led to the moon landing of 21 July 1969.

Whatever the genesis of the big two, they spread so rapidly, and footballers were so pilloried for resorting to them, that clubs actively sought to wean their players off 'football speak' by engaging professional help. When a Sheffield college instituted a communications course for footballers in the 1980s, the retired pro Jimmy Greaves was quick to respond with due eloquence: 'It's a great idea. If the course had been around in my playing days I'd have been over the moon.'

All of which absurdity suggests that football might well be 'a game of two expressions'. Not so. Football sayings and catchphrases have been around since the game began. Not that any neutral party would ever know it, because the genre has been sadly neglected by the literati.

Take the bible of popular speech, the late Eric Partridge's *Dictionary of Catchphrases*. The 1990 edition contained 'over 4,500 well-known phrases from the sixteenth century to the present day', but astonishingly there was no place for either the parrot or the moon. Nor was the new editor (Partridge died in 1979) apparently aware that 'They think it's all over. It is now' entered general currency the moment it left Kenneth Wolstenholme's lips in 1966. Yet he cheerily tells us that 'hold yer 'ush and watch thi cutlery!' was 'first heard in Sheffield at a dinner in October 1938' and 'go stick your nose up a dead bear's bum!' was 'initially recorded from an Australian infantryman during the Korean war'. So what's going on? A clue comes from the tellingly stilted comment appended to a phrase which did make the cut:

> 'AWAY THE LADS!' – sometimes rendered in print as 'Ho-waaay the laads!' it is, I think, a Geordie cry of encouragement chanted at soccer matches, especially when teams like Newcastle are engaged.

Oh dear. It seems Partridge wasn't entirely at ease with our national game. Calling it soccer was also a giveaway. Whether he snobbishly ignored football's vernacular or was merely ignorant of it (I suspect the latter), neither is forgivable for someone who supposedly had his finger on the pulse of 'everyday speech'.

Nor are today's books redressing the balance. Your search for 'Do I not like that' in the 2002 edition of *The Oxford Dictionary of Catchphrases* will be fruitless, despite it being one of *the* catchphrases of the last ten years since the hapless England manager Graham Taylor said it to camera for a Channel 4 documentary shot during England's 2–0 World Cup qualifier defeat against Holland on 13 October 1993. 'Yes boss' (Phil Neal), 'Back of the net' (Alan Partridge), 'Diabolical defending' (Alan Hansen) and 'It's a marathon not a sprint' (George Graham) are nowhere. Nor are 'Sexy football' (Ruud Gullit), 'I'll love it if we beat them, love it' (Kevin Keegan), and many others in regular currency throughout the pubs, offices and factories of Britain. David Ginola's pouted 'Because I'm worth it', does make it, but only through the back door of advertising. Yet the book includes 26 phrases from *The Fast Show* and 14 from *Dad's Army*.

The oldest popular phrase linked to football is a proverb, first used for literary effect in the 1590s in Christopher Marlowe's

The Tragedy of Dido. Rarely used today, 'All fellows at football' suggests that all men are equal in the face of adversity and that the game itself cuts across social divides. That's true, but mostly from a one-way perspective. Football has long been a 'gentleman's' way of mixing it with the *mob* (short for *mobile vulgus* = 'excitable crowd'), but the feeling hasn't always been mutual. During the 1925 England v Wales game at Swansea, the England captain Alfred George 'Baishe' Bower (Charterhouse School, Corinthians and Chelsea) had a quiet word with his over-robust team-mate at right-back: 'Now then my man, we want none of that.' The response of plain old Billy Ashurst (Notts County) is a minor classic: 'Thee! Thee fuck off.' Bower could have dredged up another centuries-old proverb to suggest to his insubordinate charge that life would pursue its inexorable course come what may, but wisely he elected not to use 'The world is round, like a football'.

The current edition of *The Oxford Dictionary Of English Proverbs* contains no football examples (are we surprised?), but if you want to do your bit there are a number of ancient sayings that can be seamlessly slipped into general conversation. 'Life is itself but a game of football' (Sir Walter Scott, 1815) and 'Lookers on see most of the game' (sixteenth century) are useful. 'The best form of defence is attack' is conveniently reversible, and 'There is nothing like leather' (seventeenth century) has a certain figurative allure.

Nor do proverbs have to be old. 'It only takes a second to score a goal' (Brian Clough) and 'It's a funny old game' (Jimmy Greaves), could both be applied to life's little ironies, as can the useful catch-all 'That's football'. You don't have to append 'Brian', but it adds a knowing touch if you do.

Others might best be avoided. Only use 'The cup's a great leveller' if you're prepared for the riposte that the Aberdeen club Bon Accord lost 36–0 to Arbroath in the 1885 Scottish Cup. Nor is it wise to rely too heavily on Cantona-isms. It's far too easy to get your seagulls, trawlers and sardines horribly muddled, although choosing something completely meaningless can sound impressive: 'When the fox plays badminton with the goose, the shuttlecock is the loser' is said to be one of Eric's.

It's worth trying 'The plastic pitch is a red herring' (Graham Taylor) or 'Only dead fish swim with the tide' (erstwhile Cambridge United boss John Beck).

Closely related to proverbs are truisms, defined by the *OED* as 'self-evident truths, statements so obviously true as not to require discussion'. 'It's a level playing field' is a good example, except for devotees of Sunderland. When they lost at Yeovil in the 1948–49 FA Cup, they blamed Huish Park's sloping pitch. Best example by far is 'It's a game of two halves', used since the Victorian age as a perfectly valid half-time reminder that things can change. Its ultimate descent into circus was sealed by Billy Wright, a bumbling sidekick to Hugh Johns on ITV's *Star Soccer* in the 1970s. Using the phrase every week for many seasons transformed a sensible truism into a much-derided cliché, something of value said so often that its worth becomes diminished.

Wright may have been a supremely confident footballer, but broadcasting wasn't his forte. There's the clue to why we're now awash with 'recent' football soundbites but bereft of truly early examples. Radio and televison have spread football into everyday speech as never before.

It's easy to forget that for the first forty years of League football, the voices of players, managers and club officials were simply not 'heard' by the public at large except through the lower-impact mediums of newspaper reports and football magazines. A limited number of catchphrases were coined in the Victorian and Edwardian eras via crowd banter and music-hall turns (at least 150 pre-First World War football-related popular songs have been traced), but few survived in the absence of media exposure.

There's only one real dinosaur. Today's 'Up the Arsenal' etc. is a shortened survival of the Victorian favourite 'Play up', widely used as a crowd exhortation, hence 'Play up Newton Heath' rather than today's 'Come on you Reds'. It embraced ancient connotations of fair play and pluck, but in football literally meant 'play upfield', the 'attack-attack . . .' of a century ago. It still survives intact for Portsmouth supporters as 'Play Up Pompey, Pompey Play Up'; the so-called 'Pompey Chimes' are the oldest known surviving football chant.

The catchphrase boom only began with football broadcasting. The first nationwide radio coverage was on 22 January 1927 when Arsenal v Sheffield United was covered by the BBC. A novel medium and a countrywide audience eager to share the experience provided perfect conditions for the birth of a catchphrase. It didn't take long. Before commentators developed good techniques to indicate spatial positioning, the BBC helped listeners by printing a pitch plan in *Radio Times* divided into eight numbered 'squares' which were referred to during commentary by 'the square man' (for years it was Derek McCulloch, better known as children's broadcaster 'Uncle Mac'). Although the idea was largely abandoned by 1940, the exposure via the nine million radio sets then in use was such that *back to square one* quickly entered everyday speech and is arguably football's most famous legacy.

In truth it was probably first used in hopscotch or snakes and ladders, but football certainly popularised the phrase that signifies 'a reluctant return to the beginning'. That meaning has confused phraseologists who haven't seen the grid. Several books assert that 'square one was the centre circle, where a side had to kick off again after conceding a goal'. Even the *OED* misunderstands it. In fact square one was in left-back territory, extending halfway across the penalty area. The phrase was simply the embodiment of an aborted attack, typically a pass back to the keeper. Anoraks will already have sussed that squares two, seven and eight carried exactly the same meaning. And super-semantic anoraks who know their pitch dimensions and geometry will have computed that the 'squares' are in fact oblongs. Football's number one offering to 'everyday English phrases' is an arrant phoney.

More influential than radio was television. Experimental football coverage began in Britain in 1936 when a German match was shown, but the first live domestic coverage on 16 September 1937 treated London viewers to the delights of Arsenal v Arsenal Reserves. The 1938 Cup Final between Preston and Huddersfield was the first final to be televised live in its entirety. The truly big date for televised footie wasn't until 22 August 1964, when BBC2 showed highlights of

Liverpool 3 Arsenal 2. They called the 45-minute programme *Match of the Day*.

Television has never looked back, introducing new words to the dictionary (*action replay, player cam, slo-mo*, etc.), and spawning scores of everyday colloquial phrases. There would be no 'look away now' without television newsreaders. Paul Whitehouse would never have conceived 'jumpers for goalposts' and 'Small boys, enduring image, isn't it?' but for seeing the mildly eccentric Fulham manager Alec Stock in interviews from the 1970s. He was the prime inspiration for Ron Manager.

Many catchphrases currently doing the rounds are from television advertising. Once the first advert was shown on 22 September 1955 (Gibbs SR toothpaste – 'Tingling Fresh') it was inevitable that companies would use footballers in commercials.

Danny Blanchflower and family ('Pass the milk, Mum') were among the first to take the plunge in the early sixties, but incongruously the first advert to create a lasting football catchphrase didn't feature the game at all. In 1972 Wonderloaf bread identified a jolly chap from Nottingham as the baker of a particularly good loaf with the tag line 'Nice one Cyril'. It was fortuitous that Tottenham's left-back at that time was Cyril Knowles, and even more so that he gave the White Hart Lane 'Shelf' reason to sing his praises by sneaking a rare and particularly deft goal while the advert was current. In no time at all 'Nice one Cyril' and its variants had been commandeered by football crowds, and the ditty 'Nice one Cyril/Nice one son/Nice one Cyril/Let's have another one' was taken to number 14 in the charts by the Cockerel Chorus. Cyril Knowles died in 1991, aged only 48, but his name lives on in the slogan, now terribly dated but still used to praise a cunningly attained achievement. Nice one Cyril.

A more short-lived slogan from the same era was 'E for B and Georgie Best', used by the Egg Marketing Board and later transmogrified to 'E for B and Charlie George'. Best's love of the product was genuine: 'I always have an Egg for Breakfast every day. They help me keep fit and in trim and I don't get that sinking feeling before dinner time.'

Lest you doubt the veracity of such claims, consider the favourite beverage of Jimmy Greaves: 'I train and win on Bovril right through the season.' Surely they weren't both telling porkies for cash? Best's embryonic affinity with ad-speak later took a literal turn. Playing in North America late in his career, he explained to the press, 'I saw a sign which said "Drink Canada Dry", so I thought I'd give it a go.'

Once players actually started to 'act' in adverts there was no stopping them. In 1975 Pat Jennings leapt around the goalmouth for Unipart, backed by the memorable slogan: 'A goalkeeper is like an oil filter'. Stops things getting past, or full of crap and soon needs replacing? Who can say? He shamelessly followed that by purring 'Great save Tony' to a cartoon tiger for Kellogg's Frosties.

Kevin Keegan's 'Splash it all over/great smell of Brut' antics with Henry Cooper really opened the floodgates. Keegan was snapped up by Shredded Wheat in 1979, and since then, Jack Charlton, Brian Clough and Glenn Hoddle have all asked 'Can you eat three?' Keegan's duplicity in matters cereal has been troublesome. He later appeared for Sugar Puffs with their mascot, which scored for Newcastle in the advert. The same mascot later appeared in goal for Manchester United, making possible the most unfair pub-quiz question of all time: 'Who is the only person to play in goal for Manchester United and score for Newcastle?' And there's no point complaining to strict quizmasters that the Honey Monster isn't a person.

Once in a while, serious lexicological inroads can be made through advertising. Who would possibly know that *isotonic* means 'it's in balance with your body fluids' but for John Barnes's Lucozade-fuelled vending machine attack during Italia '90? And without Gary Lineker's Walker's crisps stunts, 'Salt 'n' Lineker' and 'Cheese 'n' Owen' would never have passed the nation's lips.

It's tempting to ask 'Where will it all end?', but of course it won't. More adverts feature football than ever before. If we're not suffering from Adidas-related 'Footballitis' or coveting the 'Va Va Voom' of Thierry Henry, we're telling the nearest football to "Ave it!' in the style of Peter Kay. By the time you read this there will be many more.

Football's commercial value is very clear. So clear that its use in advertising has become gratuitous, not to say irritating. Appallingly choreographed action sequences are the norm and ranks of cheery fans sporting brand new scarves and bobble hats amazingly still appear. Influential people in advertising usually haven't got a clue about the game they exploit so freely.

All of which makes the occasional own goal particularly refreshing. In 1989 the American sportswear company Nike plugged its new slogan with a lavish TV ad shot in Kenya, using Samburu tribesmen. At the end, the camera closed in on a young blood speaking his native Maa language with the translation 'Just Do It' flashed on screen. Not until an anthropologist provided a true translation were Nike prepared to admit to a blooper. He'd gone off script and was actually saying, 'I don't want these. They're too small. Get me some bigger ones.' 'We thought nobody would know,' explained a spokeswoman, wiping her face clean of George Best's favourite breakfast fare.

Even great players have made unwise decisions. During the 2002 World Cup, Pelé not only made himself the champion of the 140 million worldwide sufferers of *disfuncao erectil* but also the butt of much ribald comment. He told countless millions of TV viewers: 'If my car broke down, I'd phone a mechanic. If I suffered from erectile dysfunction I'd go to see my doctor. Speak to your doctor. I would.' It was only a matter of time before someone (a Portuguese reporter) queried the vicarious use of 'if' and 'would': 'Have you had to resort to magic tablets at the moment of truth?', he asked. To which 'The Black Pearl' stiffly replied, 'Never.'

Pelé may wish he'd chosen another cause, but he certainly isn't an unintelligent man any more than today's players are the 'muddied oafs at goal' once derided by Rudyard Kipling. In any case, people who know football have long since learned to laugh at verbal slips in the face of the far more worrying ills that beset the game. What else can you do when a player earnestly declares 'It looks like it's going to be déjà vu all over again'? Even the usually articulate Gary Lineker made it into *Private Eye*'s 2002 *Colemanballs* with 'It's a tense time for managers.

They have to exhume confidence.' But we all know Gary's not daft. Nor a vampire.

At the end of the day, when half the world is well chuffed and the rest fair gutted, when the fat lady has sung and the 'we wuz robbed' quotes have been collected, football's contribution to the English vernacular should be celebrated, not ridiculed or ignored altogether.

So lobby Her Majesty to give Phil Thompson a knighthood, and next time you hear a parrotism remember the wise words of Stockport County's Uruguayan manager Danny Bergara. Having never quite mastered our tongue, he was asked by an interviewer in 1991 whether his limited grasp of English was a disadvantage in dealing with players. Bergara's reply spoke volumes: 'Football is a game – the language it don't matter. As long as you run your bollocks off.'

10

From Oxford Fellows
to Britney Spears –
The Shameful S-Word

'Biathlon. Luge. Soccer. Three of a kind.'

The Plains Dealer newspaper, Ohio,
comparing football to the Winter Olympics in
anticipation of the 1994 World Cup, 1990

Football fans are regularly roused to states of high dudgeon by 'things said'. When Manchester United lost at home to Arsenal in 2002–03, Alex Ferguson's indignant assertion that he abhorred players who 'continually surround the referee' sent all but United followers apoplectic. I was once similarly enraged by Alan Shearer's peevishly delivered diatribe along the lines of 'I don't care a stuff what the fans think, I only play football for Alan Shearer and my manager, nobody else'.

Blessedly, such gems of self-delusion are generally one-offs. There's one single word, however, used both repeatedly and knowingly without even a hint of regret, that's guaranteed to raise the hackles of more genuine domestic football-lovers than any other term in the game. It's football's most shameful word. Anyone for *soccer*?

Tradition suggests it was coined via the 'Oxford -er', a peculiar abbreviation habit beloved of late nineteenth-century Oxford undergraduates. According to this explanation, the word is just a

98

modified contraction of 'asSOCiation football'. This self-indulgent and affected '-er' practice created a rather smug and exclusive world in which the young students started the day with a hearty 'brekker', took some 'ecker' in the gym before lunch, played 'rugger' in the afternoon, 'badders' in the evening, and tried their hand at getting some nice young lady 'preggers' before lights out. There was no end to it. Queen's College was 'Quaggers', the Bodleian Library 'the Bodder', and the Prince of Wales the 'Pragger Wagger'. In 1903, one writer satirised the habit by alluding to 'the receptacle for the detritus of one's rooms' as a 'wagger pagger bagger'. Which explains one of the reasons (though not the main one) why 'soccer' is so disliked by most fans. It's traditionally used by what are perceived as 'posh people'.

Anecdotal evidence attributes the word's first utterance to Charles Wreford-Brown (known inevitably as 'Reefers' to his chums), a student at Oxford in the late 1880s. Asked if he fancied a spot of 'rugger', he supposedly replied, 'No, I'd rather play "soccer".'

Like many self-perpetuating yarns, it's never been seriously queried. Yet surely it doesn't quite ring true. Association football, after all, was born in 1863, when the '-er' practice was already well established. Documentary evidence shows that Harrow boys called football *footer* years before, so are we really to believe that it took all of twenty-five years for an upper-class wag to label the association version *soccer*? Wreford-Brown might well have shed some light on the matter, but at a time when the minutiae of football weren't as keenly examined as they are now, no one seems to have asked him. His *Times* obituary of 1951 fails to mention the soccer tale at all.

Might it be more instructive to consult the *OED*? Not much. It traces the word's first usage to 1889, spelt *socca*, which by 1891 had generally become *socker*. Only from 1895 do they suggest that *soccer* became the accepted form. Yet that's by no means chapter and verse, because *OED* citations were sourced from limited samples of known literature that didn't include the popular football newspapers and magazines of the day.

So could the term be much older than we're led to believe? Mindful of the *socker* spelling, it's tempting to look for much

more ancient roots which might render the 'Oxford -er' theory
nothing more than a fortuitous second coming. Could Wreford-
Brown have merely dredged *socker* up from his younger days as
a Charterhouse schoolboy? And might the ancient school have
in turn used it for centuries? Such alternative theories carry an
'Approach with Caution' label, but the dictionary definitions of
sock suggest a number of possibilities.

The original *sock* of the Middle Ages, from Latin *soccus* via
Old English *socc*, wasn't a 'sock' as we know it today, but 'a light
shoe of leather or cloth such as might be used for exercise and
play'. Since the *OED* traces a *footer*, a noun meaning 'a kick at
a football', to 1781, might a sock-wearing medieval footballer
have been a *socker* man? And could 'footballe-playe' have been
socking? From at least 1700, *sock* has certainly meant 'to boot
something' or 'hit very hard'.

Earlier still, from the fifteenth century, a *sock* was also a name
given to both a ploughshare and, by metaphoric linkage, 'a
muddy field'. One particularly imaginative football historian
has sought to rewrite the dictionary entry for this one by citing
an account of a football contest witnessed by Mary Queen of
Scots in 1568 while she was imprisoned at Carlisle Castle:

> Hyr grace went owte at a postern to walk on a playing-
> greene toward Scotland where 20 of her retinue played
> footballe for 2 howers, strongly, nymbily and skilfullye,
> the smalness of theyre balls accassyoning theyre fayr play.

At first glance this seems insignificant, indeed ideal fodder for
the fanzine humorist who'd doubtless conclude it must have
been a cold day and have ended in a draw, hence the 30 minutes
extra time. But maps of Carlisle contemporary with the account
reveal a curiosity, for the 'playing-greene' is clearly labelled the
'Castle Soceries'. Might a *socerie* have been a designated field
for exercise and play? And 'let's to soccer' an age-old cry?

Since other archaic meanings of *sock* also relate to leisure
pursuits, this has seductive potential. The *Scottish National
Dictionary* lists *sock* as an archaic verb meaning 'to idle or relax',
adding a citation from 1825 that 'the sockin hour was the time

of rest in the early evening before lamps were lit'. Did energetic boys of old engage in *socker* until darkness fell, just as they do now? *Routledge's Dictionary of Historical Slang* is also appealing, listing *a soccer* from the 1770s as 'a sloven, lout, simpleton or fool'. Such as might have played football, evidently. And finally, *sock* was also nineteenth-century public-school slang for 'a treat' or 'other pleasurable leisure pursuit'.

The danger in making serious claims for any of these as *soccer*'s true and much earlier derivation is that it's all too easy for amateur sleuths to 'make it all fit'. In his book *Word Ways* (1970), John McClellan coined the new word *logastellus* for such enthusiasts. Not wishing to be accused of being one, I can do no more than sit on the fence. But it's all food for thought.

Should you find a footballing reference to 'soccer' before 1887, a letter to my publishers would oblige so Wreford-Brown can be relieved of his weighty responsibility. And if you can trace the big one, a pre-1863 'soccer', get straight on to the *OED* and rewrite football's folklore.

Origin apart, what remains undisputed is *soccer*'s power to divide. Although the word didn't truly start to rankle until the 1980s, the germs of unease between the different codes of football began to multiply early. After the Rugby Football Union was founded on 26 January 1871, the oval ball 'handling' game came quickly to be known as *rugby* or *rugger*. But many of its more bloody-minded followers insisted on abbreviating 'rugby football' simply to 'football', despite the fact that use of the hands far outweighs that of the feet. This semantic battle of wits was even reflected in early sporting literature. When the Reverend F Marshall wrote the first substantial history of rugby in 1892, it wasn't clerical error that moved him to boldly title it *Football*, with the addition of *The Rugby Union Game* on the title page almost as an afterthought. This early show of obstinate elitism began a trend that is still current.

Although no publisher would sanction Marshall's title now, a recognisable breed of *rugger-bugger* still insists their game is *football* and ours is *soccer*. The appearance of more 'rugby is superior' books led James Catton, the doyen of early football writers, to fight back. His pointedly titled *The Real Football: A*

Sketch of the Development of the Association Game, published in 1900, only makes sense in the context of rugby's opposition.

The schism also extends to rugby league. On 29 August 1895 at a meeting in Huddersfield, 21 northern rugby clubs broke away from the Union to form the Northern Union, which in 1922 became the Rugby Football League. Even today *going to the football* is common parlance in Lancashire and Yorkshire for watching rugby league.

It follows that stalwarts of both union and league persist in referring to football as 'soccer', reason number two why football fans dislike it so much. For many adherents of rugby, association football is at best a secondary and at worst an inferior game, one played by 'wimps' rather than 'real men'. Rugby types often use *soccer* as a word of insult. For similar but less vehement reasons the use of *soccer* is widespread in the Irish Republic, whose own traditional football is what we term 'Gaelic football'. To emphasise the point, the Southern Irish Gaelic for association football is actually *sacar*.

Equally in Australia, whose fervently pursued *footy* played on huge oval pitches is what the British have come to call Australian Rules football, *soccer* is habitually used for the association game. Hence their national team, 'The Socceroos'. With this in mind, it might be said that the British are equally guilty of rechristening 'alien' games. That's why we call 'football' of the American variety American football, a term never used by the Americans themselves. But therein lies a significant point. The modified terms we apply to these mutated football codes have respectfully accorded them a national identity. By the same token, maybe outsiders should call our game 'British football' not 'soccer'. We could actually be proud of that.

Alas, the Americans had no such respect. Their habitual use of *soccer* is the third reason, and by far the main one, why the s-word has attained its controversial status. American football (if you really want to annoy them call it *grid-iron*, a term they hate), essentially a modified form of rugby, began to take its own peculiar shape in the early 1880s. By the time the first Rose Bowl game took place on New Year's Day 1902 in Pasadena,

California, it was recognisable as the game now played by members of the National Football League. Because of this, Americans have been calling British football *soccer* since the late 1880s. There's even a remote possibility that it was they, not Wreford-Brown, who started the fashion. Yet it was to be almost a hundred years before *soccer* began truly annoying football fans. Indeed, from the 1920s to the 1970s, many British-published books and magazines carried 'soccer' unashamedly in their titles. This was partly because chroniclers of the game were often ex-public school but also because 'soccer', like most slang terms, neatly suggested an informal and rather trendy air that 'popular' punters and journalists were happy to embrace. Television picked up the same vibes. By the 1970s ITV, who favoured a razzmatazz approach, liked 'soccer', while the BBC preferred the more traditional 'football'.

As long as Americans only dabbled in the game, something they'd done since the formation of Oneidas Football Club in Boston in 1862, thought to be the first football club founded outside England, British fans remained largely unconcerned. Only when they made a concerted effort to manufacture the popularity of the game from the late 1960s, did labels become an issue.

The North American Soccer League, founded in 1968, changed everything. It not only pursued marketing campaigns but also meddled with the game's established rules and terminology, all aimed at selling 'our' game to an American public with no feeling for its traditions and scant understanding of the way it should be played. That's really why *soccer* is now such a reviled word.

America's penchant for cultural hijacking soon became apparent. A header becomes a *head-shot*, a diagonal pass a *quarter-back ball*, a volley a *shot on the fly* and a first-time effort a *one-timer*. A penalty is a *penalty-shot*, the penalty area the *violation-zone*. Draws are *ties*, and goalkeepers *net-minders* who much prefer to *field an accelerating ground shot* than to save a low drive in the land where keeping a clean sheet isn't as much fun as *posting a shutout*.

American newspaper accounts of football matches are full of such modifications. When David Platt scored the last-minute winner in the England v Belgium 1990 World Cup game from a Gascoigne free kick, one American agency said he 'flipped in a foul shot by Paul Gascoigne in overtime'. John Harkes was one of the first American players to move into English football; the *New York Post* ran the news under the headline: 'HARKES WILL BE GOING TO SHEFFIELD, WEDNESDAY'. Television commentators are no better. Were you aware that Harkes was also 'the first American to set cleat on Wembley'?

Yet in keeping with the general creeping Americanisation of British English, football has actually begun to import some of the very terms we once scoffed at. Forty years ago we didn't have *penalty shoot-outs*, *one on one situations* and *gameplans*, nor were free kicks *set pieces* and training ground routines *drills*. Good sides looked to 'top the League' not *head the standings*. Now half-time is increasingly *the interval* and what follows is far too regularly *the second period*. The thick end of the wedge is upon us.

Lest you should be more relaxed than me about the soccerisation of football language, a few examples of how Americans relate to the game might prove sobering. Some are vaguely amusing, witness the New York Cosmos executive commenting on Franz Beckenbauer's masterful deep-lying role for the club in the 1970s: 'Tell the Kraut to get his ass up front. We don't pay a million for a guy to hang around in defence.' But far too many either carry real vitriol or are just plain dumb.

In 1990 the *Philadelphia Enquirer* said:

> Americans are masters at developing more complex and advanced games. We will watch soccer, but only in the improved form of ice-hockey, which is soccer speeded up to the point where it becomes semi-interesting.

And as early as 1967 the *Louisville Courier* was telling its readers that 'soccer is a game where mostly twenty-one guys stand around and one guy does a tap dance with the ball'.

A sign at Lime Kiln Park in Grafton, Wisconsin, says it all: 'SOCCER NOT ALLOWED. SOCCER MAY ONLY BE PLAYED IN ARCHERY RANGE'. Should you need still more convincing, consider the *Los Angeles Times*'s survey of 'America's Most Popular Sports' from 1991. Soccer came 75th out of 114, fourteen places behind beach volleyball and forty-four adrift of the 'sport' that finished 31st. Tractor pulling.

If you're tempted to think that Americans might latterly have become enlightened since their women became world champions and their men began performing admirably in World Cups, then a brief search of the internet suggests otherwise.

Among many anti-football diatribes from the States the most vitriolic must be *Soccer Sucks*, six pages of dismissive rant by one Genghis Goldberg. Starting gently with 'the game is either called soccer or football depending whether you have a life or not', he warms up with 'soccer isn't a sport, it's an exercise in mass denial, a desperate attempt by the runner-up nations of the world to protect themselves from the spread of American consumer culture by clinging to a pastime no rational person would consume'. After that comes his 'analysis of the play' which reveals that 'the offensive strategy is to get the ball as close to the goal as possible then lift it over the penalty area with a so-called crossing-pass which usually results in a botch scooped up by a jogging keeper'. His authoritative conclusions are that American football is 'much faster than soccer' which 'just isn't any fun to watch'.

All of which means we should try to ensure that *soccer* doesn't usurp *football* in the English vernacular. But word preservation isn't that easy. Some speakers of American English seem to believe that theirs is the original word and ours the impostor. In a television interview on 29 April 2002 the pop icon Britney Spears was asked, 'What do you know about football?', to which she gave the corrective reply 'You mean soccer.' To his considerable credit, the interviewer Eamonn Holmes replied with only part mock anger: 'No, I mean football.'

Another American entertainer, Andy Williams, became even more confused in a particularly embarrassing British television interview during the 2002 World Cup when he admitted: 'I don't know much about football. I think you call it soccer.'

The Japanese apparently side with the Americans by calling football *sakka*, but they have among their number at least one devotee with an eye for tradition. Step forward Mir Behrad Khamesee to present his brilliant mini-treatise entitled 'The World Game Should Be Called Soccer or Football?':

> Soccer is also known as football in different countries. In my opinion football could be the most suitable name for the sport. The word clearly explain the sport. Foot + ball isn't it? Humorously it means 'foot' kicks 'ball', but why not say feet? Because you cannot efficiency kick the ball with your pair feet simultaneously.

So that makes it clear. Yet it's ironic that Khamesee-San's preferred medium for his evangelistic campaign is the internet, which is perversely inveigling more and more British football devotees, entirely against their natural inclination, to use the word *soccer* on their websites. For search purposes it's the only effective way of distinguishing our game from American football. A trawl of the Google search engine for 'football' produces 21.5 million hits, but US domination of cyberspace dictates that nearly half relate to 'grid-iron'. Left to marketing men, this book would probably have been called *Soccer Talk*.

This is a perverse dilemma, one in which Americans could effectively preside over the slow *logocide* ('the killing off of a word') of 'football' by trapping us into doing the deed ourselves. So may all 'real football' men have the courage of their convictions and heed the game's unwritten dictum: 'Do not use the s-word as it may offend others'.

To that end, the last word goes to an anonymous Victorian whose 'Ode to Association Football' leaves no doubt that 'the only game' is a deserved epithet:

> Too sacred to name,
> With thy posts, ball and field,
> There is no winter game,
> To which thou cans't yield.

11

Ever Been Nutmegged?
– It's a Slanging Match

'All it wanted was a little eyebrows to the back stick ,
and the lad would have scored for fun.'

Ron Atkinson, TV pundit,
expertly analysing a corner kick, 1998

During my research for *Football Talk*, public response to the
subject matter has been both enthusiastic and strangely consistent. By far the most popular reactions were: 1) 'Remember
nutmeg.' 2) 'Don't forget the back stick.' 3) 'Aha, early doors.'

Others were more forthcoming. A pensioner seemed
desperate to assure me that when he kept goal in the fifties the
net was freely referred to as the *chicken run*. A six-year-old
flummoxed me completely by asking why he'd heard Andy
Townsend call the pitch *the island* when it wasn't surrounded
by sea and didn't have palm trees.

It quickly became clear that football-speak, and particularly
slang, stirs the mental faculties across the age spectrum. That
fits a leading lexicographer's assertion that 'the chief use of
slang is to show that you're one of the gang'. The message is
clear. Slang is both cool and exclusive.

And always has been. Victorian reporters confidently wrote
that 'Meredith sent in a *hot grounder* which only narrowly
failed to bisect the *sticks*', knowing that their regular readers
would understand. It's the same now. A *hot grounder* for a
strong low shot may have long fallen from use, as has the

107

thirties favourite *stinger* for a shot of uncanny velocity, but today's language is full of equivalents: *bobbler, daisycutter, shinner, fizzer, looper, scuffer, dipper, blaster, bender, purler* and *rasper*. Each conveys a clear visual image to the football lover but an equally fuzzy one to outsiders. That's where exclusivity kicks in. That rarest of rewards, true kinship, only comes to those in the know.

Consider those terms deriving from key incidents in football history. All need decoding, but thanks to television you probably won't need help with a 'Ronnie Radford', a 'Ronnie Rosenthal', a 'Nayim', a 'Frankie Wortho', a 'Scorpion Kick' or an 'Enckelman'.*

There are hundreds of these eponyms, each club having its own 'dictionary'. A 'Roger Davies' probably means nothing to most fans, but in Derby it's missing an open goal from two yards out and falling down in the process. These don't just enter the language willy-nilly; each has a precise genesis with a definite date. Some are used universally, like *doing a Beckham* for any attempt to score from near the halfway line, which simply didn't exist before David Beckham successfully performed the feat in 1996 for a huge television audience.

Yet therein lies a tale. The *OED* doesn't plan to list it in its next edition. Neither does the *OED* include the artful subterfuge which is a *Cruyff turn*. But bizarrely it does honour an American high-jumper from the 1968 Olympic Games by giving chapter and verse on the *Fosbury flop*. Once more, I'm bound to remark that our nation's lexicographers seem strangely blind to football's claims.

---

* 'Ronnie Radford' – a long-range goal in which the ball displays an uncanny homing instinct.
'Ronnie Rosenthal' – hitting the bar from an 'unmissable' open goal.
'Nayim' – a speculative goal attempt via a long-range up-and-under; it becomes a 'Seaman' when successful.
'Frankie Wortho' – a score on the volley after an audacious overhead pass to yourself.
'Scorpion Kick' – a bizarre acrobatic goalkeeping technique, saving the shot with the back of the heels.
'Enckelman' – a 'ball under foot' goalkeeping howler.

Not that it would be wise for them to suddenly become conspicuously football literate, because the true art of football slang is never to use it gratuitously. Only a dilettante would habitually refer to the net as the *onion bag* (if you've ever seen balls being carried on to the training ground in a net slung over some hapless junior's shoulder you'll appreciate the imagery), nor would a real football fan use *little eyebrows* (glancing back header) or *back stick* (far post) except in jest. It's also not a good idea (unless, like Ron Atkinson, your entire persona owes much to an inventive use of slang) to award a *spotter's badge* to any player making a perceptive pass or to describe a well-populated penalty area as a *crowd scene*. Even if you're truly desperate to be 'one of the gang', resist the temptation to describe any bit of nifty footwork as a *Joe Cole, lollipop, bunny-hop* or *stepover*. Sooner or later you'll be made to look stupid. Usually sooner.

Becoming slang proficient takes time. Starting early helps. Lexicologists have shown that children are first tempted by its risqué allure around the age of six, starting with innocent nonsense speak. Adults are generally wary of singing the praises of Beckham-peckham, Giggsy-wiggsy, Fergie-wergie or Arsy-warsy, but juveniles are quite comfortable with such whimsy. Backslang (saying words partly or fully backwards) is also a favourite that generally dies with adulthood, which is why people might look askance if you and I talked about *toofball* or *toofie*. But I clearly remember them being used in my own school playground.

Having said that, grown men do revert to childhood given half a chance. On the five-a-side pitch I've heard men earnestly discussing whether or not to allow *rush goalies*, who should have *first picksies*, and cheerily issuing an 'accounts department stick' challenge to the boys from marketing. A company's chief accountant once shamelessly pulled rank by shrieking '*bagsy* last in goal'.

Some essentially juvenile slang goes freely into adulthood. *Footie* and *footy* for the game itself are laddish favourites. *Togger*, a relic of nineteenth-century Oxford students, is much rarer. And in Scotland *fitba* is used consciously to differentiate *their* game (they perceive it as stylish, gritty and with its own distinct heritage) from that played by English softies.

This confirms football's status as a medium through which adults (men in particular) can legitimately behave in a childlike manner, if only for ninety minutes a week. Players indulge in exactly the sort of rough and tumble they first experienced in the playground, getting dirty without being told off by their mothers. The language reflects that freedom. We *play* football. Len Shackleton, Sunderland's famous England international of the 1950s, summed it up perfectly: 'When we were small boys, we knew what football meant all right. Football was what we did when they set us free.'

As for spectators, there aren't many places where fully sober adults can sing silly songs, shout their heads off, use rude words and jump up and down like mad people without being stared at. At football you can. It's regression therapy without the psychiatrist. Juvenile slang helps oil the wheels.

Then comes the adults-only hard stuff, Cockney rhyming slang. It's said to have originated as part of a criminal argot used by those wanting to talk to fellow villains in front of outsiders without being rumbled. It's certainly been popular from the mid nineteenth century. So it's no surprise to find football-related examples, although the range of those in regular use is narrow.

Football itself is sacrosanct. According to rhyming-slang dictionaries, it's never been given the treatment. In truth nothing much interesting rhymes with *football*. The pick of a miserable crop in the *Penguin Rhyming Dictionary* are *Bengal* and *bookstall*. Instead it's 'Football pools', honoured as *April Fools*, that set the ball rolling. In case you're unfamiliar with the rules, it's common for the rhyming word to be dropped in speech, so if you manage to 'come up on the Aprils' you'll be very happy indeed.

This same technique explains football's most celebrated example, used countrywide since the 1950s: *bristols* for the female breasts = 'Bristol Cities' = 'titties'. City fans consider themselves privileged, although to be better known for an association with mammarian magnificence than for on-field success must be a dubious honour. Why not invoke more successful teams? 'Manchesters' has a certain fullness about it (it's actually used in Australia), and surely someone's missed a double trick with 'Chesters'. The 'professor' of vernacular speech, Eric Partridge, approached the subject far more gravely. His *Slang* stoically asserts that 'the Bristol club were favoured purely because of an "initial" similarity to the word breasts'. How dull.

Few other clubs have made it into the Cockney dictionary, and when they do the actual usage of the terms is sporadic. The likelihood of hearing the following sentence is about as remote as Sven-Goran Eriksson not saying 'anything is possible in football' during an interview: 'Cor blimey, did you see the *screaming Alice* play the *string o' beads* last night? Talk about *West Ham reserves*, I had no nails left.' That's Crystal Palace v Leeds, a game so tense it affected the poor man's nerves. Glasgow Rangers ('strangers'), Stoke ('Stoke on Trent' = 'bent') and Barnet ('Barnet fair' = 'hair') are the only other clubs similarly honoured.

But don't expect to hear these gems every day. The idea that London's East Enders come down the *apples and pears* every morning, give the *trouble and strife* a peck on the cheek and tootle off for a day of authentic rhyming Cockney with their *chinas* ('china plates' = 'mates') is, you'll be amazed to learn, slightly wide of the mark.

Which makes it all the more pleasing to hear it for real. For the best rhyming slang in football, watch games on Hackney Marshes. Sooner or later a captain will, I promise you, bawl to his incommunicative charges: 'Come on lads, let's have some *bunny*.' *Bunny* = 'rabbit' = 'rabbit and pork' = 'talk'. Hence also the use of *rabbit* for incessant chatter.

Another dead cert is the exhortation '*up 'is arris*', directed at defenders known for their enthusiasm in the tackle. You'd be spot-on translating the phrase as 'tackle him so vigorously from behind that you might penetrate his rectal passage', but guessing the link isn't so easy. *Arris* = 'Aristotle' = 'bottle' = 'bottle and glass' = 'arse'. It's been used at least since the Football League began. Easily the most common usage of rhyming slang on the field is for 'balls'. But not the leather kind. For some odd reason, players hit in the area commentators like to call 'the lower abdomen' or 'groin area' always announce it to all and sundry. An anguished cry of something like 'aaargh, right in the balls' is typical. As if we hadn't noticed; that's why we're laughing hysterically. Popular substitutes are: *Orchestras* ('orchestra stalls'), *Henry Halls, Niagaras* ('Niagara Falls'), *town halls, cobblers* ('cobbler's awls') and *maracas* ('knackers').

And beyond rhyming slang the repertoire is endless. *Bollocks, family jewels, nads* ('gonads'), *taters, plums, cods, lunchbox, packet, pills, stones, nuts, privates, unmentionables, wedding tackle, meat and two veg, rocks, conkers, apricots, love-apples* and the foreign imports *goolies* (from Hindi for 'pellet') and *cojones* (Spanish for 'balls', first popularised by Ernest Hemingway). If you score a direct hit on an American, you'll also hear *agates*, although why they should equate their manhood with only semi-precious stones is a mystery. That's 29, and I've probably missed at least another dozen.

Listen out long enough and you'll probably hear all those because they're all in current use. Not so the more obscure examples of rhyming slang; many of those listed in dictionaries are either short-lived or deliberately contrived for effect.

No way will *Mikkel Becks* ('specs') stand the test of time. The Danish forward has already been superseded by those more illustrious rhymesters *Posh and Becks*. A few players, mostly southern based, have had their names similarly hijacked. *Sol Campbell* ('ramble'), *Steve Claridge* ('garage'), *Bobby Moore* ('score') and *Glenn Hoddle* ('doddle') have been treated gently. But surely there's a hint of malice about *Rodney Marsh* ('harsh'), *Brian Clough* ('rough'), *Dwight Yorke* ('pork') and *Don Revie* ('bevvy'). And it seems a shame that players who have done it at the highest level should have entered the English language for all the wrong reasons. *Gianluca Vialli* (= 'Charlie' = 'cocaine') might well wonder why he ever bothered to come over here. And surely England's 1966 World Cup winner *Nobby Stiles* (= 'piles') deserves better. Life has been kinder to that game's hat-trick hero. Every degree candidate now aspires to a *Geoff Hurst* (= 'first'). Regrettably we've also linked the puffed-cheeked one with the post-exam celebrations, so having a raging *Geoff Hurst* (= 'thirst') might also leave you dying for a *Geoff Hurst* (= 'burst'). Shouldn't they be allowed to sue? *Terry Butcher* ('tail-toucher' = 'homosexual') might have a case, and *Ben Cartwright* (= 'shite') must be aggrieved. But the player I feel most sorry for last kicked a ball in 1968. A hundred and eighty games at centre-half for Stoke, Oldham, Sunderland and Middlesbrough doesn't exactly make George Kinnell a legend, but it's not a bad record. Which makes it pretty unfortunate that his lasting contribution to British life will forever be as rhyming slang for 'fucking hell'. It's a cruel old game.

I'll leave rhyming slang by way of *sausage roll* ('goal'), *Hampden Roar* ('score') and *Georgie Bests* ('breasts'), but not before getting seriously to grips with *nutmeg*, the celebrated slang term for cheekily popping the ball through an opponent's legs. Cocky players sometimes shout *nuts* or *megs* when they pull it off. But it's one of those terms whose etymology is still very woolly. The accepted version is that *nutmegs* = 'nuts' which, being round, are established slang for testicles. Hence it's a sort of ribald taunt aimed at the duped victim. It's no use asking the *OED* to verify it. It lists *nutmeg* in 156 connotations, but amazingly ignores its football usage entirely. That leaves us with Jimmy Hill, who is on record as saying: 'When I was playing for Brentford in the late forties I well remember *nutmeg* coming into vogue. *Nutmegs* was simply rhyming slang for legs.' A female internet correspondent disagrees, asserting that 'it's a contraction of "not through my legs"'. Maybe we'll pass that one over. Personally I think it's a much older and more erudite term than we've previously believed.

Although it does have scrotal links (it actually means 'musk-flavoured nut', via a tortuous route from the Sanskrit *muska* for 'testicles') that's surely far too complex a connection to waste on a flat-footed full-back too stupid even to keep his legs closed.

So what of the alternatives? It's actually the *OED* that stumbles unknowingly over what's probably the true derivation. It lists *nutmegged* as a verb arising in the 1870s which in Victorian slang came to mean 'to be tricked or deceived, especially in a manner which makes the victim look foolish'. It arose because of a sharp practice used in the nutmeg trade between America and England. Nutmegs were such a valuable commodity that unscrupulous exporters were wont to pull a fast one by mixing a helping of neatly turned wooden replicas into the sacks being shipped to England. In the 1850s Connecticut, the centre of the scam, was nicknamed 'The Nutmeg State'. 'Buying a wooden nutmeg' or 'being nutmegged' soon came to imply stupidity on the part of the duped victim and cleverness on the part of the trickster. Informally, to *meg* was to swindle. Considering that so much of football's language dates from its formative years, I'll vote for that one.

Mercifully, much football-related slang is more transparent. Take the 1940s favourite *a football team*, used to taunt someone sporting a woefully sparse moustache (i.e. 11-a-side) or the name Ron Atkinson likes to use instead of the unwieldy 'angle of post and bar'. Will Beckham hit the *postage stamp*? It has been known.

There was a time when he'd have done it using the *banana shot*, now eclipsed by *curler* or *up and over*. *Banana shot* first came to be favoured by British commentators during the sixties to describe a skill for which the Brazilians were particularly noted. The imagery was perfect. The shape was right, the shot was a potential banana skin for hapless keepers, and the Brazilians even played in yellow. Nor did *banana shot* generally cause offence, although the commentator who said 'let's see what the Brazilian bender can do with this one' during the 1970 World Cup might have chosen his words better.

So why the decline? It's probably a victim of political correctness gone mad, over-fastidious broadcasters having condemned the good old banana shot to obscurity because the fruit itself has featured in shameful racial taunts.

Evidently this slang business needs approaching with caution. Jonathon Green's monumental *Dictionary of Slang* contains a number of entries which seem innocent enough but could create cross-cultural havoc. It's fine in Britain to say David James has a nice *drop-kick*, but in Australia it's rhyming slang for something else, based on its full form, 'drop-kick and punt'. Also from down under, a *footballer* is a prison warder who likes kicking the inmates. In America a *football* is a half-grain measure of a narcotic. Southend United fans are particularly advised to be careful if visiting the States, where being a devoted *Shrimper* implies a leaning towards foot fetishism, especially toe-sucking.

Even the most recently coined terms are potentially troublesome. Be careful what you wear for one of those last-day-of-the-season cliffhangers where the radio never leaves your ear. They're now officially *trannie matches*. A suitable note on which to leave the bizarre world of football slang. Please don't be too *Rodney* if I've missed your personal favourites. It's only bit of a *woolly* after all. Still baffled? *Woolly bobble hat and scarf* = 'a laugh'.

On the Island

12

Snotching and Notching –
In Search of That Elusive Goal

'Gazza said that scoring was better than an orgasm.
Lee Chapman reckoned it wasn't as good. I'll go with
Pelé – he thought it was about the same.'

Ryan Giggs, Manchester United, 1994

Scoring is the best thing a player can do, but it's not easy. Hot
favourites France exited the 2002 World Cup after failing to
score a single goal, yet their squad included the leading scorers
from the Italian, English and French leagues. One of the most
common scores in football is 0–0. The *goalless draw*, *nils*, *none-apiece*, *nought-nought*, *nil each*, *none-none*, *nil all*, *zilcho*, the *big fat zeroes*, *a pair of specs*, *naff-all*, *zip-zip*, *nowt each*, a *blank scoresheet*. Whatever the euphemism, ancient or modern,
countless matches are barren.

But that's the illogical beauty of football, and it's been
so for centuries. In Ashbourne's Shrovetide match, a celebrated prehistoric survivor, it's not unusual for the ball to be
goaled only once every few years despite the games lasting
two days. It's because the ultimate objective of football is so
difficult that the game is so popular. Anything worth
achieving, like a 'goal in life' which shares football's meaning,
has to be worked at.

Those who suggest 'making the goals bigger' (usually FIFA
representatives or Americans) don't seem to understand this.
When 13–12 becomes a typical result, the game's dead.

So it's fitting that *goal* is also an elusive word. Most dictionaries list it as 'origin unknown', merely confirming that its
earliest use denotes a 'boundary' or 'marker' at the extremity of
a territory. Written evidence dates from 1314, when it was spelt
gol. That certainly produces a football tie-in. The practice in
mass games was always to return the ball to a designated marker
on home territory, usually a well, wooden post, tree stump, mill
wheel, hole in the ground or other prominent feature.

The *OED* doesn't entirely admit defeat, listing *goal* as 'of
difficult etymology', but its editors are obviously puzzled. The
rules of descent, they say, suggest that *gol* should come from the
earlier Old English *gal*, from the verb *gálen*, meaning 'to sing,
cry out or celebrate'. But they then pose a rhetorical question:
'What link could there possibly be between a boundary marker
and unbridled acclamation?' Anyone seeing a goal celebration
Ashbourne-style as the ball is knocked three times on the pole
could certainly enlighten them. The idea of 'goal' being a
thousand-year-old metaphoric derivation from a word
encapsulating joy and abandon is an appealing one.

Other possible origins are equally seductive. *Góle* in Old
French meant 'throat, mouth or gullet'. The Old Norse for 'a
well' was *gola*. Could the Vikings have christened football's
most sacred word? *Bloomsbury's Dictionary of Word Origins*
adopts a defender's stance, suggesting the Old English verb
goelan, ('to hinder or prevent'), might have led to *gol* for a
barrier or obstacle, thence by association to the 'boundary',
'finishing line' or 'something to be breached'.

Dr Johnson's *Dictionary* (1755) takes a different tack: 'Goal
comes from the French *gaule* meaning "pole"', states the
corpulent one with absolute authority. It does mean 'pole', but
he was only cribbing from *Skinner's Etymologicon* (1671). The
OED, possibly not au fait with archaic football, rubbishes the
idea as having 'nothing to recommend it', as there is 'no
evidence to link goal and pole'.

There are more. It could be related to Old Germanic *khulaz*,
which gave us Old English *hol* for 'hole' or 'hollow', since the
idea of the ball being 'holed' or 'hidden' was central to some
ancient versions of the game. The modern Welsh for goal is still

gol, corrupted from *col*, the geographic term for a rounded hollow. Or consider the historic contests between the 'Uppies' and 'Doonies' of Workington, where a goaled ball was said to be *haled*. That's related to the Old English *geholian*, 'to acquire, hold or keep'.

The true origin of *goal* remains elusive but tantalisingly within reach. What is consistent is the idea of the ball being taken home, returned to an extremity, or otherwise 'captured'. In the latter sense *goal* has even been linked to Middle English *gaol*, now more commonly *jail*, from the Roman *gaviola* for 'cage'. There's a case for any or a combination of these. I favour the most ancient, the Old English celebratory link, but the jury remains out.

Not in dispute is that *gole, goale, gowle* and *goal* were being used in football contexts by the sixteenth century, quickly acquiring a metaphoric usage too. Take politics in 1577: 'I purpose, before he beare the ball to the goale, to trippe him if I may'. The first professional foul. And early inter-county rivalry from 1594: 'The goale is lost thou house of Lancaster'.

The first reference in a football (in the guise of 'camp-ball') context is sometimes cited to prove that 'goal meant *game* in early English'. That's not so. The playwright John Day does write in *The Blind Beggar of Bethnal Green* (1600) 'I am Tom Stroud of Hurling, I'll play a gole of camp-ball', but he merely substitutes the object of the game for the game itself, like playing 'nine holes of golf' or 'a hand of cards'.

The first really specific reference has a modern ring. In Carew's *Survey of Cornwall* (1602) he says:

> They pitch two bushes in the ground which they term their *goales*, where some indifferent person throweth up a ball, the which whosoever can catch and cary through his adversaries goale, hath wonne the game.

That's the first allusion to *goalscoring*, itself a term linked to antiquity. *Score* comes from Old Norse *skor* for 'cut' or 'notch', used from the fourteenth century for 'a mark to keep account of times or amounts, kept on a board or tally'. Farmers gave twenty sheep a single notch, hence 20 is a *score*. Games later used this system for 'keeping the score'.

Old public school slang for scoring a goal was a *snotch*, a marriage of *score* and *notch*, and today's strikers are still said to '*notch* a hat-trick' or 'add to their season's *tally*'. A last-minute goal is scored 'in the *nick* of time'. Strictly speaking, for any player to 'score' a goal is a misnomer. Victorians always referred to goals being 'won' or 'gained', as did the early rules. The only person truly to 'score a goal' is the referee, whose duty it's always been to keep the record. Teams no longer 'win' goals, but when we say 'United have just *lost* a goal' it's a definite nod to the past.

Right into the early twentieth century, *goaler* rather than *goalscorer* was being used for the man who *netted*, to recognise this semantic distinction. Today's fans subconsciously do likewise, musing not how many goals a striker will score, but how many he'll *get*.

Similarly the man *in goal*, like the employee in a job or lessee occupying a property, was known as the *goalee*. Witness the *Spectator* in 1926: 'One can imagine an indignant Cockney ejaculating as he regarded the rotundity of the Red goalee'. Only in the 1930s was he corrupted to today's *goalie*.

Every keeper strives to *keep a clean sheet*. Romantics fancy this comes from the days before goal nets (first 'invented' by the Liverpool-based engineer James Brodie in 1890), fondly imagining teams erected a sheet behind the goal. Not letting any in 'kept it clean'. Alas, nothing so lyrical. Clubs were obliged by the Football League to fill in an official scoresheet, hence the common request from managers: 'A nice clean sheet today lads, please.'

The goalscoring business can be confusing. Youngsters at their first match generally ask the chucklesome question, 'Which is our goal and which is theirs?' It's not as daft as it sounds. 'We're trying to kick the ball into *their* goal' is just a bit too simple. Mass football always required the ball to be taken from the starting point (usually the market square) back to a side's 'own' goal on home territory. Naturally each side ranged itself between their opponents' 'own' goal and the attacking force, instantly giving the game its back-to-front character still mirrored in modern football, where the market place has long been replaced by the centre circle. Echoes of the idea exist in a side's preference for attacking 'the home-end' goal where their own fans are massed, ready to verbally assist, 'suck the ball into the net', and roar acclaim. Consider too the forward who *slams the ball home*.

Only the vagaries of time have led to today's topsy-turvy terminologies, so there's no doubt now which net the ball has hit when a player commits the most shameful act in football, scoring an *own goal*. Heads are clutched, the ground beaten, men normally the epitome of confidence reduced to squirming embarrassment or stunned into shamefaced silence. It's the goal which dare not speak its name. Even abbreviating it to *o.g.* doesn't lessen the crime. It's become both a verb ('Adams o-g'd again') and a figure of speech. Scoring 'a political own goal' can be more calamitous than the real thing.

It follows that football's best goalscorers are the most revered men in the game. Every side wants a 'star striker' or 'natural goalscorer', but it takes men of special stealth to secure the prize. Chances are *taken*, goals *stolen*, *plundered* or *poached* like prize pheasants. Ronaldo *bagging a brace* is nothing to do with his dentist.

Good strikers don't dwell on past failure. They are 'never afraid to miss', always convinced that 'a rich vein of form' lies ahead. Some, like Allan 'Sniffer' Clarke, once of Leeds, have a *nose* for them. Others are *goal-hungry* or *goal grabbers*. Goals are a drug, football's very lifeblood.

The language of failure suggests that without them all life may yet cease. Forwards suffer a *barren spell*. There's a *goal drought*. When it all comes right *the floodgates open* and we drink in the pleasure that only a *goal glut* can bring. A *feast* of them sends us *goal-crazy*.

It's emotive language, and we're back to celebration. Look at a wedding photograph for a display of happiness and radiant contentment. Or a christening group for pride. But for all those and more study a photograph of a crowd the instant a goal is scored. Expressions of sheer joy, an emotion seldom encountered in any other walk of life, are everywhere.

Social commentators and some players have likened this massive release of pent-up frustration to sexual satisfaction. Since the 1970s *score* has even become established slang for a sexual conquest. The 'which is best' debate divides football, but one element of the magic moment is purely mythical. Despite cartoon strips suggesting otherwise, no one shouts 'Goal!', and certainly not 'Goooaaal!', as the ball billows the net. 'It's there', 'It's in', and 'Get in there' are popular. So are expletives. Spoof commentator Alan Partridge favours 'Eat that' or 'Twat!'. But by far the most common is the simple affirmative 'Yes!', or 'Yeeees!' if its a thirty-yarder. And the 'Yes, yes, yes!' of a goalmouth scramble can sound remarkably climactic. Watching football next to an excitable female can be quite distracting.

England's Nat Lofthouse titled his autobiography *Goals Galore*. Ronnie Allen chose *It's Goals that Count*, Roy Bentley *Going for Goal*. Jackie Milburn went for *Golden Goals*, Allan Clarke *Goals Are My Business*, Gary Lineker, *Golden Boot*, Alan Shearer *Goal Machine*. Goalscoring clichés abound. 'He knows where the back of the net is' applies to them all. They all have 'an eye for goal'. These are men who 'know the score'.

Boundary, pole, throat, hole, cage or raucous abandon? *Goal*'s origin will remain as elusive as the act it represents. As an anonymous Victorian scribe so eloquently put it: 'Time after time the leather sphere was thrust goalward, but at the call of time not a single player of either side had been able to feed that yawning, gaping mouth.'

13

Eskimos 50 Footballers 166 – A Few Words on Kicking

'Every language has areas in which it needs to be more expressive than others. The Eskimos have fifty words for types of snow, though curiously no word for just plain snow.'

Bill Bryson, *Mother Tongue*, 1990

The act of kicking is central to football's very existence. Yet like *goal*, another fundamental, the word itself is a mystery one. The *OED* tells us only that it comes from the Middle English *kike* (origin unknown), has been used since the fourteenth century, and means 'to strike with the foot'.

But beyond that simple definition is another world. It's technically possible to play and describe football without using substitute words for *kick*, but the game would be much duller for it. Nobody would *stroke, blast, place, lift, nick, hook, hammer* or *sky* it, all testimony to the subtle ability of the English language to describe things or actions by degree.

That enables us to convey instantly not only the strength with which the ball has been, or ought to be, kicked, but also the direction it moves in, the 'shape' of its course, or the distance it travels. When a defender *launches* it we know the ball has travelled high and long. *Drilling* it forward means keeping it lower, but still long. When he *slips* it we know he executed a deliberate pass rather than a general clearance, one not only shorter but along the ground. If a forward *slots* it, that immediately suggests both a goalscoring scenario and an image of the ball being pushed low, precisely and without maximum pace into one corner of the net. But if he *slams* it home or *buries* it we know the finish was just as effective but less measured, and probably from close in. If it's *slewed* wide or he *screws* it on to a post, it's a World Cup year and England are going out.

This is both a remarkable facility of English and a real testimomy to the subtlety of football itself, for players, fans, commentators and writers all use these words instinctively as a sort of code to suggest not 'roughly' what has happened but 'precisely' what has occurred. Football people select carefully between a *lob*, *chip* or *dink* to convey exactly what was done to the ball. Think about trajectory. If I asked you to draw a flight profile of each word, you probably could.

Football's language really can be that fine-tuned. Did Giggs *curl* it or simply *tonk* it? Was the pass from Scholes *pinged* from deep or *threaded* from an advanced position? 'Kick' is one word seldom used in genuine football circles. Children favour it, but only until they realise that it just doesn't do the job.

Sceptics might say this is mere embroidery, but accurate communication is vital if the game is to be played and appreciated fully. Rapid shorthand instructions to team-mates are essential. Hence *touch* it, *line* it, *knock* it, *lay* it and *slide* it all tell a man in possession what is expected of him. Commentators and reporters use similar words to paint a picture for absentees.

Such linguistic precision isn't confined to English. Most popular books about words tell us that 'the Eskimos have 50 words for types of snow but no word for plain snow itself'. The Italians apparently have 500 names for types of pasta. Natives of the Trobriand Islands of Papua New Guinea are said to have 100 words for yams, while the Maoris of New Zealand, for reasons only they must know, have 35 different terms for dung.

Fascinating as such snippets are, no proof is ever given. Bill Bryson highlighted this in *Mother Tongue*, which tells us that 'the Arabs are said to have 6,000 words for camels and camel equipment' before adding sceptically, 'a little unbelievably, perhaps'.

With that in mind I intend to break with tradition by adding concrete evidence to football's claim. So far I've used a mere 29 'kick' synonyms for ways of *addressing* the ball. That's 30 now. Only 20 behind the Eskimos. By the end of this chapter you'll no longer be marvelling at their half-century of snow words, but wondering instead why Eskimos are such dullards when it comes to expressing themselves. All the following are from genuine reports or commentary.

Particularly expressive are 'power words', especially the onomatopoeic slang words such as *thwack* and *whack*. Most are reserved for scoring opportunities:

Smash, thump, crash, ram, crack, blaze, fire, smack, lather, lammer, leather, blatter, bladder, belt, rifle, cream, lash, paste, larrup, stick, lace, hit, rasp, drive, dig, welly, thrash.

For situations requiring rather more deftness, the language is softer:

Place, tap, measure, roll, flick, tickle, waft, cushion, angle, tuck, notch, dribble, stab, poke, prod, nudge, dab, sweep, scrape.

Defenders enjoy their own special vocabulary. Forwards missing golden opportunities are occasionally said to *hoof* or *boot* the ball, but unsubtle defenders regularly do both. Erudite commentators also have them *hefting* and *heaving* the ball, while those closer to the earth describe it as variously being *lumped, humped, piled, slugged* or *punted* upfield. Only creative full-backs are accorded subtlety. Balls are *floated* in, *splashed* forward, *lofted* into the box, *hooked* goalward, *slung* long, *swung* deep, *centred* low, *crossed* early or *looped* into the danger zone.

Passers of the ball are another breed again. They *spread* it, *deliver* it, *spray* it, *send* it, *play* it, *move* it, *give* it, *release* it, or simply *pass* it. Sometimes they choose to *bend, swerve* or *spin* it, either *dispatching* it quickly or *caressing* it first before *presenting* it to a colleague. All manner of subtleties can be suggested. The deftest touches are often said to be *glanced*, but I've also known lay-offs to be *shaved, feathered* and *chamfered*, each a perfect use of imagery to convey the subtlety of an angled touch.

Commentators are ever inventive with delivery words. Passes
are *trundled, trawled, relayed, posted, conveyed, spiralled, cork-
screwed, arced, served* and *plied*. Some may sound inappropriate,
but dictionary definitions generally validate the football usage.
To *trawl* is essentially to 'drag'. To *ply* is to 'work steadily' or
'present constantly'. *Trundle* means 'to roll slowly and un-
evenly, sometimes laboriously'. A certain intellectual whose
name I forget, once asserted that 'all football commentators are
institutionally illiterate'. He was obviously wrong.

There are failure words too. Besides the obvious *miskick*,
players *shin, ankle, slice, foozle, misplace* or *scuff* it. Other kick-
words denote technique: *volley, half-volley, sidefoot, backheel,
toe-end* and *toe-poke*.

That's Eskimos 50 Footballers 141. And there are other
methods besides kicking. Take goalkeeping, where balls are
*handled, fisted, thumped, parried, fielded, gathered, collected,
received, palmed, tipped, turned, deflected, fumbled* and *punched*.
And of course the ball can be *headed, nodded, nutted, back-
headed* or even, according to Ron Atkinson, *eyebrowed*. And
chested, breasted or *kneed*.

Two things are certain about all of this. One is that if you've
got this far you'll already have thought up several contact words
I've not used. Like plain old *shoot* for one. Although it's usually
only children who say 'he shot it into the net', it must take its
place. Second is that the next commentary you listen to will
throw up some new ones, like *slivered* and *slide-ruled* for passes
made through the eye of a needle.

Enough is enough. Next time someone tries to amaze you
with tales of Eskimos and their 50 words for types of the white
stuff, here's what to do. First ask them to prove it. They won't
be able to. Then casually remark that you're surprised it's not
more. Finish by telling them there are at least 166 words in
English to describe how footballers make contact with a ball.
They might hit you, in which case I'm very sorry for starting
something. Alternatively they could ask you to prove it.
Which you will.

14

Unspeakable Cads
and Dirty Devils –
Foul Play Through the Ages

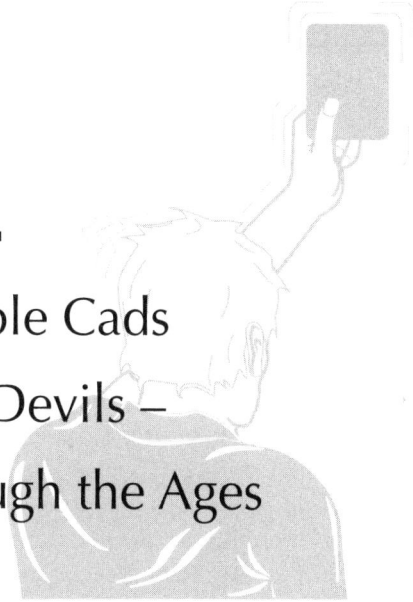

Batty would probably get himself booked playing
Handel's Largo.

David Lacey, the Guardian, after the Leeds player was
booked in the Charity Shield, 1992

Never be fooled into thinking that players of yesteryear were
angelic souls forever apologising to each other for the most minor
misdemeanour. Foul play is as old as football itself, and with a
colourful language to match. Take social commentator Philip
Stubbes in *Anatomie of Abuses in the Realme of England* (1583):

> As concerning football playing, it may rather be called a
> friendlie kinde of fyghte than a play or recreation, a bloody
> and murthering practice than a felowly sport or pastime.
> For dooth not everyone lye in waight for his adversarie,
> seeking to overthrowe him and picke him on his nose so he
> have him downe? He careth not whatever place and he that
> can serve the most of this fashion he is counted the only
> fellow, and who but he?

Indiscriminate violence graphically described. Victory for the
devious cheats. It could easily have been the Leeds United side
in the 1970s. And there's more:

So that by this means sometimes their necks, backs, legs or arms are broken, sometimes their noses gush out with blood or their eyes start out. But whosoever scapeth away the best goeth not scot-free for his adversaries have the sleights to meet one betwixt two, to dash him against the hart with their elbowes, to butt him under the short ribs with their griped fists, and with their knees to catch him on the hip and a hundred other such devices.

There we are. The *sandwich, deliberate elbow, kidney punch* and *dead-leg* fully four centuries before Jack Charlton made the first entry in his retributional 'little black book' and Vincent P Jones introduced Paul Gascoigne to that playful old device known as 'grabbinge ye gonads'.

Although the mob game described by Stubbes was 'cleaned up', like much else in British society, by the zealously fastidious Victorians (sanitation, accommodation, prostitution and education, so why not *pedipulation?*), many who played organised football did so with the determined conviction that 'rules are made to be broken'. 'Play up, play up and play the game' (from the nineteenth-century poem by Henry Newbolt, and still a rallying cry for fair play) may have been the motto of young bloods at public school, but not in the hurly-burly of League football.

This didn't go unnoticed, a late nineteenth-century chancellor of Cambridge University tartly observing that 'Football is a gentlemen's game played by ruffians and rugby a ruffians' game played by gentlemen'. Despite his perverse insinuation that ear-biting, eye-gouging and stamping are gentlemanly, he was evidently aware of football's reputation. Many times each year Victorian newspaper editors employed the headline 'Killed in a Football Match'. Even well into the twentieth century, fatalities weren't unknown. At least a dozen first-class players 'died with their boots on' between 1900 and the Second World War. Today's players are mere pussycats.

Given that ill-disciplined play was inherent in the game, no word could have been more apposite than a *foul*, a transgression of the rules. Used initially as an adjective in the ninth century, the *OED* takes 5,000 words to define its many guises, most of which suit its later adoption by football: 'Dirty, disgustingly filthy, grossly offensive to the senses, contrary to rule or custom'. Roy Keane? Robbie Savage? David Batty? Take your pick. Its root is Indo-European's *pu*, which via Latin gave us *pus*, *putrid* and possibly *pooh*, all with singularly unpleasant associations. A *fouler* meanwhile, that rather neglected word so vitriolically hurled at over-zealous playmates by generations of young footballers, is understatedly defined simply as 'one who fouls'. Yet how much it says. Don't we recoil in disgust at the merest mention of the gannet, said to *foul* its own nest? And what of poor pant-squirming souls who *foul* their underwear? So why should a footballer who *fouls* an opponent be any different?

As crowd reaction testifies, he isn't. 'Dirty bastard' and 'filthy sod', so useful for hurling at life's less sanitary folk, are as common in today's sterile super-stadia as they once were in the foulest alleys of Elizabethan England. Cue William Shakespeare, whose invention of over 2,000 words and phrases makes him the most imaginative word creator in history. I'm not claiming he was an early pioneer of Stafford Rangers, but the Bard clearly understood football's bad-boy reputation. Consider *King Lear*, Act I, Scene 4:

> *Lear:* Do you bandy looks with me, you rascal?
> *Oswald:* I'll not be strucken, my Lord.
> *Earl of Kent:* Nor tript neither, you base Foot-ball plaier (tripping his heels)
> *Lear:* I thanke thee, fellow.

Evidently the lad Ossie had a reputation for leaving his foot in.

Shakespeare's most enduring contribution to football's lexicon is *foul play*, which he invented to suggest murder in *The Tempest*: 'What fowle play had we, that came from thence?' He was also the first to use *faire playe*.

Every medieval contest had its psychos, *hammershin* and *tappertits* being two of the more evocative epithets bestowed on early wrongdoers. Serious foul play is now punishable, but some of football's pioneers positively encouraged unruly behaviour.

Indeed it was divergence of opinion regarding what was deemed 'acceptable' on the football field that prompted the formulation of first the rules and then the laws of association football which have since given English so many well-used terms.

There were indubitably cards coloured red before 1976 but not *red cards*, nor was being *shown the red card* a popular catchphrase until David Wagstaffe of Blackburn Rovers became the first to suffer the fate. Being *carded* might never have made it beyond the woollen industry but for football's law-makers, and there was a time when the only sportsmen who *walked* were cricketers. Nor would *sending off, early bath, professional foul* and a host of other phrases ever have become common staples.

This relationship between legislation and language development stretches back to the dawn of the organised game as the public schools in particular argued over the perceived rules. Rugby School allowed handling at any time while Eton forbade it completely. Harrow sat on the fence by permitting 'a fair catch off the foot'. So old school rules are replete with forgotten gems which the association game simply refused to embrace. *Mauling, piggling, shinning* and *tagging* all sound like good fun, but are no longer part of football's language. *Scrimmage* and *melée* are occasionally resurrected for frantic goalmouth action, but the *fug* and *hot* which once denoted a battle for possession are long gone.

One single term caused more heated debate than any other. Prior to 1863, *hacking* (deliberate tripping of an opponent) was perfectly above board in many football circles. Most good sides boasted a *crack-hack* in their line-up. But fierce opposition to hacking also existed. When the Football Association was formed, a serious schism arose between the hackers and those in favour of a more gentlemanly approach. On the FA's decision rested the future welfare not only of generations of players' shins but of the very word itself.

Hackers considered themselves manly and courageous. As a letter to *The Field* from the early 1860s suggests, even young boys entered the debate, although not without exaggeration: 'Girls in the crowd may squeak a bit when they see their brothers injured through hacking, but you never hear a fellow squeak even if his leg is broken.'

But such brave protests were to no avail. The FA outlawed hacking 140 years ago, although it went reluctantly. Well into the 1870s some clubs commemorated the good old days with a five-minute extra period of glorious hacking, known as a *Hallelujah*, at the end of each match. Even today, now hacking is the preserve of computer hooligans, the archaic expression lives on. Players are 'crudely *hacked down* in the penalty area', and the associated imagery of cutting still pervades the world of the dirty tackle as sundry innocents are *scythed down* or *chopped off at the ankles*.

Two stars of the foul-play dictionary merit closer scrutiny. *Penalty* and *offside* are now used worldwide. *Penalty* derives from Latin *poena* ('punishment'), which also gave us *pain* and *penance*, fitting for sinner and sinned against alike. It came late to football, entering as the new-fangled *penalty kick* in 1891, its genesis laid firmly in the guilty hands of Notts County's left-back Jack Hendry. During an 1890–91 FA Cup quarter-final against Stoke at Trent Bridge, his on-the-line handball prevented a certain goal for the visitors. County won the game, and amid great controversy the authorities quickly decided that a mere free kick (given on the goal line and smothered by the brave keeper, Thraves, who adopted a foetal position inches from the ball) had been insufficient punishment for such a dastardly deed. So ensued the first legal penalty kick to be successfully converted, calmly *planted home* by Renton's Alex McCall against Leith Athletic on 22 August 1891 in the Scottish League.

Thousands have been *put away*, *converted* or *dispatched* ever since. *Scored* is just too ordinary a word. Nor is *penalty* always sufficiently dramatic; hence the synonyms *spot kick*, the schoolboy favourite *peno* and Don Howe's strangely obsessive '*cast-iron pen*'. As an upright member of the England management hierarchy, he really ought to have known it was Victorian slang for penis.

Even the act of *conversion* spawned its own phraseology. Derby County's *penalty king* Alan Hinton always remembered his father's advice to *aim at the stanchion*. Manchester City's *spot kick specialist* Francis Lee was a *blaster*. Alan Shearer is a reliable *roof of the net* merchant. David Beckham resorts to the *driller* for a pressure kick, while those with no nerves at all calmly *place* it or are consummate *slotters*. And generations of fans have tipped off goalkeepers (usually wrongly) with the knowing observation that *he always puts it to the right.*

Penalty lore has also perpetuated the use of otherwise uncommon words, sometimes by the least likely people. I once sat behind a *yob* (said to be backslang for a 'backward boy') who watched menacingly as a disputed penalty against his side was brilliantly parried by the keeper only for the rebound to be netted on the follow-up by a trespassing forward illegally stealing a few yards. As the referee awarded a goal this inarticulate fan leapt to his feet shouting *'encroachment, encroachment'* like a man possessed.

That such a specimen should readily employ a word seldom used outside football by anyone but boundary-dispute specialists and coastal conservationists brought a lump to my throat. Regrettably his follow-up slightly took the edge off it: 'Referee you wanky-arsed toerag, that was fucking encroachment you cheating cunt.' Only Peter Reid could have put it better.

The penalty lexicon is never-ending. But the *long run-up*, *short run-up* and *interrupted run-up*, the miraculous *penalty save*, *penalty miss*, the *penalty spot* and famous *D* might never have existed at all if the famously sportsmanlike Corinthians side, founded in 1882, had had their gentlemanly way. They regarded the law as a slur on their ethos, pompously believing that none of their side would ever deliberately foul an opponent anywhere, let alone close to goal.

Their star man C B Fry pointedly explained the principle: a foul tackle in the penalty area would 'only be perpetrated by an unspeakable cad of the most unscrupulous kidney'. As a consequence their goalkeepers, even into the Edwardian era, responded to penalties by pointedly leaning against their posts, making no attempt to save, whenever a penalty was awarded against them. *Corinthian spirit* is still used as a byword for noble sporting ideals and fair play, incongruously as it happens. The original male inhabitants of Corinth in Ancient Greece, after whom the team was named, were renowned for their licentiousness.

Other big names have also condemned football's most dramatic offence. Pelé once said that 'a penalty is a cowardly way to score', something he obviously forgot when playing for Santos on 20 November 1969. As he notched his much-vaunted 1,000th goal via a spot kick he was quite happy to be carried shoulder high around the stadium, later describing the goal as 'the second favourite of my entire career'.

George Best suffered badly from PMT (post-miss trauma). Asked by the magazine *Esquire* in 1991 which one thing in his past life he would change, his answer was unequivocal: 'I took a penalty against Chelsea in 1971 and Peter Bonetti, the fucker, he saved it! I wish I'd sent it the other way!' *Penophobia* ought really to be a word.

Chris Waddle, Stuart Pearce, Gareth Southgate, Paul Ince and David Batty have all suffered chronic twelve-yarditis of the most public kind. The seeds of our foremost national angst were first sown in the semi-finals of the 1970 Watney Cup when Hull City drew 1–1 with Manchester United, only to lose out 4–3 in the first-ever penalty shoot-out. Now, after successive calamitous failures by England (and Scotland, Wales and Ireland for that matter) in tournaments of marginally wider importance, the dreaded *penalties* has attained a meaning that early law-makers could never have dreamed of.

The other star offence rivals the penalty for notoriety. Curiously it entails no violence. The ever mysterious *offside* is that unique misdemeanour which not only smacks of deliberate cheating but is also the only offence in the game effectively committed against one's own side. Players are *given offside*, *caught offside* and *stray offside*, each suggesting a shameful sense of self-infliction, as do the early slang equivalents *sneaking* and *loitering*, and the playground version, *goal-hanging*. Being a 'golanger' was even worse than being a swot at my school.

Offside was around long before it entered football, initially relating to the mounting of a horse (the opposite to the side you got on) and later to driving a carriage. It meant, literally, 'on the other or less usual side', an essence retained in cricket where the *off side* is that away from the batsman's adopted stance, and also in motoring where it is the side of the car most distant from the kerb. As an extension of that concept of 'distance' it became a nineteenth-century military reference to men who had strayed into no man's land in battle, in advance of the front line of attack. Such soldiers were therefore effectively *hors de combat*, on the wrong side. Its adopted football sense is exactly the same.

Charles W Alcock was the first man ever to suffer the chagrin of being caught offside in an official FA fixture, a match between the FA and Sheffield on 31 March 1866. He subsequently overcame his abject failure to 'look along the line' by becoming Secretary of the FA and suggesting the idea for the FA Cup. The recent trendy adoption of *offside* and *onside* by politicians and the business community to express the shifting acceptance of ideas or policies would surely have Alcock turning in his grave.

Players resorting to foul play are either roundly vilified or accorded cult status, depending which side you're on. Tommy Smith was the Anfield 'Iron Man' to Liverpool fans of the sixties and seventies but a mere *hatchet man* to everybody else. That's old American slang for 'a hired Chinese assassin'. Having seen Smith play, that seems fair enough.

Other special terms of address for habitual offenders are gloriously archaic. In football's pre-League days, northern working men playing informally in heavy wooden clogs were notoriously robust. Some still talk of *a bunch of cloggers*. Likewise the *clodhopper*, sadly no longer used as often as it was. It is an action-descriptive term dating back to 1690, the rustic definition being 'one who walks over ploughed land, a simple agricultural labourer, a country lout or clumsy awkward clown'. All teams have had one. Try using it at Portman Road. Also suggesting rural ineptitude, and rather unfair to the honest creatures concerned, are *carthorse* and *donkey*, the latter responsible for the ubiquitous 'ee-aw' chant first directed with real vigour to Arsenal's Tony Adams. It's actually the most public demonstration of dropped aitches in the English language. As any educated braying donkey knows, the correct term is *hee-haw*.

And what could be better for the heavy-browed lumberers of the football world than *neanderthals*, probably the only German borrowing ever incorporated into fanspeak? Not common now, it's true, but it was when Micky Droy, David Webb, Dave

Watson and other archetypal early men roamed free in the 1970s in search of innocent prey. Save it for Martin Keown, a late throwback. Other foully conceived terms of more recent origin have yet to be embraced by lexicographers. *Afters* appears in the *OED* as 'a vulgar term for the course of a meal which follows the main', but its well-used football counterpart in the sense of retaliation (usually of the clandestine variety) is excluded. Nor has *verbals*, the oral equivalent, yet become an automatic selection.

Dictionary-makers are, though, slowly wising up, if only haphazardly, as media coverage of football exposes its language to more people than ever before. The *OED* has recently included *handbags* in its list of words scheduled for the next edition. The modified offshoot of the old duelling term *pistols at dawn* has been traced in football to the 1970s (some say it emanates from allusions to Margaret Thatcher or the Townswomen's Guild battling sketch from *Monty Python's Flying Circus*), but it's only recently become well-known enough to have spread into general usage for any disagreement in which the protagonists' perceived ire is in truth ineffectual.

The business of word debuts can be hard to pinpoint, although invented words are easiest to place. So while *sportsmanship*, originally describing 'skill' at sport rather than a sense of fair play, came vaguely into use 'sometime in the eighteenth century', its counterpart *gamesmanship* can be reliably fixed at 1947. Every time-wasting, ref-conning, double-talking and injury-feigning player's favourite was the inspired invention of the writer Stephen Potter, who conceived it to describe a devious method for winning at tennis against more talented opponents. He first used it in his classic book *The Theory and Practice of Gamesmanship or The Art of Winning Games Without Actually Cheating* (shortly to be reissued in paperback by Wenger and Ferguson).

Not all attempts to introduce new foul words have proved successful. Match summariser Peter Taylor tried manfully to give birth to one of his own on 20 May 2002 during the televised England v Italy under-21 European Championship game. In response to a tackle by Alan Smith (there's a surprise) which went under the bottom of a bouncing ball, as opposed to the more customary *over the top*, Taylor told viewers: 'Oh dear, that was a low tackle. Yes, definitely low, very low.' Full marks for invention but it won't make the *OED*.

What Taylor's reaction does confirm is that examples of extreme or unusual foul play can provoke innovative responses from onlookers, a sort of surrogate verbal retaliation for those unable to writhe in real agony, indulge in the celebrated *Oscar-winning performance*, or go eyeball to eyeball with the perpetrator.

So next time your priceless striker is subjected to a *crude two-footed lunge, tackle from behind* or *blatant body-check*, try and be original in delivering your vitriol. 'You great lummox' is quaint but a mere ankle-tap. Likewise 'spawny-eyed wassock'. 'Dirty bugger' is all very well but so ubiquitous that the foulers of this world have long since become inured to it. 'Cheating twat' is little better, no more than a minor shirt-tug. So why not try the sharply expressive tongue of Elizabethan England. The man who gave the world *foul play* might have put it like this:

> Fackins faith. You base, proud, shallow, beggarly, filthy worsted-stockinged, lilly-livered, action-taking whoreson. You scurvy, lousy, pragging, flap-ear'd, beetle-headed, malmsy-nose, cowardly knave.

It might not result in an automatic red, but you'll feel much better for it.

15

Back Door, Johnny –
The Secret Code of Footballers

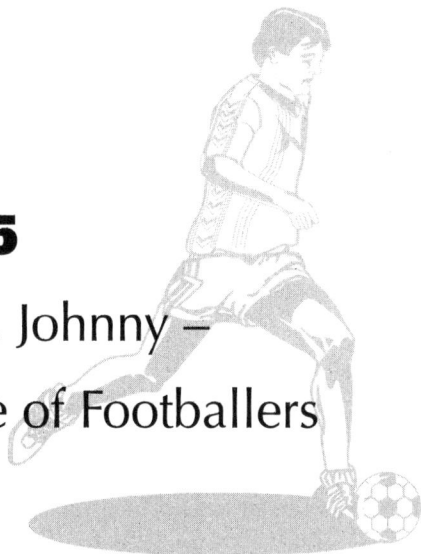

'Go on Blackie! If only we could score another one now, we'd stand a chance! Oh, no, he's sliced it wide. Maybe there's something on his mind.'

'Sorry I fluffed my shot Roy, for some reason I seem to be a bit off-target today'.

Melchester Rovers' Roy Race and Blackie Gray
in a typical example of 'pitchspeak', 1959

Air traffic controllers do it. Sea captains do it. So do keen knitters and chess players. Shipping forecasters do it so mellifluously that even outsiders take pleasure in listening to them. Text messagers do it furtively, quietly, but feverishly. Footballers do it more noisily than most.

It's called *restricted English*, not for being ineffective but because it's confined to groups of specialist users. Outsiders are necessarily disadvantaged, at best left in the dark, and at worst made to look complete fools. In football, shouting 'play it to the side' instead of '*square ball*', or 'look out' rather than '*man on*', ensures you'll be rumbled.

Spectators who have never played football are often ignorant of the constant on-pitch communication between players which is routinely drowned by the crowd. The truth is best revealed by attending a reserve match, or by playing in a park or a five-a-side game.

Playing football in silence reduces effectiveness. A manager signing a player because 'he's a *good talker*' isn't as daft as he sounds. Every team has its *quiet man* but eleven quiet men will get caught in possession more often than a team of talkers, be less creative and urgent in their passing and movement, less effective in winding up the opposition and less motivated to push for the win. In football it's not just 'good to talk', it's vital.

First essential is the warning call, telling an unaware colleague of impending danger. *Man on* suggests immediate close attention from the opposition, *man coming* a mere potential threat. *Man coming hard* is particularly disconcerting while *men coming* generally induces panic in the player on the ball. As for *men coming hard*, the brown-shorter of pitchspeak, it really shouldn't exist. Considerate colleagues should cut straight to *get rid*, football's equivalent of 'abandon ship' or 'press the ejector button'.

Such calls are necessarily short and urgent, like the lumberjack's *timber* or golfer's *fore*. 'I suggest you take evasive action as there is an opposition player approaching intent on dispossessing you of the ball and part of your leg at the same time' is just too long-winded. One of the most satisfying, even touching, moments in football, and it's a rare one, is when an entire crowd shouts 'man on' to get a player *dwelling on the ball* out of trouble.

As vital as warning, but with more creative potential, is instruction. The best players cope without it; comfortable on the ball, they are able to *play with their head up*, innately aware of the constantly shifting whereabouts of colleagues and the opposition for every split second of a game. These are that famous breed who have *vision*. It can't be taught. No one 'gave' vision to Everton's Wayne Rooney, confident enough at seventeen on his England debut to play with all the guile of a seasoned campaigner. Alas the game's 'thinkers', those with *a yard in their head*, are tragically outnumbered, even at professional level, by those needing instructions.

Asking a team-mate for the ball is fundamental, especially if he can't see you. Hence *long line* or *short line* to a man trapped in a blind alley close to touch or *back door* for 'I'm right behind you'.

Less urgently, where there's mutual visual contact, *square ball*, *one-two* and *give and go* are common staples, suggestions rather than commands. *Touch, I'll have it, give it* or simply *yes* are firmer. Ignoring them generally prompts the issuer to follow up with anything from a barely audible 'tch tch' to a full-blown 'for fuck's sake'. Offering options is much more polite. *If you want* or *if you need me* are the game's best calls. Some requests are less wise. The schoolboy favourite 'me, me, me, me, me' only irritates, as does 'I'm on'. One smacks of egotism and the other implies a team-mate's lack of awareness. The most unwise call I ever heard was from an ineffectual-looking youth making his debut for my Sunday side. Once he'd shouted 'I'm free' early in the game his days were numbered.

Selfish types call only when they want the ball themselves, but real team players are prepared to do vocal work on behalf of others who are often the game's shrinking violets, seemingly unwilling to speak even when the situation cries out for it. So 'Dave's on', 'Jim'll have it', 'Pete wants' or even, when the tempo's slow, 'Gary's available', are all valuable. This three-way link distinguishes the really good talkers. It gets a bit like chess. Grand masters occasionally employ the four-man link where John might say to Steve, 'Pete's on through Dave', Pete being the ultimate intended recipient of the ball plied by Steve via Dave. Any more than four, forget it. Just go for *lump it*.

Players sometimes call their own names. 'Pete's ball' instead of 'my ball', or the high-decibel 'keeper's ball' commonly shortened to 'keeee-pah'. It sounds pretentious, but these are merely a response to the game's laws. Confusing the opposition, either deliberately or inadvertently, is the ungentlemanly act of 'false calling', punishable by a free kick. 'My ball' is illegal, and nothing is more despicable than a forward's sly 'leave it'. But there are still defenders who buy it in the heat of the moment.

The reverse side of pitchspeak is 'coping with the opposition'. In the professional game, where 'good practice' comes naturally, much of the dialogue concerning *marking up* or *closing down* remains unsaid. It's at parks level where this comes into its own. *Find a man, man each, get goal side, let's pick up* and *get tight* are the age-old staples. Equally certain to follow as the net bulges are the blame-apportioning *who lost him?*, *he was yours* and *wrong side*. Most parks teams have one self-appointed chief caller who acts as spotter, especially at set pieces. *Runners* and *free men* are his favourites, usually shouted just before *I'll take the little lad*. He also likes 'I've got three here lads, sort it out'.

This enemy identification was made easier at a stroke when numbered shirts were introduced into the game. It wasn't until 1928 that the idea was experimented with, and shirts were first numbered (from 1 to 22) in the FA Cup Final of 1933. Only in 1939 did shirt numbering became compulsory in the English first-class game. Scotland followed suit but Celtic defiantly declined to comply, holding out until 1960 when they agreed to display numbers, but only then on their shorts.

Numbers help spectators, commentators, reporters and referees but also the opposition. That's partly why clubs objected. Helpful phrases such as 'I've got ten, you take nine' simply didn't exist for the first 76 years of the game.

This made identification by personal characteristics an integral part of pitchspeak, providing opportunities for 'legitimate' insults, still prevalent at 'playing for fun' level. 'Who's got baldie?', 'you take the lard bucket' and 'I'll deal with Saddam Hussein' can be powerful demoralisers, although there's an obvious reflected glory in having to be watched at all. Being ignored altogether is the ultimate put-down: 'Leave the plank, he's crap.' The only riposte is scoring the winner.

Most labels are kinder, even affectionate. 'You stick on ginger, I've got blondie' is harmless enough, although there's always room for mockery. Sideburns and a quiff? 'Watch Elvis.' Lumbering centre-half? 'Someone take Godzilla.' Goalkeeper with long hair and a beard? 'Get some crosses in on Jesus. He doesn't like 'em.'

More usually there's a comforting consistency in these monikers. For years I was 'the big lad with the tash', until Father Time stepped in. 'Lad' became 'bloke', then 'old bloke' and, at the age of 42, greying slightly, even 'grandad'. Oh the shame. Yet opponents can also bestow unwitting compliments when all seems lost. The sweetest words I ever heard on a football field came just before my forty-fifth birthday: 'Stick to the grey-haired guy, he's the oldest bugger on the pitch and we're letting him run the show.' Had the old bugger fallen dead from exhaustion at that very moment he'd have died happy. Even the allusion to sodomy didn't matter.

Perversely, in the game's lowest reaches, it's team-mates whose criticisms do most damage. 'Keep it simple', 'easy ball' or 'move it quicker' after an error can all sap confidence. Although rare in the top flight, there are silent equivalents. The look to the heavens, hands on hips, or withering glare, can all be deadly. Fabrizio Ravanelli's characteristic gesture, palms together as in prayer, could destroy a youngster's career.

The friendlier own-side joshing draws on colourful imagery: 'You couldn't pass water' is standard. The rather quaint 'three points to Wigan' for a shot 'high, wide and handsome' is still surprisingly popular, although 'row Z' and the subtly insulting 'don't you like that ball?' are making inroads. Strikers in particular are subjected to unusual forms of 'encouragement'. 'You couldn't score in a brothel' is damning enough, but the best I ever heard was a captain to his centre-forward: 'You're about as much use as a condom in a nunnery and a chocolate teapot put together. You couldn't hit a pig's arse with a banjo, and a big 'un at that.' The art of motivation South Derbyshire style. There might be something in it: a few minutes later he scored the winner.

So for humour watch parks football. And for misdirected verbal effort. 'Did you pull that bird last night Bazza?' isn't untypical, even in the thick of the action. The theory that professionals talk more than amateurs is flawed. They actually talk less but say more. What they impart is useful. There's a world of difference.

And what professionals ask for is usually realistic. At 1–0 down with five minutes left, 'come on lads, big push, last five' is a valid call. So is 'have a dig' from the edge of the box. Park-level exhortations ring more hollow. A team-mate of mine only ever said one thing, but constantly: 'Come on lads, let's get some shots in.' By means of leading by example he'd then shoot, from seventy yards. 'Come on reds, we can win this one' at 5–0 down after 20 minutes has rarely proved prophetic. 'Let's get at these, they're rubbish' generally follows a brief rally at around 4–0 down with minutes to go. One of the wiser souls will usually try and dupe the less cerebral elements at this stage by disguising the real task in hand: 'Just one goal lads, then a quick couple, and we're one off a draw.'

The centre-half in one of my less athletic sides never said 'out' or 'push up' when he wanted the back four to play the offside trap. Instead he yelled 'spring', giving the manoeuvre that finely coiled urgency which is the watchword of any well-drilled defence. Considering the combined weight of our two full-backs was 32 stone (and that's being kind) it was probably the wrong word of command. 'Amble' they might have coped with.

Should you be unconvinced that good communication really matters, confirmation comes from a well-qualified source. *Deaf United: A History of Football in the British Deaf Community* (2000) presents some telling statistics. Approximately one in a thousand people are profoundly deaf. Ninety-two English League teams field a minimum of 1,012 players each week. Crude extrapolation suggests that at least one of them on any Saturday in football's entire history should have been deaf. Yet the authors were able to trace a mere dozen with League experience, and most of those had very average careers. No profoundly deaf player (from birth or an early age) has played in the League for almost fifty years. Ray Drake of Stockport County (1953–57) was the last example.

Some players have become partially deaf during their careers and coped well. Rodney Marsh and Jimmy Case are two post-war examples. England's Cliff Bastin became partially deaf through illness after signing for Arsenal in 1929. He largely kept his condition secret, making 353 appearances, winning five Championships and two FA Cup winner's medals, although he still professed that his deafness had been 'a grave handicap as far as playing to my full ability was concerned'. Bastin performed wonders but he was the exception. Today, with ever more refined coaching techniques and playing systems, the need to be able to hear and speak unimpeded is more vital than ever.

So at the risk of sounding like Gary Lineker, here's a spot of advice to budding young footballers. Use your mouth, eyes and ears as much as your feet. Practise in front of a mirror if necessary. *'Worth a poke'*, *'jockey'*, *'stand up keeper'*, *'jump it'*, *'yards, linesman'*, *'going nowhere'*, *'grab a shirt'*, *'no left foot'*, *'man over'*. They'll come in useful, so learn the lingo before it's too late. And don't *get sucked in* by popular misconceptions. No one says 'On me 'ead, son', except in jest. Above all, learn to use the words that win matches. The over-used favourite, 'Get stuck in', is mere huff and puff. It guarantees nothing. Better by far to follow the mantra of the best sides in the world. You'll be difficult to beat if you remember the three most important words in pitchspeak: *'Keep the ball'*.

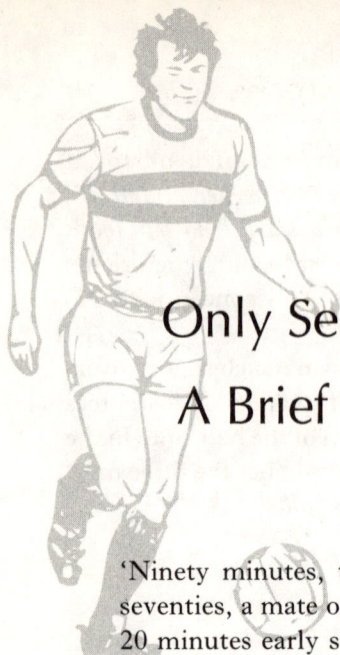

16

Only Seconds Remain –
A Brief History of Time

'Ninety minutes, that's the tradition. In the early
seventies, a mate of mine suggested we leave a game
20 minutes early so we could "get home for *Disney
Time*". Our friendship never really recovered.'

Frank Skinner, West Bromwich Albion devotee,
The Times, 2003

Football people live by different time rules from the rest of the
world. For years, when half-time was just a ten-minute break
and traditional kick-off times still reigned, near-mystical
significance was attached to the otherwise mundane time of
'twenty to five', when the three o'clock starts terminated. 'Ten
past nine' for the 7.30 kick-offs, so often associated with
thrilling cup replays, wasn't far behind.

Men pressed into Saturday shopping were prone to strange
unease at around 4.25, as 'getting back for the results' surpassed
all other considerations. Loitering outside television shops was
a well-used emergency option.

Women wise to football's time zones used this to advantage,
half past four being the optimum moment for getting partner
approval for expensive new outfits or household luxuries that
wouldn't have stood a chance any other time in the week.

My own family folklore has it that during the choosing of my
mother's engagement ring my father was straining to listen to a
radio commentary coming from the back room of the jewellers.

Any ring in the shop could have been hers. To her eternal credit she declined to abuse the privilege. Countless 'other halves' are intimately aware of the differences between an ordinary clock and a football clock. Rules need to be followed. Monday night 8 p.m. till 9.45 is a Sky zone. No talking allowed. Similar scenarios, sometimes extending to open conflict, occur in millions of homes every day.

Not everybody is fully adjusted to today's flexi-time. Diehard managers still say, 'I'll let you know come twenty to five on Saturday,' if asked for a prediction. But that magic time has long passed into obsolescence.

Fifteen minutes half-time and a predilection for digital clocks has made 4.45 the new twenty to five, but with vastly reduced status. Overbearing policing and commercial considerations now dictate that games kick off at all times of the day, and every day of the week. Much of football's old rhythm has been lost, and with it some of the ritual significance of 'kick-off time'. Even accounts of medieval mob football describe the ball being thrown up 'at the appointed hour'. Now that's all gone.

What has remained sacrosanct is the playing time itself, and this has infiltrated our language. We have the Football Association to thank for this, although the first draft laws of November 1863 ignored duration completely. This implied adherence to the Cambridge University Rules, published a month earlier, which stated: 'the time during which the game shall last is to be settled by the heads of the sides.'

By 1866, when the first representative match under Football Association rules was played, a duration of ninety minutes seems to have gained currency, for newspaper announcements confirmed that play was 'to commence at 3 p.m. and terminate at half past 4 p.m.' In 1871 the first FA Cup Rules stated unequivocally that 'the duration of each match shall be one hour and a half'. This became universally accepted well before League games began in 1888, although only in June 1897 was it officially incorporated into the FA Laws.

Note, however, that in football vocabulary, a game lasts *ninety minutes*. 'An hour and a half' doesn't exist. No team has ever been 'under the cosh for the full hour and a half'. But why ninety minutes? It's rather a riddle.

Football scholars with an eye for precedent have pointed excitedly to the celebrated contests between Selkirk and Yarrow played on 5 December 1815 at Carterhaugh. Accounts seductively confirm that 'the first game lasted an hour and a half'. Alas that's pure coincidence, for 'the second game lasted twice as long'.

The more likely origin of the ninety-minute duration is its correlation to public-school timetables in the early nineteenth century, when a 'double period' allotted to 'games' was typically two hours. Allowing for changing into and out of 'togs', that left ninety minutes or so for football itself. The *Rules for the Football House Matches* printed at Uppingham School on 16 November 1863 certainly specified that 'each game last one hour and a half'. After lunch but before prep. It makes sense.

Because of the required level of exertion, football was never going to be an all-day game like cricket. Later on, as working men took to it, an hour and a half on a Wednesday or Saturday half-holiday (still the 'traditional' fixture days) before going home for tea was both feasible and, in truth, sufficient: 'Much more of this and I'll be knackered' has ever been a football adage.

Aside from practicality there has long been a comforting symmetry attached to forms of measurement divisible into quarter hours or units of fifteen, something which Victorian rulemakers would be aware of by acquired convention. In everyday speech 'I'll only be fifteen minutes' is normal, despite it being an odd number, but 'seventeen minutes' is unheard of. And when was the last time you heard someone say 'I'm just popping out for eleven minutes'?

This obsession with 'quarters' sprang from the division of a clockface into 60 minutes. That number enjoyed special significance in the Middle Ages, often representing entirety just as 100 does now. Although circles have 360 degrees, each was made up of six sextants of 60 degrees. Each degree had 60 minutes and each minute 60 seconds. Six hundred years ago 60 was king of numbers.

Sport latched on to this. Tennis historians hold that it explains the otherwise illogical scoring system in lawn tennis, which in its original 'real tennis' form in the early fifteenth century was 15, 30, 45 and game (i.e. 60), the 45 later being shortened to 40 purely on the grounds of laziness. The relevance of this to football is rather oblique, but let's just say that fifteen-minute divisions, or multiples thereof, are historically 'tidy'. Even today, phases of the game tend to be measured in quarter hours. Managers insist that 'we must stay solid for the first fifteen minutes'. Commentators tell us 'we're into the last fifteen'. Make no mistake, football's ninety minutes is logical and well 'rounded'. Rugby's eighty minutes, like its misshapen 'ball', is not.

Players are immune to such niceties, but they certainly know the value of time. Football's finite lifespan makes every minute a rare commodity, each match a desperate struggle to achieve objectives in 'the allotted time'. Not surprisingly, metaphors for life, death and ninety-minutes football are interchangeable. The *last gasp* equaliser. Conceding *at the death* after *surviving* for so long. The *seconds ticking away*. One last chance to *stay alive* in the Cup. The *final whistle beckons*. *It's all over*. Not phrases much used in cricket or golf.

It's because time is so precious in football, as in life, that referees and players are roundly vilified for manipulating it. No one suffers physical harm from *time-wasting* but it remains one of the game's most detestable offences. And of all the privileges given to referees, perhaps the greatest is that enabling him to extend a game beyond its natural end. Call it what you will – *injury time, added time, time allowed, additional time*, or the horribly Americanised *overtime* – it's a God-given bonus. Personally I prefer *stoppage time*, a medievalism in danger of being killed off altogether. And never call it *extra time*. That's a different thing again.

Some officials abuse their timekeeping privilege. Early in his controversial career, Clive 'The Book' Thomas let a match run on for 35 additional minutes to allow for 'ball retrieval'. The pitch was on the edge of a hillside in the Rhondda valley.

Players are technically incapable of extending time (although the most composed can certainly *make* it) so confine themselves to wastage instead, sometimes with lasting consequences. In

1892 Aston Villa's goalkeeper Bill Dunning, angered by a last-minute penalty awarded to Stoke when Villa led by a single goal, hit on the novel idea of booting the ball clean out of the ground so that by the time it was retrieved the referee had already blown for time. It's thanks to Dunning that the laws were swiftly revised to allow for a penalty kick to be taken come what may.

Such shenanigans soon gave rise to clockwatching. Alex Ferguson's dual-purpose wrist-tapping technique is nothing new. After Uppingham School played the Old Boys on 15 December 1865, the match account in the school magazine was quick to report the Old Boys' sour grapes concerning the scholars' equaliser, their captain having 'cruelly insinuated that the Uppingham clock had already pealed its last note of the hour when the goal was won'.

Such *late sickeners* are less likely to be suffered if you can score a couple *early doors*. The footballer's favourite is an odd one, because it's easier just to say 'early'. Doubtless they imagine it originates from laddish pub culture, an 'early doors beer' being one shortly after opening time. In fact it's more cultured.

Correctly it means something occurring 'prematurely'. It originates from nineteenth-century theatrical jargon, theatre doors being opened early for patrons willing to pay a premium price in order to nab the best seats. Goals towards the end of a game, on the other hand, are scored *late on*, never 'late doors'.

If *ninety minutes* is football's micro-time, its macro equivalent is the *season*. As everybody should know, there are five seasons in a year – spring, summer, autumn, winter and the football season. It's from Latin *sation*, 'to sow or scatter seed', originally used by the Romans to refer to the ideal 'sowing period' which in time simply became the 'season' itself. Scattering salt or spices on food is *seasoning* for the same reason.

The football writer Dr Percy Young demonstrated his keen understanding of the 'fifth season' in *The Football Year* (1958): 'In August regrets are buried and hopes renewed, for then the year begins.' The essence of supportership encapsulated in just thirteen words. Dr Young was evidently the Nick Hornby of his age. But not as rich.

He's right about the year not beginning in January. Central to it all is the *fixture list* (the *fikkies*), around which all football lives revolve. The Victorians sagely labelled them 'the football calendar'. For supporters these can never come out too soon, hence the evergreen observation 'surely the fixtures should be out by now'.

Poor souls who live by a traditional calendar do so at their peril. The church holding its annual fete on Cup Final day will wait longer for its steeple restoration than the one whose vicar knows his football. And haven't we all had inconsiderate friends who insist on getting married on a matchday? We know the drill. The best man announces the latest score when he should be reading telegrams. Rumours circulate that cousin Wayne had a radio on in church. The bride spots someone rigging up a television in the bar. All too often it ends in tears. If only they'd consulted the fixtures first it could have been such a perfect day.

Fans sometimes avert such fixture clashes in dramatic ways. In 1991, Hereford fan Kevin McCall called off his wedding the night before the big day to watch his side play Aylesbury in the FA Cup. He told the press: 'I know it sounds awful, but it just hit me halfway through my stag night that I'd rather be going to the match with the lads than marrying Nicola.'

Nick Hornby also cited lost love in *Fever Pitch*, famously illustrating football's capacity to serve as a marker of time:

> I have measured out my life in Arsenal fixtures, and any event of significance has a football shadow. When did my first real love affair end? The day after a disappointing 2–2 draw at home to Coventry.

Such examples illustrate an undeniable truth. Because football is so irrevocably organised around dates, passing seasons, and times, and because it arouses so much emotion and reaction, it serves as a permanent reference point. No one knows the exact moment at which Suffolk's John Constable put the last brush stroke to *The Hay Wain*, but football history records that much of that county's population leapt into the air at 4.26 p.m. on 6 May 1978 after precisely 76 minutes and 45 seconds of the FA

Cup Final between Arsenal and Ipswich Town as Suffolk's real favourite son, Roger Osborne, scored the Ipswich winner.

Only major historical incidents, disasters, deaths and births are similarly treated, but then only on an ad hoc basis. I can't recall the moment at which Winston Churchill died, or even the precise time on 11 September 2001 when New York's twin towers were attacked. I am completely ignorant of the time of my own birth. But I do know, courtesy of a memorable radio commentary, that at seven minutes past nine on Friday 9 May 1986 Derby County's Trevor Christie scored the penalty against Rotherham that gained the Rams promotion to the Second Division.

This phenomenon has been apparent since the game began. Every goal and incident has been assiduously chronicled. Through that medium, we can pinpoint precisely what happened in almost any town in the country at one particular moment on a matchday, right back to the Victorian age.

As such, football 'cheats' time to a degree that few activities can match. That's why nostalgia is so central to football supportership. Fans looking back to football's 'Golden Age', which is really whenever you want it to be, are sometimes accused of over-sentimentalism, but the propensity to reminisce begins very young. The seven-year-old child at his second game who says 'it wasn't as good as last week's' is from just the same school as the oldster who says 'I'll never forget the day I saw George Best get six'.

Football can even deliver what humankind has been seeking for generations, the secret of eternal youth. Witness the reaction of a West Bromwich Albion fan moments after their 2002 promotion to the Premiership: 'Brilliant. I've just turned fifty and I'm crying my eyes out. I feel like a ten-year-old again'.

Assuming you want to feel ten again, and admittedly not everybody does, that's a pretty good testimony to football's role as a rejuvenation drug. Nor is that only a modern sentiment, for football has long been a refuge from the dark days that 'being grown up' demands we endure. Consider this poignant reminiscence of a British prisoner of war in Germany during the First World War:

There were terrible times and good times, which all those who experienced them will never forget. Make no mistake, boys became men in that Hell-hole, but it's far more pleasant to recall the better days when we were allowed to play football, and men became boys again.

Football can be frenetic and painful, but the permanence of its past continues to seduce. Will the game still be going in five hundred or a thousand years? Will the world end? Nobody knows. But who beat Cardiff City 3–0 in the 1929 Welsh Cup Final? Connah's Quay Nomads. In Arthur Conan Doyle's *His Last Bow*, the master detective Sherlock Holmes says to his trusty sidekick: 'Good old Watson. You are the one fixed point in a changing age.' For many of us, football is our Watson.

Supporters seldom articulate this clearly, but it's the game's sense of time and place that keeps them coming back for more. Even when it pains them to go on, the ever-alluring sirens of hope are irresistible. Gordon Jeffery's poem 'Men on the Terraces' encapsulates that spirit. To him I give the last words:

> Surely there are better places?
> More admirable ways of using
> Saturday afternoon, than choosing
> To watch men playing a game they're paid for?
> (Is that what Englishmen were made for?)
>
> But sometimes during the dullest play
> Something comes back from an earlier day.
> A fleeting moment, a hint of grace,
> Brings back a feeling, a time, a place . . .
>
> We are more than what we seem
> Men on the terraces soaking wet.
> We have glimpsed part of our golden dream,
> Our April glory. Together, yet
> Private, as the thoughts recall
> The hopes and dreams of what we were,
> Or wanted to be, in the far-off days.

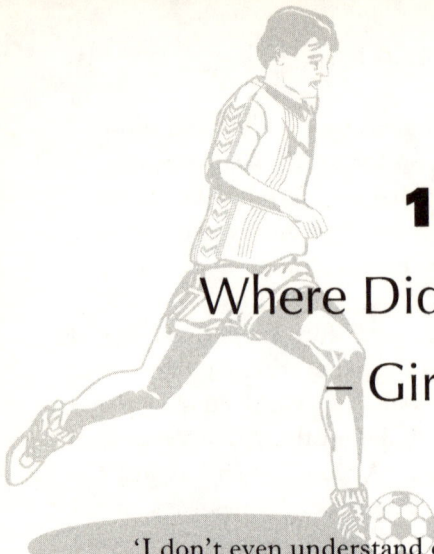

17

Where Did I Get You?
– Girl Talk

'I don't even understand offside, so I'm not likely to understand a Manchester United contract.'

Victoria Beckham, during delicate
renegotiations for David, 2002

Over two million British schoolgirls play football, and many more in the United States. The Women's Football Association, founded in England in 1969, promotes the senior game more vigorously than ever before. A national league formed in 1991 with a modest 24 clubs now flourishes, with around 4,500 teams competing in a United Kingdom pyramid structure topped by the FA Women's Premier League. In 2000 Fulham became the first professional women's team in England, and the FA are currently pushing towards a Women's Professional League.

The third Women's World Cup, staged in America in 1999, achieved ticket sales of 600,000. The final between USA and China, won 5–4 on penalties by the home nation, attracted a crowd of 90,185. Before the game, FIFA president Sepp Blatter asserted that 'the future of football is feminine'. That alliterative soundbite may prove to be an overstatement but, with more than 30 million registered female players worldwide, it's safe to say that 'feminine football has a future'.

That doesn't please everyone. In 1989 Ron Atkinson, then Sheffield Wednesday manager, said: 'Women should be in the kitchen, discotheque and boutique, but not in football.'

154

Atkinson's use of 'discotheque' and 'boutique' twenty years after they'd ceased to be fashionable suggests a marked inability to keep abreast of trends, but he wasn't alone.

In 1990 the revered (though not by everybody) football journalist Brian Glanville, one of the women's game's fiercest critics, sneeringly proclaimed that 'it should only be played by consenting adults in private'. Football's history is littered with similar 'keep the game male' pronouncements. Even those accepting that distaff sides had a place in football often did so in bitingly condemnatory fashion. Oscar Wilde certainly lacked even a hint of Victorian chivalry when he observed that 'football is all very well for rough girls, but hardly suitable for delicate boys'.

Others of that male-dominant age cited 'health issues' to justify their opposition. In 1894 the *British Medical Journal* stated: 'We can in no way sanction the reckless exposure to violence of organs which the common experience of women has led them in every way to protect.' Even in the 1920s the Arsenal manager Leslie Knighton was pursuing the same theme: 'Anyone acquainted with the nature of the injuries received by men could not help but think, looking at girls playing, that should they get similar knocks and buffeting their future duties as mothers would be seriously impaired.'

Although the Blatter–Atkinson dichotomy illustrates the diversity of feeling surrounding women's place in football, it's equally evident that the female game has provoked a diverse usage of language beyond that generated by the male game alone.

Consider words to describe female participants. *Footballer* ought really to be a cross-gender term, but while 'he is a footballer' is common, 'she is a footballer' is rare. 'She plays football', however, is widely used. That's partly understandable, because labelling someone a *footballer* generally implies professional status. But there's surely a sexist vein to it as well. Although English doesn't assign gender to its nouns, it's still regarded as somehow odd or even improper to suggest that *footballer* is a unisex word.

There are parallels in other professions. *Hairdresser*, now gender-liberated, was once almost exclusively female but *nurse* still hasn't broken free, hence *male nurse* to solve the problem.

I've never encountered a male *typist*, and even in today's PC society a *secretary* can still marry a *butcher* without too much confusion over which one wears the dress.

Women 'footballers' were first depicted on Chinese frescoes from AD 200, and first written of in the sixteenth century. In *Dialogue Between Two Shepherds* the statesman and poet Sir Philip Sidney (1554–86) wrote:

> A tyme there is for all, my mother often sayes,
> When she, with skirt tuckt very high,
> With girls at football playes.

In the seventeenth century Thomas D'Urfey again confirmed the female propensity to try out the 'men's game', albeit introducing a note of gender uncertainty:

> Her was the prettiest *fellow*,
> At Foot-ball or at Cricket.

Eighteenth-century records describe women's football as folk ritual linked to local marriage customs. In Inverness, single women annually played married women while prospective husbands watched from the sidelines mindful of selecting a suitable bride. And that women have long fulfilled their traditional supporting role is romantically illustrated in a verse by Robert Greene from 1587 in which Carnela sends her footballing hero into action with a lucky charm:

> Ah leave my toe, and kiss my lippes, my love,
> My lippes and thine, for I have given them thee:
> Within thy cap 'tis thou shalt weare my glove,
> At football sport, thou shalt my champion be.

Detailed nineteenth-century accounts describe the first official women's fixture played to association rules. On 23 March 1895 at Crouch End Athletic ground in north London, two teams of middle- and upper-class schoolgirls faced each other in a game organised by Nettie Honeyball, secretary and captain of the

British Ladies' Football Club. In Scotland the same promotional role was performed by Lady Florence Dixie, the youngest daughter of the Marquis of Queensbury.

Such novel matches were promoted under the banner 'a manly game that can be womanly as well', and the preferred terms *ladies' football* and *lady footballers* prevailed into the first heyday of the female game in the early 1920s. The First World War did much to boost ladies' football by placing men and women on a more common footing than ever before. Women were expected to enter male spheres in the workplace as part of the war effort, and by May 1918 there were over a million in the munitions industry alone. The authorities became acutely aware that social activities were vital if these 'new women' were to lead fulfilled, respectable and healthy lives, and many well-organised works football clubs were formed to that end, foremost among them the Dick Kerr engineering factory team. Dick Kerr's Ladies (often erroneously thought to be named after a chap called Dick Kerr), otherwise known as Preston Ladies, attained huge celebrity status playing charity matches at home and abroad. On Boxing Day 1920, 53,000 watched them play St Helens Ladies at Everton's Goodison Park. In 1921, with ladies' football at the height of its popularity, they played 67 charity games in front of 900,000 spectators. The star of that era, a member of Pioneer Ladies, gloried in the name Ada Anscombe.

The women's game today might have been much more advanced had the dinosaur tendencies of the male-dominated Football Association not emerged in that very same era. The FA had already forbidden 'mixed football' in 1902, but on 6 December 1921 ladies' football was banned altogether from the grounds of FA member clubs amid trumped-up allegations of financial corruption regarding allocation of gate money to charities. The tone of their statement, though, made their more general distaste abundantly clear:

The council feel impelled to express their strong opinion that the game of football is unsuitable for females and ought not to be encouraged.

That put back the development of the game at a stroke. Ladies'
football entered its wilderness years, failing to make a sustained
revival until the 1980s. But even in 1988 the FA chief executive
Ted Croker became squeamish at the prospect of girls playing
with boys in school teams: 'We just don't like males and females
playing together. I like feminine girls. Anyway, it's not natural.'

The uncertainty surrounding the ladies' game in that sixty-
year hiatus was mirrored in the nomenclature applied to the
players. Various labels were given to 'lady footballers' from the
fifties until the eighties but most reflected the public perception
of the game as something akin to a circus act. Brian Glanville
once passed judgement on female footballers by paraphrasing a
famous quotation: 'Like the dog which walks on its hind legs,
one is surprised not that they do it badly but rather that they are
able to do it at all'. In that climate of opinion, *soccerettes*,
footballinas, *footballettes*, *footballistas*, *soccerinas*, *footerbelles*,
footerettes and even *ladyballers* and *she-footballers* were invented
by journalists in a seemingly desperate effort to give the girls
their own distinguishing, but certainly not distinguished, label.
Some terms were more crass still. A game involving teams of
models in the 1970s was described by one hack as 'The battle of
the footballing dolly-birds' and another dubbed the players 'the
catwalk kickers'.

The sixties and seventies, the age of 'joke' games in women's
football, was certainly its low point. Poor standards in
technique, fitness and knowledge put the game back years.
Photographic images from that period did little to help its cause.
Those not showing blonde models wincing at the approach of
the nasty ball depicted beefy girls with huge pink-marbled
thighs and disconcertingly manly haircuts. As a result women's
football experienced a crisis of sexuality in which it was
regarded by 'the public' as the preserve either of hot-panted
showbiz bimbos or pint-swilling lesbians. The shift back
towards 'acceptance' and the vastly improved athleticism and
skill levels of today began in the midst of that crisis when the
Women's Football Association was formed in 1969. The title
they chose has seen the more feisty term *women's football* finally
usurp the rather genteel *ladies' football*.

Curiously, though, many women's clubs retain 'ladies' in their titles. 'Arsenal Ladies' sounds right, 'Arsenal Women' doesn't. Some clubs solved the titular problem more imaginatively, notably the most famous side of recent years, Doncaster Belles. Millwall Lionesses are another. Others attempted touches of levity but encountered resistance. In 1996 a Camberwell women's side re-christened themselves the Old Fallopians Women's Football Club, their fans adopting the rallying cry 'Up the Tubes'. Alas the Women's FA spoilt the fun, insisting they remain Camberwell WFC.

The clubs themselves are much less concerned about political correctness than many off the field, or outside the game completely, would like them to be. Most female players willingly embrace the game's linguistic conventions by shouting '*man on*' instead of the ludicrous equivalent 'woman on', and they still go down to *ten men*, mark *man to man* and *find a man*.

Although *player on* and other substitute phrases are creeping in, most players are unconcerned about such niceties. Even at the highest level the game has been slow to adopt gender-adjusted language. When Arsenal Ladies beat Doncaster Belles in the 1993 Women's FA Cup Final, Arsenal's Lesley Shipp was amused but certainly not annoyed when she said, 'I never expected to get the *man*-of-the-match award.'

In truth, the core vocabulary of women's football differs little from that of the male game. *Skirt* replaced *shorts* in many kit-bags between the thirties and fifties and *sports bras* (famously exposed by USA's Brandi Chastain in her 1999 World Cup Final goal celebration) understandably out-number *jockstraps*, but there the fundamental differences end. Most women players spurn gender-adjusted language because they want to play football as far as possible on equal terms with the men. Preserving a common tongue is integral to that desire.

Language used by women writing books about 'their' game reflects that determined stance. Consider the titles: *Can Play Will Play*, *One of the Lads*, *Women on the Ball* and *Kicking the Boys' Balls*. Contrast that with one written by a man, the rather patronising *Belles of the Ball* from 1991.

Although a fighting spirit within the women's game is evident, it doesn't follow that the on-pitch vernacular of the players exactly mirrors that of the males. A television documentary about the Doncaster Belles (*I Lost My Heart to the Belles*) and the drama series *Playing the Field*, featuring the Castlefield Blues, both illustrated that footballing girls can be given to the excesses of coarseness that characterise so-called *ladette culture*, but the prevailing linguistic trend in women's football is towards less aggression.

Having watched from the touchline I can personally confirm that, compared to the male game, there is less swearing, personal criticism of team-mates and abuse of opponents and officials. Indeed most coaches actively discourage inflammatory language.

Things are heard during a women's match that are rare indeed from the men. 'Hard luck', 'Good try', 'Keep going', 'Nice attempt' and 'Never mind' are surprisingly common, as is 'Well done, you were the best side' at the end of a game. The quaint schoolboy custom of 'three cheers for the opposition' also survives in some quarters.

Even 'bad language' often belies that title. 'Sugar!' and 'Shoot!' after missed chances are favourites. I've heard 'Ecky thump ref' following a bad decision, but most expressive of all, after a clearance sliced horribly into touch, was the self-admonishment 'Tits and bums!'

Much of it may be the sort of dialogue typical of a 1950s *Roy of the Rovers* strip but that's one reason why the women's game can be so entertaining and fulfilling to watch. Levels of enthusiasm and sportsmanship are high. The game is less cynical. In a sense, it's altogether more 'pure' than its male counterpart. And there is certainly skill. During his time as England manager, Kevin Keegan mirthfully confirmed as much to the *Guardian*: 'Some of the girls can do things men find very difficult. When I coached at the Centre of Excellence one girl had a trick I'd never seen any professional do before.'

Occasionally a real verbal gem wafts to the touchline. I once witnessed a big strong defender leave a winger in a crumpled heap, then offer a hand with the apology, 'Sorry, where did I get you?' The day Roy Keane says that has yet to arrive.

So while the core vocabulary of the women's and men's game is essentially identical, styles of speech differ. This is equally marked in supportership. Many women really know their football and are word perfect. But those not fully conversant with its jargon can easily betray themselves. No true supporter has ever said 'Beckham kicked a penalty shot' or 'Seaman saved loads of goals'. And hands up who has tried in vain to explain how simple the concept of the European Cup Winners' Cup really is? Or the 'away goals count double' rule.

Certain women, it seems, actually have a form of football dyslexia. A friend of mine about to settle down to a recorded TV match implored his wife, 'Don't tell me how many goals there were.' She failed to understand why her candid reply, 'Don't worry, there weren't any,' ruined his entire evening.

The same chap, evidently surrounded by football-blind women, tells the tale of his mother, scrutinising a televised match which used the latest on-screen projection technology, being moved to remark: 'Don't those big badges on the pitch put the players off?'

Yet occasionally that very naïvety hits the mark better than exhaustive analysis. Millions of words were expended by experts seeking to rationalise England's 2002 World Cup defeat against Brazil, but none were more succinct than those casually tossed into the debate by my aged aunt: 'Brazil kicked it better than we did and had a goalkeeper who could jump.' Maybe male football language has simply become too sophisticated for its own good. We're all disappearing up our own inside channels.

The roll-call of famous names from women's football is also idiosyncratic. While men's football is replete with thousands, most fans would be hard pressed to nominate more than a dozen women of note. Nettie Honeyball has gained some currency as an early pioneer, but can you name players from the sixties or seventies? Football's most famous women from that era were Cissie Charlton (Bobby and Jack's mother), George Best's landlady Mrs Fullaway, and Joy Beverley, showbiz wife of Billy Wright. In the modern game England's Kaz Walker is one of few domestic names readily recalled. Most fans will have heard of the American Mia Hamm, currently rated the most famous female player, but beyond that it's a struggle. Off the field Wendy Toms is offered up regularly on the refereeing front and Karren Brady and Delia Smith represent the boardroom. There are a number of very talented journalists and broadcasters, but still no mainstream female commentators in radio or television. And it says much about how far women have still to progress that the word *manageress* has only been used in the first-class British game in fiction. Cherie Lunghi played *The Manageress* Gabriella Benson in the 1990 television series.

It's significant that the most famous woman 'in football' today is Victoria Beckham, figurehead of that much-maligned group *footballers' wives*. Such has been the stereotyping of this 'accessory' to the game that the breed has entered the English language in a wider sense. Observing that someone would 'make a good footballer's wife' isn't a compliment.

Feminising influences in football language have a way to go yet, but significant steps in the evolutionary process are being made apace. Sometimes support comes from unlikely sources. In the *Independent* in 1996, arch-feminist Germaine Greer was moved to write: 'Football is an art more central to our culture than anything the Arts Council deigns to recognise.' More recently, two sentences never before articulated in the history of the English language were given wide press coverage. In September 2002 Fulham's 20-year-old midfielder Katie Chapman was the first person ever to say, 'I'm pulling out of the England football squad. I'm three months' pregnant.' The *Daily Mail* also confirmed what in the men's game would have to be a misprint by labelling her 'a £20,000-a-year star international'.

Even more of a stir was caused early in 2003 by the celebrity cook Delia Smith. Many of her fans were first shocked and then terribly disorientated when Norwich City's highest profile supporter uttered one of the most startling sentences in history: 'I'm giving up cooking to concentrate on football.'

Some Deliaphiles, both male and female, felt cruelly betrayed. The rest of us loved it, wondering if 'get it in the mixer' was her favourite call. As much as the FA's damning 1921 proclamation had retarded the cause of women in football, so Delia's bombshell advanced it. More girls and women than ever before now want, in the words of the film, to *Bend It Like Beckham*.

Perhaps after all there is some symbolic significance in the little-known story behind the first-ever recorded appearance of the word *football* in England. I've mentioned elsewhere that this was a 1486 glossary entry in *The Book of St Albans*. The printed line 'It is calde in Latyn *pila pedalis*, a fotebal' began the game's written history.

What I omitted to say is that the author is thought to have been a woman, although there's some doubt about her identity. The British Library lists her variously as Dame Juliana Barnes or Berners. Some historians say she was prioress of Sopwell nunnery, near St Albans. Others suggest she was male and the name was a pseudonym – probably for Brian de Glanville. That would be a pity. The possibility of a fifteenth-century nun setting the ball rolling on football's monumental word industry is an appealing one.

Whether the language of the game was truly blessed by 'a woman's touch' at its very genesis, we shall never know. What is certain, six centuries later, is that the 'ladies of football' are sharpening their pencils, tongues, wits and skills as never before.

18

Nomads v Real Ale Madrid – Christening the Club

'We were going to fly out for my stag night from East Midlands Airport. Now they've changed its name to Nottingham we've all cancelled. They're Derby's biggest rivals. It's unthinkable.'

Steve Elliot, Derby County defender, who was born and bred in the city, 2004

Contemplate for a moment a world in which all fixtures were billed Team A v Team B. All home sides would be Team A, all away sides Team B. What could be simpler? But would it work? Consider the drama of the cup draw: 'Number 31, Team A, give the drum a whirl, will play . . . number 17. . .' You already know the next two words. Where's the suspense in that?

Teams must have names, not just because of the sense of identity which has been football's rationale since antiquity, but for the simple avoidance of utter confusion. Since the first football club was formed, deciding a name has been item one on the agenda. No one truly knows who was first, but the oldest club to have ultimately adopted 'association' rules is generally accepted to be Sheffield Football Club, whose first constitution was issued on 24 October 1857. They were closely followed by Forest Football Club, formed in 1859.

Both opted for basic christenings. Sheffield, unsurprisingly, comprised men from that city, actually members of Sheffield Cricket Club. Forest Football Club (no relation to the 'Tricky

167

Trees' from Nottingham) were formed in Snaresbrook, East London, by former pupils of Harrow School. Their home ground was in Epping Forest, where a clearance wasn't so much a useful defensive device as a vital prerequisite.

Both titles embody that proud sense of geographical identity since incorporated into almost every football club's name. Where you come from, who you represent, or where you play, is paramount.

Even teams with nowhere to call their own made a play of their very homelessness. When Forest were denied use of their Epping turf, they agreed for a time to play all their games away, adopting the name Wanderers to reflect their new status. It did them no harm. On 16 March 1872 they won the first-ever Football Association Challenge Cup (the FA Cup), and went on to lift it five times in its first seven years.

Bolton, Wycombe, Wolverhampton and others of the displacement breed followed suit, as did those carefree clubs who advertised loudly that they were willing to 'go anywhere for a game'. A case of 'have leather, will travel' in the pre-League days when fixtures could be hard to come by.

As such, in the 1860s and 1870s, football was replete with Strollers, Ramblers, Nomads and Vagabonds. Two sides chose foreign names to press the point home. Alas Gitanos and I Zingari, from the Spanish and Italian for 'Gypsies', no longer grace the first-class game.

Others of the footloose breed survive. Glasgow and Queen's Park *Rangers*, Blackburn and Tranmere *Rovers*. And Bristol Rovers, who by the time they adopted the name in 1898 had already had five grounds and been Purdown Poachers, the Black Arabs, Eastville Rovers and Bristol Eastville Rovers.

Wimbledon's controversial move to Milton Keynes in 2003 may have prompted debate about what they should be called, but football today is stability itself compared to its first thirty years. The early days are littered with clubs changing names and grounds, going bust, re-forming under different guises or amalgamating with rivals. That's why so many names are no longer in the mainstream. Consider these pre-League entrants to the FA Cup between 1871 and 1883: Harrow Chequers, Civil

Service, Royal Engineers, Oxford University, 1st Surrey Rifles, Old Etonians, Old Wykehamists, Old Salopians, Old Harrovians and Old Carthusians. The aristocratic air of the line-up simply reflects the fact that former public schoolboys were prime movers in setting up most of the early clubs, but their domination was not to last.

Not that the era wasn't capable of more light-hearted imagery. Imagine the speed and agility of Swifts and Panthers, the persistent attacks of Mosquitoes and Hornets, the work-rate of Trojans, the pioneering spirit of Pilgrims and the steely resolve of Phoenix Bessemer. Druids v Church sounds an interesting fixture, and wouldn't we have marvelled at the way the rabble known as Remnants miraculously overcame the sharp-eyed Hawks in the FA Cup?

For the current crop of familiar names to come into being (the Town, City, United and County set) the toffs needed to be superseded by ordinary working men. Clubs representing 'establishments' had to be either joined or replaced by those representing whole urban communities.

The small Lancashire town club, Darwen, were the first 'industrial' team to make inroads. This impoverished side, who sometimes relied on donations from their upper-class opposition to fulfil away fixtures, created a cup sensation in 1879 when they took mighty Old Etonians, that year's winners, to two replays in the quarter-finals. It's indicative of the ensuing shift in power that Darwen later gained access to the Football League (they were members from 1891 to 1899) while Old Etonians never had that privilege.

Etonians were again the fall guys when they lost 2–1 after extra time in the 1883 Cup Final to Blackburn Olympic, the first provincial side ever to win the Cup. The northerners included five textile workers, a picture framer, an iron worker, a dentist's assistant, a plumber and two shameless men who, rumour had it, were actually being illegally paid for their services.

Urban clubs were on the march. Every single FA Cup winner since has been a recognised name still playing first-class football today. Virtually overnight the gentlemen were eclipsed as professionalism was officially sanctioned in England in 1885 and the Football League kicked off on 8 September 1888. The new working man's craze sparked a veritable explosion of club formations at every level.

Most leading clubs were keen to adopt their town or county name, but therein lay a problem. Take my own home town. Derby County were formed in 1884, but active at the same time were Derby Junction, Derby Town, Derby Midland, Derby Wanderers, Derby Swifts, Derby St Lukes, Derby Ramblers, Derby West End, Derby Nomads and plain old Derby, to name but a few.

The titles illustrate the solution. The adoption of 'added names' (we'll call them *suffixes*) for purposes of differentiation created the household names of today. The biggest-thinking clubs looked to bag 'County' where possible, but local authority approvals for such a privileged moniker were rarely granted. The oldest Football League club, formed in 1862, did pull it off by shrewdly calling themselves 'The Notts. Foot Ball Club' in their initial constitution. Including the abbreviation for Nottinghamshire in their title made it kosher for the name Notts County to be quickly but quietly adopted. That hasn't pleased followers of Nottingham's 'bigger' club, who took their more unusual name from their early playing area, the Forest Recreation Ground in Sherwood, formerly the mythical playground of Robin Hood.

That *County* is the holy grail of 'territorial' names is borne out by its rarity. Of the 92 English league teams for 2003–04, only Notts, Derby and Stockport are so blessed.

Others have contented themselves with narrower patronage, on a sliding scale by size. Of the boundary-related names, *City* leads the way in the Football League with 14, followed by *Town* with 10. Peterborough fly the flag for the rather more archaic *Borough*, with two other clubs supporting them through an adaptation of the word incorporated into their titles. That's Middlesbrough and Bury, both corruptions of the Old English *burg* for town, from the Germanic meaning 'protect'. As for smaller settlements still, the non-league scene duly obliges with the lowly West Sussex side Crawley Village and the illustrious amateur side Dulwich Hamlet. Kings of geographical minimalism, though, are Port Vale, named after the single dwelling in Longport where they were formed in 1876.

Natural selection seems to have regulated affairs down the years to the degree that *Town* and *Borough* clubs are regarded as quaint survivals of a bygone age. The Premiership, as I write, contains no *Town* club and the last to win the title were Ipswich Town in 1962, regarded then, as it would be now, as quite a sensation. Prior to that, only Huddersfield Town, who secured three titles in a row in the twenties, really dominated.

As for *Borough* sides, they seem most comfortable in the Conference League, the tautologous Farnborough Town keeping company with Nuneaton Borough, Scarborough and Stevenage Borough. Of their fellow members only Chester City boast a really grown-up name.

A significant number of clubs chose not to represent entire settlements, but instead adopted a separatist approach by flying the flag for a particular suburb, 'end' of town, or even a single street. On the latter front, Plymouth Argyle score well by perpetuating the name of Argyle Avenue, close to where they were founded in 1886, as do the former League members Bradford Park Avenue, while Preston North End are only marginally less parochial.

But the most favoured way of marking a territory without actually using the town name was to choose an area within it. That's why – perhaps no one dares to take on the responsibility – no first-class clubs use *London* in their name. Fulham and Chelsea are good examples of 'locality' clubs, each maintaining something of the village about them despite being large clubs in the Premiership. Everton are another, but therein lies a tale. They surely scored the greatest own goal of all time. Having had ample opportunity to adopt the name of the city itself, they chose instead that of the district in which their original headquarters was situated. They were the city's pre-eminent club when along came a team of upstarts who promptly christened themselves *Liverpool*, achieving the pinnacle of single-namedom at a stroke.

Liverpool remains the biggest settlement in the British Isles to be so blessed, and as such Liverpool Football Club are probably the most 'representative' of all. Everton fans have never lived it down. Others of the 'name's the same as the town' breed include Sunderland, Southampton, Portsmouth, Blackpool and Burnley. There are 25 single-namers in the 92 clubs.

If you're following this trail assiduously, you'll by now be screaming, 'What about *United*?' It beats *City* to overall top spot in the suffix league by a narrow 16 to 14. While not a territorial title, it's the most evocative of add-ons, used world-wide in its naked form 'United' to refer rather presumptuously to one of the Manchester clubs, and slavishly borrowed by fiction writers and schoolboys as a generic name for any team supposed to be 'good'.

Many clubs adopting the tag are arguably mongrels, since they did so because of a merger. Newcastle United, the result of a shameless coupling between rivals Newcastle West End and Newcastle East End in 1892, are typical.

Others adopted *United* to reflect both a pooling of resources and a sense that all members were pulling together for the common good. Employees of the Lancashire and Yorkshire Railway based at Newton Heath in Manchester founded a club in 1878 and were proud at first to call themselves Newton Heath Lancashire and Yorkshire Cricket and Football Club. When they gained entry into the Football League in 1892 the more streamlined Newton Heath was felt sufficient to identify them, but after a ground move in 1893, as their status grew, a name change was mooted. It took until 1902, precipitated by the club's slide into liquidation, to effect it. From a number of suggestions, Manchester Central was a favourite but was ultimately rejected. The name they did choose reflected the club's union with a rescue group of business investors. The club became Manchester United. That was how close the mother tongue came to having Manchester Central as a global celebrity. Instead it was a mere railway station, now long since closed.

United may be first-class football's top name, but others are more original. Hotspur FC were founded in North London in 1882 by a group of romantically inclined cricketers. Harry Hotspur was a fiery character from Shakespeare's *Henry IV, Part 1*, based on the real-life Harry Percy (1364–1403), son of the first

Earl of Northumberland, whose family had large land holdings in the Tottenham area. As the club's first enclosed ground was at Northumberland Park it was a neat if rather arty device to forge the link. The prefix *Tottenham* was added in 1885.

Crystal Palace not surprisingly have direct links with the building which housed the Great Exhibition of 1851. It was relocated from Hyde Park to Sydenham where, on the football arena in its grounds, a professional club formed in 1905 chose to play its games. It was natural they should take the name of the giant glass edifice itself.

Isn't this name game easy when you get the hang of it? Leyton Orient must be so called because they play in East London. If they played in West London they'd be Leyton Occident, just a keyboard error away from perpetual misfortune. Right? No. It was because some of their early players were employed by the Orient Steam Navigation Shipping Line. They began as Glyn Cricket Club in 1881, but became Orient Football Club in 1888, thence Clapton Orient, and eventually Leyton Orient in 1946.

Another cricket-inspired origin, dating to 1816, is better known. If members of a club meet on their half-day holiday, a Wednesday, why shouldn't they call themselves the Wednesday Club? *Sheffield* wasn't officially appended until 1929.

Three current League teams, Charlton, Oldham and Wigan, might sound fitter than the rest, but their choice of *Athletic* (from Greek for 'contending for a prize') was merely the appropriation for effect of a word long connected to sporting vigour. But directly linked to track and field is a club formed originally for athletics in 1877. They share their name both with that of a hound used for hunting hares and a type of falcon, each noted for speed and agility, as are Kidderminster Harriers on a good day.

Perhaps the most 'British' of all first-class clubs are Brighton & Hove Albion and West Bromwich Albion. *Albion* is the ancient but now little-used poetical name for Great Britain, thought to derive from the Latin *albus* (white) and said to be linked to the first sight of Dover's distinctive cliffs which was so powerfully impressed on the memories of ancient voyagers to

Britain. The clubs adopted it purely as a romantic notion, although Brighton, at least being on the coast, might have the better claim.

If that pair personify Britishness, one club stands out for looking all too foreign. But for the *s* it's a Spanish holiday resort. The name itself comes from a mix of Italian, French and Arabic. Love them or loathe them, there's no denying Arsenal the etymology league's top spot.

Formed in Woolwich in 1886 by workers at the government munitions factory, the Royal Arsenal, they initially took the name Dial Square, a mere workshop in the complex. They quickly adopted Royal Arsenal, which they retained until 1891, before further reflecting their expansion by changing to Woolwich Arsenal. They retained that until 1914, dropping the prefix when they moved to a new ground in North London, ten miles distant from their Woolwich roots.

There they became known first as The Arsenal, and from 1927 simply Arsenal, the only club in the Football League playing as a suffix. One–nil to the Arsenal. As if that wasn't enough, the name itself has an interesting etymology, deriving from the Arabic original *dar-as-sina ah*, literally 'house of the manufacture'. That passed into Venetian Italian as *arzana* for the name of the large naval dockyard in Venice, known to this day as the *Arzenale*. English borrowed it either from that or the French equivalent *arsenal*, initially using the word purely for dockyards before it came into general use for 'a military storehouse' late in the sixteenth century.

While Arsenal's name can be accurately traced, some clubs have lived a lie for years. Until recently Crewe Alexandra, formed in 1877, were said to have been so called because the team met at a public house named the Alexandra, an explanation tacitly accepted until detailed research revealed that no hostelry of that name existed in the town.

The club is now thought to have been named in honour of the then Princess of Wales, the Danish Princess Alexandra, wife of the future King Edward VII. Similarly named after a revered female personage were the former League club Northwich Victoria.

Alexandra and *Victoria* are two of English football's oddities, but they are nothing compared to those in Scotland. You'll look in vain for even a single *Town* in the main leagues, nor are there any *Wanderers*, and only Elgin and Brechin use *City*. No one lives in Hibernian or Celtic, allusions respectively to the ancient names for Ireland and the Irish, to which the clubs owe their origins. There is a team in Dumfries, but don't go asking for Dumfries Athletic. The side representing that fair town opted instead for the settlement's nickname, Queen of the South.

There is only one senior club in the United Kingdom named after a school. Hamilton Academy gave birth to Hamilton Academical in 1875. And only one has named itself after a prison, the jail immortalised in Walter Scott's eponymous 1818 novel *Heart of Midlothian*, which the Edinburgh club adopted in 1874 on a purely romantic whim.

One Scottish team goes one better than Arsenal by employing a double suffix as their title. Albion Rovers play in Coatbridge, just east of Glasgow. Another boasts the shortest first name in first-class British football, Ayr United.

It's clear that Scottish nomenclature is both delightfully quirky and a minefield for the unwary. Deciding who plays where can be difficult. Raith Rovers, founded in 1883, were named after the Lord of Raith and Novar who leased them their first ground on the shores of the Firth of Forth, over the water from Edinburgh. But you'll search for Raith for ever. No such town exists. They play in Kirkcaldy, all of which led to much mirth at the expense of the English television presenter who, after one of the club's rare triumphs, confidently informed viewers that 'they'll be dancing in the streets of Raith tonight'. David Coleman is thought to have been the culprit and it's since become the club's catchphrase. There's even a record called 'Dancing in the Streets of Raith'.

Only the English non-league scene competes with Scotland for idiosyncrasies. Their own suffix heaven includes Progressive, Welfare, Gabriels, Friday, Snooker, Cricketers, Constabulary, Ancients, Castle, Cross and hundreds more. Vosper Thorneycroft and Marston Montgomery (not the Edwardian actors) play to the crowds, McGinty's Nicholians take on British Sugar Fonnereau and St George Easton-in-Gordano contemplate facing Grimethorpe Miners' Welfare in the cup. It's a world where Guru Nanak, Ibis, Frome Collegians, Old Latymerians and Cray Valley Paper Mills Reserves battle week in week out for their own bit of glory.

The *Non-League Yearbook* lists several thousand teams, each uniquely named. The Premiership champions may currently top football's pyramid, but below that the base broadens to apparent infinity: parks teams, church teams, gay teams, works teams, ladies' teams, even parliamentary teams, each playing for the honour of their name. There are literally hundreds of thousands.

Not surprisingly, the grassroots level has produced some tongue-in-cheek namings. It's a pity their results aren't given on radio as the reading could be more entertaining than the games themselves:

Borussia Munchenflapjack 6 Bacon Sandwich 4
PSV Licence 2 Aston Vanilla 1
Colin's Forgotten to Come Again 0 Surreal Madrid 9
Old Shambolics 3 Bring Elvis On 5
And Today They've Scored 14 Grampus 8 My Hamster 0
Athletic Supporters 1 Real Ale Madrid 5
Fruits of the Forest 2 Atletico Getrid 0

That's par for the course at playing-for-fun level.

Even some first-class clubs have attempted to achieve distinction by devious means. The acronym FC ought to be sacrosanct, but in 1971 Bournemouth decided not only to use AFC (Association Football Club) but to place it before their name in a shameless bid to gain alphabetic ascendancy in listings. At least a dozen non-league clubs followed their lead but were snubbed by the statisticians and handbook editors who stoically ignored their blatant attempts to steal a march. Changing their name to Aardvark FC might have been wiser.

Others have also used unconventional combinations. Rugby United confused people for many years as VS Rugby, which stood for Valley Sports. Leigh RMI are the Railway Mechanics

Institute. At base level there seems to be an unofficial acronymic battle going on. Leek CSOB FC (County School Old Boys), formed in 1945, led the way for years, only to be overhauled in 1994 following a merger of Beaconsfield United and Slough Youth Centre Old Boys who now play as Beaconsfield SYCOB FC. It's a cruel world.

Nor are distinctive club names confined to the domestic scene. Such has been the influence of British football on world language that hundreds of overseas clubs sport English names. Robin Hood were champions of Surinam seven times in a row, Shooting Stars are legends of the Nigerian league, and there are Uniteds all over the world. Some of the oldest clubs owe their origins to British influence and reflect that in their names. In Brazil the leading São Paulo club formed in 1910 is Corinthians. Argentina's famous Buenos Aires club River Plate would be playing as Rio de la Plata but for English influence. Racing Club and Boca Juniors also sound familiar, and what could be more English than Newell's Old Boys, founded in Rosario in 1903?

Club Blooming in Bolivia, Young Boys and Grasshoppers in Switzerland, and Red Star Differdange in Luxembourg all follow suit. Liverpool were Kenyan champions in 1965, Arsenal won the cup in Lesotho in 1991, and Mighty Blackpool FC are a towering force in Sierra Leone. Ghana's oldest club is Hearts of Oak. Even in Italy, so proud of its own football traditions, Athletic Club Milan (not AC Milano) and Genoa (not Genova) have adhered to anglicised names given them by their English founders in the 1890s. So too have Athletic Club de Bilbao from the fiercely independent Basque region of Spain, who prefer the English prefix to the Spanish 'Atletico'. But it's not always wise to attribute Englishness to overseas names. The Zimbabwean club Wankie are not a particularly inept side. They play in the town of that name.

There's a reverse effect to this trend. Some overseas supporters have such difficulty pronouncing the names of English sides they rename them to suit. This is at its most entertaining in the frenetic betting world in China, where according to Graham Sharpe of the bookmakers William Hill, the following Cantonese versions are standard. To test your linguistic aptitude cover up the left-hand column.

Arsenal	Ah Sin No
Aston Villa	Ah Shi Ton Wai Lai
Charlton	Cha Yi Tun
Chelsea	Chea Lo Si
Coventry	Koeh Wan Tei Ley
Derby County	Tah Pei Gan
Everton	Oi Wah Tun
Leicester City	Lei Si Tat Sing
Liverpool	Lei Mut Poh
Manchester United	Marn Luen
Middlesbrough	Mei Toeh Si Poeh
Newcastle	Ngau Kah So
Nottingham Forest	Lok Ting Ham Su Lam

If you romped through those try Sek Chou Sam, Lik Si Luen and Poeh Lik Pun Lau Lorng. If you said 'Sheffield Wednesday' and 'Leeds United' to the first two you'd do well behind the counter in a Chinese bookie's. If you said 'Blackburn Rovers' to the third, you are Chinese.

That's a difficult act to follow. Let's just say that throughout British football history, at all levels, there have been several million football clubs, most of them uniquely named. That's quite a testimony to both the ingenuity of the clubs' founders and the flexibility of the English language.

What they do have in common is that they are all both a *club* and a *team*, two of the most used words in football. *Team* comes from Old Norse *taumr*, the name given to a chain for yoking working animals together. It came in time to mean 'rein' and was applied to any group of animals pulling together in an act of labour, hence 'a team of oxen'. It gained its modern sense of 'a group of people acting together' in the sixteenth century. As such Oxford United, the most bovine club in the League, could claim to be the most appropriately named 'team' in existence.

As for *club*, its sense as 'a group of people with a common interest' first arose as a verb in 1674 when Nathaniel Fairfax wrote that 'two such worlds must club together and become one'. It literally meant 'forming into a mass like the thickened end of a club', soon becoming the noun we use today to refer to the whole entity which is the focus of our support.

In that sense, supporters who have suffered so much pain at the hands of their heroes might appreciate the older meaning. The *Bloomsbury Dictionary of Word Origins* leaves us in little doubt: '*Club* is borrowed from the Old Norse *klubba*. Its original meaning is "a thick heavy stick for hitting people".'

19

One David Beckham –
The Men Who Made it

'We all end up yesterday's men in this business.
You're very quickly forgotten.'

Jock Stein, former Celtic manager, modestly
misunderstanding his legendary status, 1989

Most football followers are keen students of *anthroponomastics* without knowing it. In plain English, that's 'an interest in personal names'. From the most accomplished players to the dullest journeymen, we revere them and revile them, but above all we remember them. For me, Dave Mackay, Charlie George and Colin Todd leap to the fore as Derby's best players, but lurching alongside them are Bobby Saxton, Steve Biggins, John McAlle, and a host of others I associate purely with gross ineptitude.

I also know the names of hundreds whom I never saw kick a ball. Mostly they're dead. Frankly, it's slightly strange, but we all do it. There's something refreshingly democratic about the whole business. Stanley Matthews and Albert Smith take up roughly the same space in *Football League Players' Records*, but one played 697 League games and 54 times for England, while the other's League career began and ended with a solitary appearance for Loughborough Town in a 12–0 defeat one March afternoon in 1900.

Many fans even remember at least one entire team without even having to try. These dream teams occupy the same subconscious territory as Co-op 'divi' numbers, army numbers and car registrations. Mine is Green, Webster, Robson, Durban, McFarland, Mackay, McGovern, Carlin, O'Hare, Hector, Hinton, from the 1969–70 season when Derby County used only seventeen players. It comes tumbling out at the oddest moments, yet I'd struggle to name the current side to order. I suspect these things may never leave us. My father, well into his eighties, was still name-perfect on Bolton's FA Cup Final side of 1953, although they lost. It's just there. It's a sobering thought that, should I progressively lose my faculties, the last word I ever speak might be 'Hinton'.

Curiously this also embraces fiction. Someone out there could doubtless chant the names of the Melchester Rovers side graced by Roy Race in the 1974 Cup Final win over Burndean. If you are he (this is largely a male phenomenon), here's a checklist with my profound admiration. If not, save it as a chat-up line: Tubby Morton, Ralph Derry, Noel Baxter, Geoff Giles, Jimmy Slade, Lofty Peak, Merv Wallace, Blackie Gray, Roy Race, Jumbo Trudgeon, Vernon Eliot. Manager, Tony Storme. General manager, Ben Galloway.

More famous still is Barnstoneworth United's 1922 side. Thanks to inspired comedic writing by Michael Palin in *Ripping Yarns*, designer T-shirts listing the heroic line-up are currently being worn in some of the world's ritziest holiday spots: Hagerty F, Hagerty R, Tomkins, Noble, Carrick, Dobson, Crapper, Dewhurst, Macintyre, Treadmore, Davitt. It confuses the Germans no end. And I've not even touched on 'Iron' Charlie Barr (Darbury Rangers), 'Hotshot' Hamish Balfour (Princes Park) and Jimi 'Raven on the Wing', the gypsy boy signed by Baldy Hagan for First Division Highboro United.

When comic characters have 'careers', we know we're into serious territory. The game is so inherently personal that anonymous football just couldn't work. Who's in the starting line-up, who's on the bench, who you direct your abuse at, who you will never criticise even if he has an absolute 'stinker'. Identification tags are key.

Fascination for names isn't exclusive to the British, but we take it further than most. Try telling an Italian that one of their greatest composers, Giuseppe Verdi, would be plain old Joe

Green in English, and you probably won't get a belly laugh. But tell an Evertonian that the surname of Liverpool's former left-back, Alan Kennedy, means 'ugly head' in Gaelic, and he'll probably stand you a pint.

Thus the sheer variety of British surnames helps things along. In South Korea, where twenty per cent of the population are called Lee, there just isn't the scope. And where's the fun in a Bulgarian side with at least nine players ending in 'ov'? Contrast the Wanderers XI which won the very first FA Cup in 1872: C W Alcock, A G Bonsor, 'A H Chequer' (pseudonym), W P Crake, T C Hooman, E Lubbock, A C Thompson, R C Welch, Revd R W S Vidal, C H R Wollaston and E E Bowen. Even the initials suggest mystique. A good team line-up delivered with just the right rhythm and timbre is surely poetry.

The *Oxford Dictionary of English Surnames* is enlightening on the subject. Eight hundred years ago, that line-up wouldn't have been possible. Before the thirteenth century, Britons were identified only by first or given names. Add-ons based on character or parental origin were sometimes used, but seldom passed on. So two Roberts living in close proximity might be termed Robert the Savage and Robert son of Will, but their offspring wouldn't take the names.

Gradually surnames did evolve, and by 1450 the foundation for today's system was in place. The huge variety reflects Britain's history as a land often invaded. Until football enjoyed its own foreign influx in the 1990s, a typical team line-up would include elements from Old English, Middle English, Old French, Old Norse, Irish, Gaelic, Celtic, Pictish, Welsh, Germanic, Gaulish, Latin, Greek and Hebrew. We were a mixed bag long before Chelsea fielded the first entirely continental line-up in 1999.

Close to 40,000 men have played professional football in England since the League began. It isn't actually very many. In a typical week, around 1,600 professionals participate in English and Scottish League games. That's roughly 1 in 20,000 of Britain's male population. Which is why we envy them, and why an otherwise unremarkable work colleague who 'had trials with Rochdale' is spoken of in hushed tones around the photocopier. And why two of the saddest words in the entire English language are *ex pro*. Even the substitution of *former* for *ex* fails to reduce the poignancy.

Despite an overall bias towards 'the working classes', those who 'made it' are a good cross-section to use for a potted history of surname origins.

All native British surnames come from one of four basic sources. *Patronymics*, those based on the first name of the ancestor's father, are very common. Alex Ferguson is 'son of Fergus', Bobby Robson 'son of Robert', and so on. All the 'Macs' and 'Mcs' also denote 'son of', and the 'O' in Martin O'Neill and his ilk means 'grandson of'. Manchester United's ragamuffin from the 1960s, John Fitzpatrick, a Scot, probably had ancestors who settled in Ireland soon after the Norman Conquest. He was 'son of Patrick', from the French *fils* for son. *Fitz* in England, meanwhile, often denoted bastard status. Fitzroy (from French *Fils de Roi*) was the illegitimate son of the King. The suffix *kin* also denoted a paternal link. Ray Wilkins is 'Little William', the 'kin' of Will. The surnames Richards, Roberts, Stevens, Peters, and countless more, also generally point to the father's Christian name. Gary Neville's dad, Neville Neville, somewhat overdoes it.

All this begs the question whether the FA were fully aware that the patronymic trend is particularly prevalent in Scandinavia. Sven-Goran Eriksson may have sounded super cool in Swedish, but would they have appointed 'Boy George, Son of Eric' with quite the same confidence?

The biggest group of names are those deriving from place names or topographical features. Few inhabitants of the Norfolk village of Beckham, originally *Becca's Ham*, could ever have imagined it would become a lucrative global brand, but the small settlement (*ham*) once renowned for its manufacture of *beccas* (pickaxes), probably named the man himself. The village (*ham*) on the stream (*beck*) is a more general possibility, but either way it seems David Robert Joseph Beckham is but a simple rustic at heart. And there really is only 'one' in football's entire history. His agent may well claim for effect that, like Beecham, the name came from the French *Beauchamp*, meaning 'beautiful field', but even a superstar's life isn't that perfect. It didn't.

Some in football do boast Gallic roots. Venables is a small parish in Normandy. Gascoigne is a man of Gascony. Matt Le Tissier, appropriately enough, was Matthew the weaver. But most British names are closer to home. Six of England's 1966 World Cup side were *toponymic*: Banks ('dweller on a bank'), Moore ('moor'), Hurst ('a wooded hill'), Stiles ('dweller by a stile or slope'), and the two Charlton brothers, from a village of that name. Football is awash with these locational indicators. Gareth Southgate hails from a certain part of town. Everton's Gordon West wasn't from East Anglia, but George Eastham might have been. Players ending in *ton, land, ville, ham, don, burg, berg, borg, bury, berry, field, by, fort, caster, chester, thorpe, dorf, hoff, dam, veld*, or *stead*, can generally be found in an atlas as well as in the programme.

But you'll need to search hard for examples of players who actually bear their team name. Surnames such as Manchester, Liverpool, Sheffield, Nottingham and Leeds are very uncommon. Most surnames only perpetuate small settlements, since they were generally only bestowed when someone moved away. Henry de Manecester, from the thirteenth century, only became known by that name when he left Manchester and arrived somewhere else. As most movement was from smaller rural settlements into the cities, not vice versa, big city names are scarce. *Postlethwaite*, a small north-country settlement, is a much more common surname than *London*. And only five players named *England* have played League football. As if to prove the point, the most successful, Spurs' Mike England, played for Wales. One player rather over-celebrated the rare occurrence of playing for his 'own' club. Arthur Blackburn was born in Blackburn in 1877, signed for Blackburn Rovers in 1894, again in 1899 and yet again in 1901. He died a happy man, in Blackburn.

Second only to place-name derivations are occupational surnames. David Seaman, Graham Taylor, Alan Smith and Kieron Dyer are exactly what they seem. So, too, players named Saddler, Clarke, Butcher, Baker, Glover, Potter, Forrester,

Falconer, Miller, Weaver, Shepherd, Glazier, Tiler, Stoneman, Woodman, Carter, and many more. Others celebrate near-obsolete trades. Cooper, Cartwright and Fletcher still entertain the crowds, but makers of barrels, carts, and arrows are in decline. Former England manager, Joe Mercer, never 'traded in fabrics', but his is one of an astonishing 165 British surnames related to the medieval cloth industry. Robbie Fowler no longer 'hunts wildfowl' for a living. Jim Baxter had a female baker, a *bakester*, somewhere in his ancestral line. Shaun 'Feed the Goat' Goater would be delighted to know that he's named from the Old English for 'goatherd'.

Lastly there are surnames derived from nicknames that describe physical, mental or moral characteristics. These were common in medieval records, but few gave rise to modern surnames, although football's records include a smattering. Craig Short, Brian Little, Graeme Sharp, Alex Young, Geoff Strong, Frank Large, Robbie Savage, Roy Keane, Wes Brown and Dennis Wise are all descriptive names. Others are less obvious. Bill Shankly's ancestors were strong in the legs (*shanks*), George Armstrong's higher up. Norman Whiteside's clan were a pale lot. Ryan Giggs has kept strangely quiet. *Giggs* comes from the Middle English *gigge*, meaning 'a flighty, giddy girl'. Others are more obscure still. Well spotted if you guess that a mangled contraction of Gaelic's *Caoimhin Mac Taidhgin* gave us 'the beloved son of little Tadhg the poet' known as Kevin Keegan.

Of course, this isn't a precise science. How appropriate, I hear you say, that one of the greats should be named George Best. No, actually. But then, considering his more recent antics, perhaps it is: *Best* comes from the Old French *beste*, meaning 'beast', used of 'a wild man, often suggesting stupidity or folly'. I could go on, but won't. Suffice to say that should the relentless round of hot dates and fast living ever begin to pale, great sport is to be had with a footie reference book in one hand and a dictionary of anthroponometrics in the other.

Football's records also reflect trends in Christian names and the game's social structure. Will men christened Caleb, Almeric, Theophilus, Levi, Septimus, Ephraim, Lycurgus and

Claude ever make the line-up again? They did before the Second World War. In the nineteenth century, the prefixes Major, Reverend, Captain, Doctor and Sir were not unknown in football. The suffix MP appears twice in pre-war League records. Derby County fielded a cleric who later became the Bishop of Sudan. Blackpool's right-back in 1908 was Herbert Ernest Saxon Bertie Cordey Lyon, who, modest to a fault, preferred to be known as Bert Lyon. Even as late as 1938, Chester's right-half was Arthur Stanley Sackville Redvers Trevor Boscawen Griffith Trevis. The fans called him 'Bos'.

Most of the players from 1900 to 1939, though, were from patently humbler stock. Most pre-war teams included three or four named Alf, Bert, Jack, Bill, Harry or Sid, none of which is widespread in today's Premiership. The zenith for Wilfreds was 1935–36 when twenty appeared in the League, but *Wilf* has been in decline ever since. Wilf Rostron's retirement in 1992 might well have signalled the end of an era. The long-forgotten Barney Battles and Billy Brawn sound purely fictional, but weren't, although neither beats Kilmarnock's current Australian midfielder, Danny Invincible. And would Manchester United's public relations arm permit them to sign any of this pre-1950 selection? Henry Clutterbuck, Fred Crump, Bert Badger, Billy Spittle, Fred Didymus, Fred Biggar and Gerald Cakebread. Could Arsenal be sure not to brick it in defence with a back five of Bert Diaper, Tom Fillingham, Alf Messer, Tommy Smelt and Christopher Crapper? Grand days.

Today's dearth of 'old-fashioned' surnames suggests football has become increasingly 'middle class', and we may never see the Cakebreads of this world strut their stuff again. Fashions in Christian names though, being cyclical, are a different matter. The top ten names given to boys in England and Wales in 1980 – the players we're watching now – were Christopher, Matthew, David, James, Daniel, Andrew, Steven, Michael, Mark and Paul. Only two of these appeared in the lists for 1900 and 1950. But by 2025 the League may be sporting a retro look. The 2002 top ten were Jack, Joshua, Thomas, James, Daniel, Benjamin, William, Samuel, Joseph and Oliver. It seems that Shane, Carl, Wayne, Craig, Lee, Luke and Scott may be football's dying breed. Exceptional odds are to be had on a Joshua lifting the World Cup for England in 2030, but it could be worth a punt. Not that today's line-ups are devoid of exoticisms. The single biggest change in the linguistic face of British football was brought about by the flood of 'foreign' players entering our game since the 1990s. Even the *OED* has been affected, the journeyman Jean Marc Bosman taking pride of place in the new additions for the next edition. His 1995 legal challenge regarding freedom of movement in the European Union helped transform British football. Listed under the entries 'a Bosman' and 'on a Bosman', he's the only footballer eponymously celebrated in the *OED*. Another for the 'famous Belgians' list.

Of course there were non-indigenous players long before the 1990s, but in such meagre numbers that they stood out as curiosities. Arthur Wharton, the Ghanaian-born Rotherham United goalkeeper of the 1890s, was regarded in the same way as we might look at a white blackbird in the garden, or a pigeon with one leg. Early reference books say he was 'generally known as "Darkie"', an attitude prevailing for many years. Some say the great William Ralph 'Dixie' Dean, the Birkenhead-born Tranmere, Everton and England legend of the 1930s, acquired his unusual nickname because he had, as they used to say then, 'been touched by the tar brush'. Even in the sixties, players with non-British names were such a novelty that they stood out. Albert Johanneson, Leeds United's South African-born left-winger, made a great impression on me. Likewise Villa's John Sleeuwenhoek, despite being born in Wednesfield. Colin Viljoen, Arnold Muhren and Alberto Tarantini were later part of the same tight-knit group. When the Argentinians Ricardo Villa and Osvaldo Ardiles signed for Spurs in 1978, it was quite a sensation. Even in the early eighties, West Bromwich Albion's Cyrille Regis looked unusual on a team sheet. Now it's Alan Smith who seems oddly out of place.

Chelsea were at the forefront of the revolution. On 26 December 1999 they won 2–1 at Southampton with the first League team made up entirely of non-British players: De Goey (Netherlands), Ferrer (Spain), Thome (Brazil), Leboeuf (France), Babayaro (Nigeria), Petrescu (Romania), Deschamps

(France), Di Matteo (Italy), Ambrosetti (Italy), Poyet (Uruguay), Flo (Norway). For good measure they were managed by Gianluca Vialli (Italy).

That's a far cry from Chelsea's 1938–39 season when their outside-left, Adolf Hanson, wisely insisted that 'from now on I'll be known as "Alf"'. At the same time, Millwall's Reg Schmidt decided he'd be happier as Reg Smith. The same had happened following the First World War when Ashington's Ernest Hoffman succumbed to a sudden urge to turn out as Ernie Holt.

Football's pseudonymous history throws up a number of other curiosities. The game was so tainted by the spectre of 'professionalism' in its early days that 'men of standing' were sometimes uncomfortable playing as themselves. The first man to score a goal in an FA Cup Final (1872) was Morton Peto Betts, but he played in the game as A H Chequer, 'a Harrow Chequer', inspired by having played for that team in an earlier round. Sherlock Holmes's creator, Arthur Conan Doyle, played in goal 'as an amateur' for the original Portsmouth Football Club of the 1880s when he was a struggling medical practitioner in Southsea. It seems likely he took a backhander, as he always appeared as A C Smith. Not as imaginative as his plots, perhaps, but certainly a wiser choice than some. Norwich City's 1930 Argentinian signing, Francisco Enrique Gonsalez, was surely set up by his team-mates. With Britain's entire heritage of names at his disposal, he elected to go through life as Frank Peed. Some players who might have been tempted to adopt pseudonyms had they been playing now, were spared the relentless leg-pulling simply due to the vagaries of time. Not once was 'You should have stuck to Quidditch' directed by a wag in the crowd at Rochdale's full-back of the early fifties. Harry Potter was just a very dull name back then. Likewise Arthur Fowler, Harry Hill and many more were fortunate to play in the pre-television age.

It's a short step from pseudonyms to nicknames, which only schoolboys use as much as footballers. That figures: many players admit that the mollycoddling nature of the profession never really allows them to grow up. Does a High Court judge named Giggs get called 'Giggsy' by his colleagues in the corridors of justice? Probably not, but if he did, 'Giggsy' it would have to be. There'll never be a 'Giggso' any more than a 'Barnso'. It has to be 'Barnsey'. But Phil Thompson is 'Thommo', not 'Thompsony'.

Players don't actually consult a book called *The Grammatical Rules of Nicknamedom*, but they seem to know the drill. Sibilants (*s*, *sh*) generally take a 'y': Scholesy, Rushy, Banksy. So do *d*, *t* and *p*: Bouldy, Wrighty, Sharpy. And Motson is shortened to Motty. But why is Beckham Becks and not Becky? *N*, *m* and *b* seem to like 'o' endings: Keano, Tommo, Robbo. But what about Browny, Poomy and Webby? OK, so there aren't any rules, just guidelines.

Nor are these names reserved for the dressing room; many attain general currency. If you've got this far in the book, I'm sure you'll put full names to at least an eleven from this seventeen-man squad, even though some of them retired years ago: Sniffer, Sparky, Crazy Horse, Bruno, Psycho, Razor, Butch, The Giraffe, Sir Les, Mighty Mouse, Supermac, The Kaiser, The Guvnor, Der Bomber, Chopper, Chippy and The Black Pearl.*

Let's delve still deeper into football's canon of trivia. Bob Wilson's middle name is Primrose, Gary Lineker's is Winston. Emile Heskey has two, William and Ivanhoe. Shaka Hislop changed his name from Neil in honour of the King of the Zulus. Australia's goalkeeper when they lost 17–0 to an English FA touring XI in 1951 was Norman Conquest. In 1992, his last year as manager of Spurs, Peter Shreeves bravely came out of the closet to reveal his real name. It was a small closet: he was actually Peter Shreeve. Tony Goodgame played for Orient, Tommy Fairfoul for Liverpool and Ted Passmore for Swansea. Charlie Faultless and Segar Bastard were both top referees. Officials named French and Saunders were once teamed at the same game.

---

* Allan Clarke, Mark Hughes, Emlyn Hughes, Emile Heskey, Stuart Pearce, Neil Ruddock, Ray Wilkins, Jack Charlton, Les Ferdinand, Kevin Keegan, Malcolm MacDonald, Franz Beckenbauer, Paul Ince, Gerd Muller, Ron Harris, Liam Brady and Pelé.

Consider on the other hand what happens when names are taken as read. In November 1999 *The Times* was the embarrassed victim of a hoax when it reported that Liverpool were keen to sign the £3.5 million French World Cup star Didier Baptiste, actually a soap character from Sky TV's *Dream Team*.

Yet there are still those who insist names don't matter. The last word can only go to the all-time leading advocate of that creed, Jack Charlton. At a Republic of Ireland press conference during the 1990 World Cup, taking the art of management straight back to the Middle Ages, he not only demonstrated why his side didn't lift the trophy, but also what football talk would be like without its labels:

Interviewer: Jack, which of the Egyptians impressed you?
Charlton: I couldn't tell you, I don't know their names. There was the boy with the beard, the dark lad in midfield, the keeper, the little dark lad who played centre-midfield, the very coloured boy and the boy who played up front – Hassan, Hussain?

20

Where Do You Want Me? – Humpty Dumpty's Guide to Keeping the Shape

'Shelbourne are obviously having trouble with Bohemians' five-man back four.'

Eamonn Gregg, Irish TV analyst, 1995

There are only so many ways eleven men can line up to play effective football against another eleven committed to stopping them. The idea of ten left-wingers and a goalkeeper-sweeper sounds interesting but as the French philosopher Jean-Paul Sartre so perceptively noted, such surreal formations are unlikely to succeed: 'In a football match, everything is complicated by the presence of the opposite team.'

Managers of lowly clubs habitually seek to pretend otherwise when facing better opposition by resorting to a cliché: 'At the end of the day it's still eleven against eleven.' That being the case, it might be expected that there would be a limited number of names for the positional deployments and tactical formations that managers ask their players to assume. But not so. Making things sound more scientific than they really are is an art form in football. Having just checked my research files on the subject (life really can be that exciting), I find I've listed 93 formal or colloquial names for the eleven positions since the Football Association was formed.

The uninitiated might be forgiven for feeling a tad bamboozled by such a disparate nomenclature, one apparently straight from the Humpty Dumpty school of linguistics. In *Through the Looking Glass*, the ovoid one was at great pains to point out that 'when I use a word it means just what I choose it to mean, no more no less.'

Take the man whose role is so specific that *goalkeeper* really ought to say it all. Yet he's been *goals, basekeeper, netminder, custodian, sentinel, guardian, goalee, goalie, keeper, keeps, the number one* and *numero uno*. Victorian reporters, paid by the word, were apt to further over-egg his title, hence *the man between the sticks, the man under the bar, the line patrol-man, the man with the cap* and even, for maximum pecuniary gain, *the wearer of the goalkeeper's gloves. Lone sentry, the acrobat, the duty-man* and *the last line of defence* make 22 so far.

The idea of the keeper as 'a breed apart' (remember he does have his own 'Goalkeepers' Union' and is the only player allowed to handle) is also perpetuated in *The Sportsman's Glossary* (1960) in which Frederick Avis tells us that *stiffie* has long been 'the generic name for the goalkeeper'. That little gem (which I was wary of researching on the internet for fear of what might pop up) derives from a popular Edwardian music-hall sketch featuring Harry Weldon as 'Stiffy' the Goalkeeper, a *stiff* being Victorian slang not only for a corpse but for any person thought to be lacking vitality, particularly an unskilled labourer or honest plodder. A club's reserve side is still called the *stiffs* for the same reason.

It seems unfair that goalkeepers should be thus regarded but the idea of the weakest link 'going in goal' is long established. In *Football at Westminster School*, charting the 1840s, goalkeepers were referred to as *funk-sticks*, which implied they were too cowardly to play in the outfield.

The idea of positional labels was first implemented by the Romans in their football-related game *harpastum* as early as the fourth century BC. Writing 800 years later, the Gallo-Roman chronicler Sidonius Apollinaris (c. AD 430–479) describes defenders playing near the baseline taking their places on the *locus stantium* ('the position of the standing players') and gives a particularly lively account of a player called in Latin the *medicurrens* ('in-between man' or 'middle runner'), the world's first *midfielder*, whose role was to intercept the ball *praetervolantem aut superiactem*, 'as it flies past or is thrown over'.

The true genesis of *positions* (Latin *positio* = 'put in place') lay in man's natural inclination to engage in teamwork in the performance of any task. Even in mass football, as soon as one participant suggested to another, 'You push yourself into the *hug* and I'll back you up behind,' the concept of forwards and backs was born. But it was in the smaller and equal-sided games that such differentiation would have been even more necessary. Most standard football histories insist that such games were unknown until the 1800s, but they were certainly played many centuries before.

In *Football's Secret History* (2001) John Goulstone has traced written evidence of 'a football playing' in May 1595 at Bewcastle in Cumberland between 'six men of Bewcastle' and 'six of a Border family named Armstrong', just one of many such records. In 1810 the *Book of Games* describes a friendly 'two v two' between boys of Kingston Academy, and the *Poor Robin Almanack* for 1683 contains the line: 'Sometimes football for the men. To try their strength ten against ten'. More famously, the antiquary Joseph Strutt described 'civil football' as opposed to 'mass football' in his *Sports and Pastimes of the People of England* (1801):

When a match at football is made an equal number of competitors take the field and stand between two goals placed at a distance of eighty or an hundred yards the one from the other.

As for eleven-a-side matches, these appear to have been fairly common by the early years of Victoria's reign although it wasn't until 1871, in the first *FA Cup Rules*, that eleven was officially specified as the required size of a team.

Why eleven no one knows; it's an odd number in both senses. Some scholars link it to the ancient fancy that odd numbers were considered lucky and the fact that they seem to figure prominently in the 'natural' world (five digits on each hand and foot, seven days in a week, 365 in a year, seven musical notes, nine planets, five senses). Certainly the two rugby codes, cricket, hockey, netball, basketball, baseball and many other team games settled on odd numbers.

Another possible reason lies in the illogical belief that odd numbers made a result more likely. Or, more practically, that all internal team affairs could readily be resolved by a vote. A further theory offered by those linking football's ancient roots to religion and magic cites the old English folk song 'Green Grow the Rushes O', which includes the line 'Eleven for the eleven, that went up to heaven', a reference to the number of apostles remaining once Judas Iscariot had done away with himself. In old ecclesiastical symbolism this was thought of as a propitious number, one perfect for a 'faithful team'.

Whatever the reason, an *eleven* (as we noted earlier, still often referred to as an *XI*) became the generic name for a football team around 150 years ago. Positional names since then have been influenced by four major forces: changes in styles of play, modification of the offside law, managerial whim and the inventiveness of the media.

The earliest records, from the 1850s, show nine *forwards* and two *behinds*, one playing further back than the other; hence the distinction *long behind* (literally 'a long way behind') and *short behind*.

By 1865 the wisdom of using a specialist goalkeeper had been accepted and the standard formation adjusted to a *goalkeeper*, with a *goal cover* in front of him, one *back* and eight *forwards*, what would now be termed a 1-1-8 formation. Note the keeper, due to his fixed status, is never included in team notations.

By 1870 this had again been refined to 1-2-7, that's seven forwards with two *half-backs* (literally 'half-way back'), one *full-back* ('fully back') and the keeper.

These changes marked a gradual shift towards defensive strengthening, but the presence of seven forwards still reflected the *dribbling* (thought to be related to Dutch *dribbelen* = 'to toddle') style of play prevalent before 1875, in which the man on the ball made straight for goal in a 'cavalry charge' style known as the *rush*, a term now surviving only in the informal *rush-keeper* of five-a-side games granted special dispensation to join the outfield players in forward forays. In the dribbling era the art of passing was little used and in football's first ten years, it was often accorded the epithet 'the dribbling game' to distinguish it from the passing codes favoured by adherents to rugby.

By 1875 further defensive entrenchment had made six forwards, two half-backs, two full-backs and a goalkeeper the norm, which remained as standard into the early 1880s. As players began to adopt specialist roles, so the need to apply clarifying labels arose. The six forwards comprised two *outsides*, two *insides* and two *centres* each designated *right* or *left*. Behind them were *right half-back* and *left half-back* and bringing up the rear a *right full-back* and *left full-back*.

This increasing arrangement of players in 'ranks', allied to a change to the offside rule which at last made forward passing legal (it's still not permitted in rugby), made the concept of working the ball forward from man to man a viable one, and by 1885 *passing* (originally 'passing on') was fully established. The Victorians termed the new style *combination* and a succession of passes a *combine* or *combined movement*, shortened today to *move*.

With passing, the increased importance of *marking* and *closing down* space became obvious and *tactics* became a vital part of the game. It comes from the Greek *taktos* ('arranged'), originally applied to military formations in the phrase *taktike tekhne*, the 'technique of arrangement'. Not that some element of planning hadn't always been around in British football. Even as early as 1602 the antiquary Richard Carew in his *Survey of Cornwall* was at pains to point out that there was method in football's madness:

> The play is verilie both rude and rough yet such as is not destitute of policies, for you shall have companies laid out before on the one side to encounter them that come with the ball and of the other party to succour them in the manner of the fore-ward.

Only one more post-1875 refinement was necessary for positional names to take on a form still used by many fans today, despite later changes effectively rendering some of them misnomers. England adopted that refinement when they played Scotland in 1884, dropping one of the centres into a midfield role at the heart of the half-back line to form a 2-3-5 line-up which remained popular for almost fifty years. He naturally became the *centre half-back*, soon shortened to *centre-half*. In turn the centre remaining up front was logically christened the *centre-front* and then quickly the *centre-forward*. To make room for the third half-back the other two moved further apart towards the touchline to become *wing-halves*, again soon abbreviated to *right-half* and *left-half*.

That formation might have remained unchanged for much more than half a century had not the offside law been modified again in 1925. Prior to that date an attacker needed to keep three men (including the keeper) between himself and the goal line in order to remain *onside*. This meant that two intelligent full-backs could readily set an *offside trap* simply by one of them springing forward on command, a tactic also known as the *one back game*. Pioneered as early as the 1890s, it was perfected by Newcastle United's right-back Bill McCracken and his sidekick Frank Hudspeth shortly before the First World War, and taken up by many sides by the early 1920s. As a result, thirty or so offsides per game was not unusual.

To counter this negativity the offside amendment changed the 'three men' requirement to 'two men', as it remains now, rendering the art of catching a forward offside far more difficult. As a consequence, rampaging centre-forwards found it far easier to dash between the two spreadeagled full-backs and were able to plunder goals as never before, something which certainly helped Everton's Dixie Dean to his record-breaking 60 goals in 1927–28.

Suitably alarmed, managers realised the central gap needed plugging and responded by pushing the centre-half deeper. The old centre-half position had come informally to be known as the *pivot* because it was a *midfield play-making* role on which much depended, filled by some of the most talented footballers in the game. But the Arsenal manager Herbert Chapman changed all that, ushering in the donkey days by pioneering the withdrawal of his centre-half to play between but slightly ahead of the full-backs. The tactic came to be known as the *third back game* and the new 'deep-lying centre-half' was informally christened the *stopper*. It was a metaphoric link to his namesake in a bottle, leak prevention being their common function. Arsenal's first stopper was Jack Butler but the first to really make the role his own was Bert Roberts, whose relentless headed clearances helped Arsenal to five Championships in the thirties.

Many fans, especially those of senior years, still call a *central defender* or *centre-back* the 'centre-half', despite the *half* part of his name becoming obsolete nearly eighty years ago.

As a consequence of the half-back line being reduced again to two by the centre-half's desertion, the *inside-right* and *inside-left* from the flat forward line previously known as the *five in a line* formation tended to drop back slightly to compensate. The forward layout then resembled the points of a letter 'W' and the rest of the side the points of a letter 'M', or vice versa looked at upside down. Hence the mysterious 'W-M' formation often referred to in older football books before numerical notations such as '4-2-4' became prevalent from the 1960s.

Although further refinements have taken place since the 1930s, the basic spatial plan of modern football was established by then and the W-M formation, in truth, was not too dissimilar to the 3-4-3 played by some of today's sides. Nor was the worrying-sounding *no back game* of the 1930s as cavalier as its name implied. Frederick Avis defined it as 'a method of playing the backs close to the half-backs with the intention of luring the opposing forwards into offside positions'. It sounds suspiciously like today's *flat* defensive systems. Everything since is essentially a variation on a theme.

Although most changes have resulted gradually by combined input there have been, like Herbert Chapman, a number of key tinkerers who have ushered new terminology into our language. Take *wingers*, originally known as *sides* and colloquially as *flanksters*. We'd never be calling them *old fashioned* or *orthodox* but for Alf Ramsey having changed their traditional role.

As manager of Ipswich Town in the late fifties and early sixties Ramsey experimented by turning his left-winger into a wide-left midfielder briefed to deliver early diagonal balls into the box from deep rather than strive obsessively to reach the legendary bye-line. Jimmy Leadbetter filled the role admirably and Ipswich won the League in 1961–62. Ramsey became so enamoured of the system that he controversially adopted it on both wings to create the 'Wingless Wonders' formation which helped England win the 1966 World Cup.

By that time Chapman's 'third back' had generally been joined by a fourth so that most clubs played a *back four* and Ramsey's starting formation in 1966 was therefore termed a 4-3-3 system. This began something of an obsession with numerical notation. Shifting from 4-3-3 by pushing a midfielder forward created an attack-minded 4-2-4. Pulling an extra forward back, as Jack Charlton was one of the first to do when he managed Middlesbrough to a runaway Second Division title in 1973–74, created a more defence-minded 4-4-2.

Many of today's sides play what is sometimes termed *five at the back* in a 5-3-2 system, also termed 3-5-2 because the two widest defenders (*wing-backs*) are encouraged to push forward to join forces with the midfield and attack. If that doesn't work there's always the option of a *lone front-man* backed up by five midfielders and four defenders, the triangular 4-3-2-1 formation known as the 'Christmas Tree' and used by Terry Venables for England in the run-up to Euro '96. Failing that, why not try the 'Diamond', which has four midfielders making the *shape* which is so often said to be '*lost*' when things don't go well. And there's always the retro approach. The *echelon* formation sounds suitably progressive even though it's actually from the 1950s.

And nothing is more certain than that there will be more. Derby County played 'the colander' for much of 2003–04. My adage that there are 'only so many combinations of eleven men' begins to look thin indeed.

When I played Sunday football I adopted a deliberately pragmatic approach to positional matters. Either I asked the captain 'Where do you want me?' or, if he actually asked where

I played, invented the utilitarian 'general midfield'. But knowing how to describe yourself as a player now isn't that easy. Being a *predominantly right-sided wide left* midfielder capable of *pushing on, drifting in* to *play off the front two*, or even willing to *drop deep* to assume a *holding role*, sounds much better than 'general midfield', but maybe that's why so many of today's players look confused.

Centre-forwards were the first to suffer an identity crisis, in the seventies, when *target man, striker, front man, leader of the line* and even *attacking spearhead* became fashionable. More recently a playmaker occupying territory between the forwards and midfield, the famous Teddy Sheringham role, is said to be *in the hole*. Nor were defenders spared new labels in that same era. Astute readers of the game, detailed to patrol watchfully in order to snuff out threatening attacks, became *sweepers* (a dual allusion to 'minesweepers' and 'sweeping up'), who simultaneously averted danger and kept things tidy. Full-backs once played *wide* but in a game where every blade of grass now carries a label they can also play *narrow*. We used to call it *drifting infield*, which was generally a serious offence.

As for the midfield player, variously tagged *general, dynamo, supremo, maestro, mastermind* or *playmaker*, he's now encouraged – on a pitch which is still flat – to explore the *channels* and *gullies* by playing *high*.

Cricket fielding positions were once commonly held to be the most confusing to the uninitiated, but football is surely making a stand. Of course the truth is that any formation is fixed only for that fleeting moment when the players line up. Once a game starts, flexibility is the key and the field of play is as ever-changing as a kaleidoscope. Look at the players before a goal kick and you'll often catch them doing what every sportsmaster told us not to ('no bunching') in an area not much bigger than the centre circle.

The other favourite bit of 'sportsmasterese', 'stick to your positions', just can't be taken literally, although I do remember a couple of full-backs at school (Harpur and Hitchcock) who were so petrified in form games that they did exactly that, literally jogging on the spot while the game went on around them. It took the famously relaxed Dutch to openly declare the idea of rigid systems a complete nonsense. In the early seventies the Ajax manager Rinus Michels played 4-3-3, but allowed his players freedom to roam and interchange. In 1974 he took Holland to the World Cup Final using the same system, termed in Dutch *totaal voetbal*. *Total football* has since become something of a cliché to describe attractive football. In a neat parody by comedian Steve Coogan, spoof commentator Alan Partridge's own 'That's liquid football!' has achieved catch-phrase status.

A number of other names for 'styles of play' have been coined over the years. The Spurs side that won successive Second and First Division titles in 1950 and 1951 under Arthur Rowe did so using an exaggerated quick-passing style in which off-the-ball movement was key. The press dubbed it *push and run*, a style now taken for granted by any team of quality.

Its opposite was the direct approach used to such good effect by Wolverhampton Wanderers in the forties and fifties, coined the *long ball game*. The same 'lump it forward' tactic, particularly attributed to Wimbledon in the seventies and eighties, was re-christened *route one* football, a term which owes its origin to the 1970s television show *Quiz Ball*. Choosing 'route one' enabled the footballer contestants to score direct from the back by answering just one 'difficult' question instead of the more laborious but easier option of 'route four'. Cerebrally challenged players, of whom there were many, often chose route one to get their turn over with quickly. It's the same on the pitch.

The game's spatial vocabulary will continue to develop. Fresh terms will be invented by new generations and old ones recycled by those who think they've discovered something revolutionary. Sooner or later some defence-obsessed coach might suggest a second deep-lying sweeper and christen him the *long behind*. *Custodian* is certainly making a comeback in the commentary world. I am still waiting for *funk-stick*, but John Motson might oblige.

Many of the words and phrases have never made it into the *OED*. Incongruously they remain part of a 'specialist' language used by millions. Most fans know deep down that football really is just 'eleven v eleven' but they continue to hope that one day the manager will hit on that magic formula which comprises the most elusive two-word combination in football. The *right blend*. As for the managers, they'll keep trying to make a simple game sound complex. They have to justify their contracts somehow. It was Ron Atkinson who once said 'the back four were at sixes and sevens', but it might just as well have been Humpty Dumpty.

21

Quaking and Shaking –
A Schoolboy Guide to Nicknames

'Why the nickname "Blue Brazil"? Easy. Cowden
play in blue and have the same debt as a Third World
country.'

Cowdenbeath stalwart Big Bob, with his personal
take on the club's nickname, 1993

There were two types of boy at my school in the late sixties:
those who knew the nicknames of every League club, and those
who didn't. Far more *kudos* (Greek = 'praise') was to be had
from knowing that Crystal Palace were 'The Glaziers' than
from being able to solve quadratic equations or decline irregular
French verbs. Really wise boys, though, kept some of their
knowledge under wraps, because being able to give a faultless
discourse on the linkage between Palace and Britain's biggest-
ever 'greenhouse' was the quickest route to a summary duffing
up at the hands of less intellectually adept boys whose faculties
didn't quite extend to recalling 129 nicknames to order. It was
129 rather than 92 because the two Scottish divisions, naturally,
were part of all the best-honed repertoires.

Falkirk, 'The Bairns', Scots dialect for youngsters. Origin in
the old saying 'Better meddle wi' the Devil than the Bairns o'
Falkirk'. Partick Thistle, 'The Jags', Scots slang for a thistle.
Montrose, 'The Gable Endies', the name of the town itself on
account of the proliferation of dwellings displaying that
architectural feature. It was like rote learning. Remember the
memory man in John Buchan's *The Thirty-Nine Steps*? Boys

202

who could hardly recall their names at exam time could readily have doubled for him on the nickname front. How it comes flooding back: even the odd Welsh one thrown in for show. Caernarfon Town? 'The Canaries', yellow shirts obviously. Shared with Hitchin Town and Norwich City, the latter not *because* they played in yellow, but apropos Norwich being a centre for breeding cage-birds. A rare case of colour imitating name rather than vice versa. They initially turned out in blue and white. That well-rehearsed little mantra (Sanskrit = 'thought') earned me more than a few dead-legs and Chinese burns. Once I started an overseas act I knew I had a pernicious disease. Atletico Madrid, red and white stripes, 'Los Colchomeros', 'The Mattress Makers'.

But then it all changed. Palace's go-ahead manager Malcolm Allison declared 'The Glaziers' outmoded, ditching it for the high-flying 'Eagles'. Boys became confused. Those still peddling 'The Glaziers' patter exposed themselves to cruel mockery. In 1975–76 Brighton also pursued an avian route, this time at the behest of the fans. Sick and tired of 'Flipper' taunts from rival supporters, they ceased to be 'The Dolphins', rose majestically from the East Sussex waters and transmogrified overnight into 'The Seagulls'. By then I was away at university, my brain too addled from an unprecedented intake of fresh knowledge and amber liquid to really keep track.

With the waters thus muddied, *nomenologists* who'd been club-perfect in their prime were thrown into a maelstrom (whirlpool in the Arctic Ocean off Norway = 'a whirling stream') of doubt. Edges thus blurred, the great days of nicknamedom seemed to have passed. Can anyone out there still do the full set with absolute assurance?

So this is for old times' sake. A nickname isn't a name that's been nicked. It was originally an *eke-name*, *eke* meaning 'additional' or 'also' from the Old English *eac*. It became 'nickname' in the fifteenth century by the process of mis-hearing and mis-writing called *metanalysis. An eke-name* simply became *a nickname* via the 'n' forward-shift. The same process gave us *newt* from *an ewt*, and in reverse *a napron, a nadder* and *a numpire* turned into the words we use today.

But why use nicknames at all? To convey a sense of place, identity, individuality and intimacy. To imbue a team with characteristics thought to be laudable or otherwise appropriate.

Many clubs, formed at a time when urban settlements were developing apace in a competitive economic climate, chose to celebrate local industries or crafts. Or rather journalists chose for them, since most nicknames were initially informal tags bestowed by the press.

Stoke, for example, were regularly 'the team from the Potteries' or 'the men from the land of kilns'. No imaginative hack wanted to repeat 'Stoke' over and over. Soon 'The Potters' became official. The 'cutlery-men' of Sheffield United were christened 'The Blades' (although Wednesday had it first) and Arsenal, formed by munitions workers, became 'The Gunners'. Football writers loved it, and linked metaphors have abounded ever since. Stoke have been 'fired' with enthusiasm so many times you'd think they'd be shattered by now. Sheffield United are forever 'razor-sharp' or 'blunting' the opposition. Arsenal will be 'shooting down their rivals' ad infinitum.

Others duly followed, hence 'The Cobblers' (Northampton Town), 'The Mariners' (Grimsby Town) and 'The Railwaymen' (Crewe Alexandra). But because times change, some labels no longer elicit the knowing recognition they once did. Don't expect to see hordes of boater-waving 'Hatters' in Luton and Stockport. And when was murder on the high seas last advanced as a serious career option in the southwest? Yet Bristol Rovers are still 'The Pirates'.

Wycombe Wanderers are 'The Chairboys' despite a decline in the town's age-old furniture industry, just as Walsall remain 'The Saddlers' long after the horseless carriage took a chunk out of the leather goods market.

Because of these economic vagaries, some clubs have judiciously sidelined long-standing monikers in favour of something less prone to obsolescence. Barnsley were once proud to be 'The Colliers', but decline in the South Yorkshire mining industry saw them sheepishly dabble with 'The Reds' before taking refuge in 'The Tykes' from Yorkshire dialect for 'a fellow'. They like to translate this as 'a really good, honest bloke with a great sense of humour and all that being a proud Yorkshireman entails', but if you're not of the Parkinsonian persuasion, and actually couldn't care less that Sidney 'Skinner' Normanton played 123 games at half-back for Barnsley between 1947 and 1953, alternative translations may come to mind.

West Ham resolved the same difficulty more neatly. Founded in 1895 as Thames Ironworks, named after an East End shipyard, their early nickname was 'The Iron'. That original amateur club disbanded in 1900, re-forming as West Ham United, named after the locality they then played in. It was pure luck that their revised nickname, 'The Hammers', reflected both the club's new name and the tools of the shipbuilding trade. Shouts of 'Up the Iron' still transcend the years at Upton Park. (Strictly speaking the Boleyn Ground, Upton Park merely being the district it's in.)

There's a guaranteed way of avoiding obsolescence. Like property companies who trade under names such as Badger Estates and Kingfisher Homes (although there just could be a Mr Badger and a Mr Kingfisher), many football clubs realised early on that it's generally wise to associate with God's creatures.

They followed an ancient tradition. Every society has either revered or demonised animals and birds, which came to symbolise emotions, abilities, thoughts, strengths and weaknesses. Ancient Egyptians were famously fond of cats. Hindus hold the cow to be sacred. Many Britons happily admit to liking dogs more than their fellow men. The lamb, pelican and unicorn are symbols of Christ. Satan tends towards the dragon, serpent and swine. Few men have kind leanings towards the vampire bat or common toad. The slug is nature's outcast.

As a result, many British settlements incorporated living things in their arms, and football clubs followed suit. As Malcolm Allison so shrewdly recognised, high-flying birds are pretty good copy, as are plucky ones and cute varieties. Torquay United are 'The Gulls' for seasidey reasons, Bradford City 'The Bantams' because their claret and amber strip reflects the bird's coloration. Bradford also collect a bonus by way of character association. The bantam, traditionally linked with the Javanese town of that name, is defined in *Brewer's Phrase and Fable* as 'a plucky little fellow that will not be bullied by a person bigger than himself'. *Brewer's* adds for good measure that 'the bantam cock will encounter a dunghill cock five times his own weight and is therefore said to have a great soul in a little body'. Perfect nickname imagery for football.

Not far behind is the cheeky strutting magpie (literally 'pied [= "black and white"] Margaret'), long regarded in folklore as an uncanny old bird. Newcastle United and Notts County sport its colours, both happily ignoring the bird's association with witchcraft, ill-luck and petty larceny by playing as 'The Magpies'.

Bristol City, Swindon Town and Cheltenham Town, all playing in red, are equally comfortable as 'The Robins', the Robin Redbreast being symbolic of confiding trust. Swansea City, 'The Swans', merely pun on their name.

You don't have to be an ornithologist to follow this feathered trail, but in the case of West Bromwich Albion it helps. Traditionally they're 'The Throstles', from the old name for a song thrush. *The Rise of the Leaguers* (1897) obligingly enlightens:

> It is almost a proverb among the folk of South Staffordshire that 'If you want a throstle get a Bromwich throstle'. So when Mr. Tom Smith became the secretary of the club in 1884 his pretty wit suggested a crest which took the form of a throstle perched on the crossbar of a goal.

A throstle still graces Albion's crest although it has long flown the crossbar for the cover of a bramble thicket. Most fans now prefer to call them 'The Baggies', said to relate to their once voluminous shorts.

What Albion's quaint story demonstrates is the role of folklore and yarn-spinning in nickname-ology. Not even the most assiduous 'twitcher' would claim to have spotted the subject of Cardiff City's nickname, although Vera Lynn did predict that the mythical birds symbolising happiness would be flying over the white cliffs of Dover. Cardiff are 'The Bluebirds'.

Nor should you expect a flush of birds wearing mortar boards and bookish spectacles in the vicinity of Hillsborough. Sheffield

Wednesday are 'The Owls' only because their famous ground was originally called Owlerton after the district it was built in. Beasts are equally popular. Hull City's black and amber strip naturally makes them 'The Tigers'. Likewise Watford became 'The Hornets' and Alloa 'The Wasps'. But there are traps. Don't Brentford, 'The Bees', play in red and white stripes? The nickname may in truth be 'The Bs', after the club's initial, but it's worth recalling that from 1889 to 1922, when the nickname first surfaced, Brentford sported deep yellow and ink-blue stripes.

Those creatures suggest qualities which would reasonably be expected to create a modicum of anxiety in opposition camps, which is the underlying rationale of good nickname tactics. There are enough arachnophobes around for the famous Scottish amateur club Queen's Park to remain loyal to 'The Spiders', which originated from their unusual black and white spindly-hooped shirts. If you're dubious, check out their website.

Millwall, 'The Lions', and Hudderfield Town, 'The Terriers', also understood this. But sometimes it just doesn't work. Wolverhampton Wanderers were on safe ground when they punned on their name to become 'The Wolves', but Shrewsbury Town acquired what was arguably the most ineffectual nickname in history by following suit. However many times journalists have either had them 'tamed' or doing the taming, it's hopeless. No matter that this small mouse-like mammal was held in ancient folklore to be venomous, or that its name derived from the Middle High German *schrawaz* meaning 'devil', it all counts for nothing. 'The Shrews' just didn't cut the mustard, which is why they now prefer 'Town' or 'Blues', or the rather more interesting colloquial name for Shropshire which accounts for the unusual cry 'Come on Salop' still heard at Gay Meadow today. It's from *Salopesberia*, the eleventh-century Anglo-Norman name for Shrewsbury.

Local tradition is responsible for other animal nicknames. Leicester are 'The Foxes' because Leicestershire is a renowned hunting county, Mansfield 'The Stags' because herds of them once roamed nearby Sherwood Forest. And Derby are 'The Rams' in honour of the 100ft-tall legendary creature made

famous by the eighteenth-century folk ballad 'The Derby
Ram', which tells us that

> The little boys of Derby sir, they came to beg his eyes,
> To kick around the streets sir, for they were football size.

Note that animals renowned for speed, cunning, strength and
virility are often favoured. No club has yet sought to ally itself
with the three-toed sloth.

While Derby's is one of the most ancient and romantic
nicknames, some are less inspiring. Spurning the living world
in favour of nothing more interesting than an initial letter link
are Oxford United, Leyton Orient and Queen's Park Rangers.
Only marginally more imaginative than 'The U's', 'The O's'
and 'The R's' are 'The Dale', 'The Dons', 'The 'Gers', 'The
Gills' and 'The 'Well', which serve as thinly disguised code for
Rochdale, Wimbledon, Rangers, Gillingham and Motherwell.

Even the greats can lack imagination. Liverpool, variously
'The Pool' or 'The Reds', ought surely to be 'The Liver Birds',
'Scousers' or 'Merseymen', but doubtless reason they need no
identification beyond their famous club colours. Others seem to
agree. Birmingham City and Carlisle United are officially
'The Blues'. Coventry City introduce a hint of gaiety as 'The
Sky Blues' and Dundee shade in the opposite direction as 'The
Dark Blues', but it's all rather dull. And what a pity the Stamford
Bridge powers-that-be have actively sought to distance the club
from its traditional 'Pensioners' nickname. The red-uniformed
veteran soldiers of the Royal Chelsea Hospital seemed once to
encapsulate the spirit of football itself, brave and decent
guardians of time-honoured British tradition. But do they fill
hotel rooms in Chelsea Village? Would the transfer-printed
image of an old soldier standing proud on the crotch of 'these
stylish briefs for the female fan' really help the club's
merchandising arm maximise its turnover? Time to deny the
ancients that rare pleasure and become 'The Blues' instead.
Even nicknames are prey to the game's business demands.

Thank goodness some camps still hold with tradition.
Everton's first headquarters was the Queen's Head Hotel close

to 'Ye Anciente Everton Toffee House'. The club are still 'The Toffees', and rival fans partial to a bag of matchday sweets pay them unthinking homage when their selection includes 'Everton Mints', first launched in the Victorian age by Mother Noblett's Toffee Shop near Goodison Park.

Other structures of even greater status than confectionery emporia have also stood the test of time. York's magnificent thirteenth-century cathedral made York City 'The Minstermen', and a much-loved but grotesque carving in Lincoln Cathedral (said to have been a devil turned to stone after misbehaving in the Angel Choir) gave Lincoln City a good excuse to become 'The Red Imps'. And the famously twisted spire on the fourteenth-century St Mary and All Saints parish church in Chesterfield explains why the town's club are proud to be 'The Spireites'.

Willingness to perpetuate links between football and religious faith should come as no surprise. A number of clubs began as church or Sunday School teams playing as 'The Saints', but only one first-class English club kept the name. Southampton were formed as Southampton St Mary's in 1885, becoming plain old Southampton when they turned professional seven years later. Another saintly club is the Scottish side St Johnstone, who play in Perth, a town long well-disposed to St John the Baptist. It's literally 'St John's town'.

Darlington carry both a religious and wordworthy link. Over two hundred years before the club's foundation, their future nickname entered the English language in its current sense on account of George Fox founding the organisation known as the Society of Friends. He began preaching his controversial doctrine in 1647 and, three years later, when he told Justice Bennet of Derby that he should 'tremble at the word of the Lord', the censorious judge disdainfully dismissed the organisation as a bunch of 'quakers'. That off-the-cuff remark not only christened a religious movement but gave Darlington their alternative name at the behest of one of their early benefactors, John B Pease, a zealous member of the Society of Friends.

'The Quakers'' tremblesome encounters with Bury over the years have always provided headline writers with scope for fun. Either Darlington 'quake' or Bury 'shake'. Stability reigns only after a draw. Again it was a chance remark that led to Bury becoming 'The Shakers'. During their triumphant run in the Lancashire Senior Cup in 1891–92, their upbeat chairman Mr J T Ingham boasted before one of the games that 'We'll give them a shaking up; in fact we are "The Shakers".' The press reported it. The fans liked it. It stuck.

A number of other clubs merit etymological scrutiny. Bolton Wanderers are generally assumed to be 'The Trotters' because pigs' feet are consumables held in surprisingly high esteem in Lancashire. But objectors assert that it was because the earliest Bolton sides were required to 'trot' from their headquarters to the ground. In fact, according to the club's historian Simon Marland, it was because both the team and its fans were wont to have a jolly time of it. A 'trotter' in Victorian Lancashire slang was a 'prankster', a chap like a 'cherry knocker' who had fun at someone else's expense before showing the victim a clean pair of heels.

Absence of definitive proof characterises a number of nick-names, sometimes resulting in serious debate. Most reference books say Oldham, Charlton and Wigan are 'The Latics' because it's a lazy corruption of 'Athletic', the second part of their names. Fair enough, but it's only a short step from there to the 'send three and fourpence we're going to a dance' world of Chinese whispers. Charlton are also known as 'The Addicks', which some sources assert is again short for Athletic. It's getting woolly. Those really in the know disprove the point by citing early printed matter listing Charlton as 'The Haddocks'. That name develops into 'Addicks', South London vernacular for the fish in question. Theories vary as to why they were thus christened. One website cops out with 'it was due to the original team's love of eating haddock', but the club's historians are more convincing. Their early team changed in a room above a fish and chip shop whose proud owner habitually arrived at matches waving a haddock nailed to a wooden placard. It sounds fair enough, although fans preferring something con-crete simply call Charlton 'The Valiants', in punning honour of their residency at 'The Valley'.

Peterborough's nickname is shrouded in mystery, on two fronts. Custom suggests they're 'The Posh' because they looked so dandy turning out in a brand new strip against Gainsborough Trinity in 1934, but no one has ever provided chapter and verse. Now even the long-accepted derivation of the word *posh* has been exposed as a myth. It was purportedly an acronym for 'Port Outward Starboard Home', the supposed cabin preference requested by wealthy travellers aboard the P&O steamship service from England to India.

As such it came to represent anything or anybody exuding an air of luxury. But in his 2002 edition of *Word and Phrase Origins*, Nigel Rees upsets the apple cart by revealing that the historic booking records of P&O contain not a single 'P.O.S.H.' request. The etymology is now widely thought incorrect, the true source being that *posh* was nineteenth-century Romany slang for both 'a dandy' and 'money'. None of which would concern Peterborough, although they value their name sufficiently to have victoriously contested the haughty claim of Victoria Beckham in a 2002 law suit that the club, who used the name sixty years before 'Posh Spice' achieved her dubious fame, were 'in breach of copyright'.

Without a basic knowledge of dialect or slang, some nicknames appear confusing. Arbroath are 'The Red Lichties' in honour of the warning signalled by the famous Bell Rock lighthouse built there by Robert Stevenson. Anglicised, they're simply 'The Red Lighters', which also happens to be slang for 'prostitutes'. Newcastle United are increasingly spurning 'Magpies' in favour of 'Toon', Geordie dialect for their 'town'. Heart of Midlothian, long 'The Hearts', are also 'The Jambos' or 'Jammies', 'Jam Tarts' being Scots rhyming slang for 'hearts'. Queen of the South, geographically closer to many English clubs than they are to their nearest Scottish rivals, are 'The Doonhamers', a Celtic variant of 'down homers'.

These exploratory excursions can be troubling. Fulham are 'The Cottagers', in honour of the ancient dwelling which once occupied the site of their Craven Cottage ground. Romanticism personified. It mattered not that a *cottage* was also Victorian slang for public conveniences, until some retro word bandit hijacked it in the 1950s. Now *cottagers* graces the dictionary as slang for 'gay men who frequent public lavatories in pursuit of

sexual encounters'. That makes Fulham v Arbroath the most
lascivious fixture in football, should they ever meet. What price
Fulham do a Chelsea and stealthily effect a change?

This all suggests that the world of nicknames isn't half as
straightforward or innocent as my schoolboy patter once fooled
others into thinking. Some 'football sociologists' have even
suggested that 'the cult of nicknamedom' is a bad influence on
the game, having been vitriolically misappropriated by today's
fans as a means of widening divisions between supporters.

Arsenal call Spurs fans 'The Yids' on account of the Jewish
support in the locality. The highlanders of Aberdeen and Derby
County's ram worshippers are greeted everywhere by shouts of
'Sheepshaggers' (strangely revelled in by their own 'Sheepshag
Army' who have perversely embraced the mantle of bestiality
with fervent good humour). Fans of Liverpool, Manchester
United and Bolton now habitually hurl at each other a
sixteenth-century epithet which the *OED* defines as 'impurities
rising to the surface of a liquid, also applied to people regarded
as the most worthless sector of the population'. There are few
redeeming qualities in 'The *Scum*', now being adopted by many
more fans as a generic insult word for close rivals. Portsmouth
supporters employ a modified version of that foul term by
labelling Southampton 'The *Scummers*', slang for what dogs
leave on pavements. Age-old divisions in perceived economic
prosperity and social standing on Wearside and Tyneside are
perpetuated even today. Shipbuilding has long since declined,
but Sunderland are informally 'The Mackems' (they 'make
'em') and Newcastle 'The Tackems' (they 'take 'em').

Even managers have been guilty of coining uncomplimen-
tary nicknames. Liverpool's Bill Shankly was so angered by a
robust Southampton performance in the 1970s that he dubbed
them 'The Ale House Brawlers', which stuck for some years.
At least one has had a lasting effect on the English tongue. Prior
to Saturday 23 July 1966 *animals* (Latin *animalis* = 'having
breath') was just another word. But once Alf Ramsey had lost
his cool by applying it to the Argentinians after England's
World Cup quarter-final win, no football fan could hear that
word without thinking of the Argentine captain Antonio

Rattin, breathing fire, becoming the first man in World Cup history to be sent off. Even the press has pursued the insult route: 'Arsenal Scramble Through – Sheffield Miss Many Chances', said *The Times*'s headline after their 1–0 win against Sheffield United in the 1936 Cup Final. 'Lucky Arsenal' has stuck with them ever since.

The press have also been responsible for the upside of team labelling by creating epithets which define eras. Most score high on alliteration. Wolves in the 1930s started the idea of the manager as the parent of young talent. 'The Buckley Babes', nurtured by Major Frank Buckley, were followed by 'Drake's Ducklings', Chelsea's 1955 Championship side. And at Old Trafford 'The Busby Babes', tragically decimated by the 1958 Munich air crash, were followed by 'Sexton's Soldiers' and 'Fergie's Fledglings'. The Scottish side who beat England 5–1 at Wembley in 1928 will forever be 'The Wembley Wizards', the Hungarians of the 1950s 'The Magnificent Magyars' and Ramsey's England World Cup winners 'The Wingless Wonders'.

So where does that leave us? It's clear that these formal and informal varieties render nicknames both laudatory and derogatory. Should a casting vote be needed to justify their existence, look no further than a body of intermediaries representing both ends of the spectrum: cuddly but also mischievous. But for nicknames, there would be no football mascots. Which means some of the game's most memorable moments would never have occurred.

Barnsley's 'Toby Tyke', a seven-foot bulldog, could never have provoked outrage among Manchester City's travelling fans on Boxing Day 1996 by cocking his leg at the visiting supporters. 'Sammy the Seagull' of Scarborough wouldn't have displayed the bare-faced cheek to moon at Brentford fans two years later. And several of Stoke City's squad would have been spared the embarrassment of being beaten by a hippo in the club's 1997–98 Footballer of the Year poll. 'Pottermus' was voted into seventh place by supporters not entirely satisfied by that season's relegation.

And what of 'Wolfie', psychopathic representative of Wolves? His violent record began in 1998 with a spot of bother at Bristol

City involving three little pigs, promoting the double glazing firm Coldseal. Stewards intervened as trotters and paws flew, then fur as Bristol's 'City Cat' entered the fray. Avon and Somerset police duly took a statement from Paddy Kelly, one of the pigs: 'Wolfie told me to fuck off,' he squealed. A police spokesman meanwhile, not one of the official pigs, defused the situation by declaring: 'We understand there was a lot of huffing and puffing.' But Wolfie remained unrepentant. In 1999 he allegedly attacked West Bromwich Albion's 'Baggie Bird' and was promptly reported to the FA by an Albion diehard.

These were problems that football's 'suits' could never have imagined having to face, but Wolfie proved merely to be the warm-up act for the game's most excitable mascot. If Swansea were not 'The Swans' there would be no 'Cyril the Swan'. Fully nine feet of feathered mischief, Cyril stuck his neck out too far on too many occasions. February 1999 saw him officially reported by killjoy referee Steve Dunn for 'inappropriate celebrations' after a cup goal against Millwall. Cyril had merely run on to the pitch, as swans do, to hug the scorer, for which Swansea were fined £1,000 by the Welsh FA, with a touchline ban for Cyril thrown in. That was after the *Sun* had given him their Man of the Match award against Derby in January of the same season. He was also nominated for the BBC TV Wales Sports Personality of the Year award, was invited to make the National Lottery draw, wrote his autobiography, and sold 2,000 copies of his CD 'Nice Swan Cyril'. The word *mascot* derives from *mascotto*, the diminutive of the Italian *masco*. Cyril evidently knew it means 'little witch'.

It's difficult to conclude categorically what it says about football and its fans when a team's nickname and mascot becomes more famous than the players and club. Probably that football, which the vastly over-quoted Bill Shankly once suggested might be 'much more serious' than 'a matter of life and death', is actually nothing of the sort.

Taken seriously, yes. But, thanks in no small measure to team nicknames, a game shot through with tradition and humour. Often partisan, sometimes pantomimic, but always a vehicle for the childish fun which is a bigger part of football's appeal than we overgrown schoolkids sometimes care to admit.

Talking a Good Game

22

And He's Gone For the Chip –
Why Commentators Talk Funny

'There's only one team looking like scoring.
Scunthorpe have had all the play. Burnley look very
tired all of a sudden. Hang on – Burnley have scored.'

Alan Mullery, Talk Radio summariser, 2001

Only commentators attract both genuine affection and merci-
less mockery from the same quarters. Managers, players and
officials polarise opinion; we either love them or hate them. Not
so the 'mike-men'. We may seize on their every blooper, but
still we can't help liking them. Imagine televised football
without commentary. OK, they make verbal slips. Sure, they
can be infuriatingly opinionated, often plain wrong. But we
need them. Radio football would be particularly low-key
without them.

So this isn't a hatchet job, full of *Colemanballs* (coined by
Private Eye in honour of David 'One-nil' Coleman). Having
tried commentary, I assure you it isn't easy. John Motson did
say, 'We're back to one-all' and 'The game is balanced in
Arsenal's favour', but that doesn't mean he's not a consummate
professional and a national treasure to boot. We can all be word
perfect in hindsight.

Jimmy Hill's 'Don't forget to put your cocks back before
going to bed tonight' was, it's true, somewhat more overt, as
was the (linked?) promise delivered by Barry Davies to an
expectant male viewership late one Saturday evening: 'More

217

League action soon, but first we're going to show you a few snatches from the Ladies' Cup Final.' From Kenneth Wolstenholme to Jonathan Pearce, Gerald Sinstadt to Alan Green, Brian Moore to Alan Parry, they've all done it. The only surprise is that they haven't done it more often.

So let's concentrate on what they do well, and why. It can't have escaped your notice that these men use words differently from how we speak and write them in everyday life. It's possible Martin Tyler might say 'and he's gone for the gravy' as he reaches out to enhance his Sunday roast, but probably not. In a nutshell, commentators talk funny.

That's not surprising considering the weird and wonderful techniques they draw on for effect. To a man they have mastered *ellipsis*. Most use *synecdoche* as readily as *prosody*. *Passive construction*, *inversion* and *deictics* come naturally. *Alliteration* is as essential as *tempo*. All of them use *jargon*, which in the fourteenth century simply meant 'the twittering or chattering of birds'. And those who fail to master the art of *intonation contour* can forget about ever reading the results on radio to a nation hanging on every subtle change of pitch.

Quite simply, commentators and their sidekicks are linguistic wizards. The Latin derivation confirms it. *Cum* ('with') + *mens* ('mind') gave *commentum* ('invention' or 'interpretation'). All those years I thought David Coleman and Barry Davies were useless, and they were geniuses all along.

Tense is the first obstacle. Only commentators earn a living describing something that's actually happened, but so recently as to be almost in the present. To get round this subtle problem they use what grammarians call the *instantaneous present*. No live commentator would presume to tell us that Beckham has passed the ball to Owen until he's actually done it, but you'll never hear him describe it in the past tense. Instead of 'Beckham passed to Owen', he'll say 'Beckham passes to Owen'. Children at play mimic this 'commentator's present' in monologues of their own: 'Here comes Seddon, beats one, beats two, goes round a third, and it's there!' That was me crossing the road. The most mundane occurrences are rendered exciting through the magic of commentary.

The next problem is time, epitomised by every commentator's nightmare, tennis on radio. The legendary 'Voice of Wimbledon', Max Robertson tackled this by talking soquicklythatitbecamealmostimpossibletovisualisetheaction. Football commentators have more time, but need to make more of it still. Good ones know how. Omission of 'unnecessaries' is the key, known as *ellipsis*. So 'Beckham passes to Owen, who moves it on to Rooney' becomes simply 'Beckham to Owen, on to Rooney', a forty per cent economy at a stroke. 'The ball' and impersonal constructions such as 'it is' are hardly ever used, hence verbal shorthand like 'Rooney has a go, fisted out, in again by Cole, banged away upfield', which is never used in ordinary speech.

Television commentators, in contrast to those on radio, are masters of minimalisation. In 1974, when Martin Tyler was about to do his first live TV game, John Motson advised him, 'Talk little, but say a lot.' Sometimes 'Beckham, Owen, Rooney' does the entire job, simply because the commentator knows the viewer can see the action. Not so with radio commentators, where longer constructions are maintained, mainly because they must avoid silence at all costs. If commentators were paid by the word, the radio boys would come out on top. The build-up to Alan Shearer's Euro '96 goal in the semi-final against Germany was described in 270 words on BBC television and 473 on radio.

Several other subtle time-making devices come in handy. Having to ensure split-second recognition of players, commentators have learnt to buy themselves fractions of extra time by using passive constructions and word order inversion. Misidentification cock-ups can be dramatically reduced if 'Scholes puts in the early cross' conveniently becomes 'The early cross put in by Scholes'. Before your very eyes 'Rio Ferdinand slipping away from the training ground now' becomes 'slipping away from the training ground now, Rio Ferdinand'. There ought to be a name for this specialised language, say 'Motsonese' or 'Mottish', but it's yet to advance beyond 'commentator speak'. The humorist Clive James once attempted to gatecrash the dictionary with his own uncharitable creation: 'A *colemantator* is someone who tells you something you don't want to know. A *commentator* is someone who tells you something you do.' It failed to make the *OED*.

Last but not least of the time-saving devices is *synecdoche*, a short figure of speech describing a more complex whole. 'The management team and substitutes sitting on the bench' becomes simply '*the bench*', an inanimate object which nevertheless 'leaps into the air', 'looks crestfallen' or 'gesticulates wildly' as is its wont. No commentator asks if a player is 'ready to assume the responsibility and leadership that being a captain entails'. Far quicker to ask 'Is he *captain's armband* material?'

Synecdoche isn't quite the commentator's best friend. That honour goes to his co-commentator, originally called *colour commentator* because their embellishment added vibrancy to the occasion. When they first began to be widely used in the 1960s, they were also termed *summarisers*, superseded today by expert *pundits* as their role now embraces the sort of incisive insight that only managers or ex-players can provide. When Ron Atkinson says 'You know what Clive, I rather fancy Owen's limping,' only years of managerial experience qualify him to make the observation. You and I just couldn't tell! Great players aren't always so perceptive. Consider this from the 1990 World Cup:

> *John Motson:* I'm trying to be referee, mathematician and commentator. Now it's your turn, Bobby.
> *Bobby Charlton:* The game is nicely poised, it could go either way.

Charlton went the way of not being offered much more work as a pundit.

Apart from *kebab* (Arabic = 'skewer') and *lager* (German = 'store house' for keeping beer), *pundit* is one of only a handful of foreign words current in British football. Whether it accurately describes Alan Hansen and his ilk depends on which dictionaries you consult. Most say it's from the Hindi *pandit*, via Sanskrit, for 'a learned man or scholar', but *Hobson-Jobson: The Anglo-Indian Dictionary* is more insightful: 'In India, the correct pronunciation of *pandits* is "pants".'

In fairness, co-commentating isn't always easy. It has its own tense problems. Having to talk through, for a second time, action that has already happened and been described once before, is easy on radio, where the simple past tense suffices: 'Owen drove into the box, beat the defender, gave him a little nudge which the ref didn't see, and stroked it home.' No problem. But doing the same over a television action replay sends everything haywire. Most players performing this peculiar skill take refuge in a nether world between the past and present, so what comes out is a unique brand of English: 'Owen's driven into the box, he's went past the defender, done him with a little nudge which the ref never seen, and he's stroked it home,' is how Chris Waddle, in particular, would describe the action.

This might have something to do with having once worked in a sausage factory, but even football's more educated fraternity are inclined to follow Waddle's dictum. The replacement of 'was' for 'were' in the past tense of the verb 'to be' is one of the most celebrated forms of this metamorphosis. 'We wuz robbed' was first said by a disgruntled American boxer in the 1920s, but football has since adapted it for all occasions. 'We just wasn't ourselves today' is a great favourite of Terry Venables, otherwise a thoroughly articulate speaker. Although it's a trait common in many speakers of Southern English, it's spread to all regions in football.

Venables is also an adept of its only serious rival, the use of 'done' instead of 'did', as in 'the lad done great'. 'Brilliant', rather than 'brilliantly', is often substituted for 'great' to further compound the error. This caused such ire to one amateur grammarian that he wrote to the *Guardian* suggesting a declension of the verb 'to do great':

I done great
You done great
He done great
We done great
They done great
The boy Lineker done great

What prompted this minor classic was the creative grammar of pundit Mike Channon during the 1986 World Cup. Even his fellow ITV panellist Brian Clough, a stickler for correctness, couldn't help extracting something from Michael.

> *Channon:* We've got to get bodies in the box. The French
> done it, the Italians done it, the Brazilians done it . . .
> *Clough:* Even educated bees done it.

Perhaps it's as well commentators do most of the talking. They have the skills to cope. For years, David Coleman demonstrated a passion for *prosody* before several million viewers without once being arrested. That is 'the use of pitch, loudness, tempo and rhythm to create a particular effect'. It's especially effective on radio, where every late attack can be made to spell mounting danger even if the keeper never has a save to make. It's the sort of con trick that makes radio games legendary. Alan Green is the current master, but no one has ever topped Peter Jones, who could have made the proverbial drying paint a compulsive event.

Top of the skill chart for difficulty is the *intonation contour*, not commentator-speak as such, but a close relative. We're talking about 'the reading of the classified results'. James Alexander Gordon, known as 'JAG', has performed the task on BBC Radio's *Sports Report* for so long now (he started in 1972) that his 'result-speak' is legendary. How many Saturday nights have been made or ruined by the rise or fall in voice pitch that betrays the result of a match before he's finished reading it? Little may he know it, but Gordon is one of the most powerful men in Britain, hardly ever clocked in the street but often 'recognised' by his voice. In surveys of 'quintessential Englishness' he's up there with fish and chips and cricket on the village green. Yet he's Scottish, born in Edinburgh in 1931, though rather spookily – at least to the eye – he now lives in Reading. It's virtually impossible to convey his skill in print, but if I write 'Manchester United 2, Arsenal 2', I know exactly how you'll say it if you know *Gordonese*.

Incorrect application of score-intonation is the biggest crime in broadcasting. Something like 'Manchester United 1, BURTON

ALBION . . . 0' deserves instant dismissal. Strangely, former football front man Eamonn Andrews got away with something similar for years. The genial Irishman with the permanently sheepish grin unfortunately pronounced 'won' and 'one' identically (rhyming both with 'gun'), which gave every stand-up comedian in the north (where 'won' is pronounced 'wun' and the number 'wohn') at least one (or 'won') guaranteed guffaw per gig with the hackneyed line 'Liverpool won, Everton lost'.

Use of football results for comedic effect has always been around. Many assume the oft-quoted 'Forfar 5, East Fife 4' is fictitious, but it actually happened in the Scottish Second Division in 1963–64. *Monty Python*'s Michael Palin once credited Wrexham with an incredible home win without actually reading the scoreline: 'Tonight is European Cup night. One result already in from Munich. First round, second leg. Bayern Munchen 4397, Wrexham 1. So Wrexham going through on aggregate there.' Another I like is 'Real Madrid 3, Surreal Madrid Fish'.

It will be a sad day when J A G utters his last intonation. Hopefully he'll contrive an interesting death-bed speech, so we'll know he's going a fraction of a second before he actually does. Something like 'I think I'm going 2, breathe my last 1' would do a decent job, or for a real cliffhanger 'What has it all been 4, it must be something I 8.'

It's all too easy to dismiss broadcasterese as a specialist *argot* (also known as *cant*) understood only by lovers of the game, but as that number stretches to millions we'd have to say that commentator-speak far outstrips the verbal peculiarities of shipping forecasters, airline pilots, railway announcers and other masters of distinctive styles. So much so that a piece of football commentary arguably claims to be the most recognised sentence ever spoken in the English language.

'England expects that every man will do his duty' (Lord Nelson) and 'We shall fight on the beaches . . . we shall never surrender' (Winston Churchill) are certainly up there. Even 'Not a lot of people know that' (Michael Caine) makes a claim, although Caine himself didn't coin 'his' catchphrase. It was Peter Sellers doing an impression of him on the *Parkinson* show.

'Elementary, my dear Watson' (Sherlock Holmes), and 'Play it again Sam' (Humphrey Bogart) are also disqualified on the grounds that they too are *mythquotes*. So can anything really top Kenneth Wolstenholme's 'They think it's all over. It is now', which achieved instant fame on 30 July 1966? Even the moon landing's 'One small step for man . . .' isn't so often repeated. And Ken's World Cup Final classic has entered the language well beyond its original football context. If indeed it's the best-known English sentence, it deserves a closer look.

Although the late and great Kenneth claimed he was absolutely in control of that epoch-defining moment, it's difficult not to conclude that he was just a tad fortunate in the way it all worked out: 'I saw some people on the pitch and I said "Some people are on the pitch," and I had a stop-watch and thought, any second now the referee's got to blow. He put his whistle in his mouth, and I made the excuse for the fans that they thought it was all over, and while I said that Geoff Hurst hit it. It was obvious it was the end, and I'm proud of the fact that I said "It is now" before the ball went into the net. I knew if Geoff had missed, it would still have been over because there's twenty or so yards behind the goal and by the time they got it back to the goalie the referee would have whistled anyway.'

I have an irresistible urge to say 'Hmmm' at this point. What if Hurst had scuffed it weakly into Tilkowski's hands? Only the fact that he scored made Wolstenholme's comment legendary. It's true that Ken said 'It is now' a fraction before the ball actually hit the net, but it was clearly 'in' as he spoke the words. So even Ken himself has embellished the moment further. And in fact it was he who thought it was all over. Seconds before his greatest moment, he'd spluttered 'It's all over, I think . . . no, it's . . .'. If the whistle had blown then, what a lame finish that would have been. Imagine, too, if the clinching moment had actually been Hurst's previous goal, the famous 'over the line' one which made it 3–2. Would dear old Ken's commentary still have been used to name a television programme? 'Yes! Yes! No! No! The linesman says no! The linesman says no! It's a goal! It's a goal! Oh and the Germans go mad at the referee.' A bit of a 'mare' to be frank.

Wolstenholme deserved his bit of luck, but one must feel a trifle sorry for the two forgotten men of that memorable moment, the commentators for ITV and BBC radio. On ITV Hugh Johns was saying, 'Geoff Hurst goes forward. He might make it three. He has, he has. And that's it, that's it.' Not a classic, but not noticeably worse than Wolstenholme. Arguably better than both was Peter Lloyd's BBC radio commentary. He's not exactly a household name, and few Englishmen will recall his words, but I defy any fan to listen to the recording (preserved on a double LP) without experiencing an emotional reaction: 'Yes, yes, it's a goal! A wonderful, wonderful goal. Good ol' England! England who couldn't play football! They've got it in the bag! And the whole stadium has gone mad, absolutely mad!' He only needed to add 'we've beaten the Hun, we've beaten the rotten Hun' and it would have been perfect. In the event, his Welsh co-commentator, 'Geevers' Wynne-Jones, finished the job admirably in a voice choked with emotion: 'It's a magnificent victory, the result of years of planning, this enormous crowd, standing, cheering madly, and the sun shines brightly on this treasured isle. England's such a happy place, Wembley such a wonderful spot on this World Cup afternoon.'

I'm sorry. I can't go on. So let's give commentators the benefit of the doubt. Next time you hear a slip of the tongue, let it go. At least the first one. If they do it twice, get straight on to *Private Eye*. And if they make the hat-trick, remember the perceptive words of Jimmy Greaves, ace pundit speaking live to millions in 1991: 'I don't know what's going on out there, but whatever it is, it's diabolical.'

23

Welcome to Our Visitors –
The Cosy World of Proggie Chat

We are now into a new season and I have no doubt
that George and Mildred are delighted to be selling
their cheese rolls in the Fourth Division.

Colin Murphy, Lincoln City manager,
in his 'Murph's Message' programme column, 1988

On Tuesday 18 February 2003 Sotheby's sold the Spurs v
Sheffield United 1901 Cup Final programme for a world-record
auction price of £14,400. Apart from suggesting that football
memorabilia collectors have more money than sense, this
confirms beyond doubt that humble football programmes, once
single sheets of card or flimsy paper, now hold a significance far
beyond the ephemeral purpose for which they were intended.

Nostalgia and football go hand in hand. Long after games are
consigned to history, it's still possible, through tactile contact with
the match programme, to be there in spirit. It's the missing link,
laid down like a fine wine, to consume another day. Look at it
longingly, read it feverishly, fondle it lovingly, or deposit it in a
bank vault and simply think about it before you go to sleep at
night. It doesn't matter which. You've got it and they haven't. It's
what collecting is all about. Serious money for a piece of paper is
ludicrous. But for a whiff of the game itself? Who's to say?

Men and boys are the main culprits, obsessively preserving
that time when, for at least ninety minutes of their lives, all
seemed right with the world. Something to fall back on. Few

226

women save football programmes. Yet how many order-of-service cards from weddings and christenings are secreted in dressing table drawers? It has to be a gender thing. Stoke v Aston Villa, Midland Cup Final 21 April 1945, slight fold, minor edge wear, teacup stain to rear, score written on front and team changes pencilled in, otherwise very good for age. Or your name card from the table setting at your second cousin's third marriage? The choice is yours.

Programme language is suitably cosy. Apart from *pirate issue* (unofficial publications usually sold at Cup Finals to gullible day-trippers) and the recent *reprographic copy* or outright *forgery* which have ominously entered the world of collecting, it's virtually impossible to detect anything overtly nasty in the sanitised world of programme-speak.

Unless, that is, the scrupulous control that officials exercise over the 'club organ' can itself be construed as sinister. Many believe it is, hence the rise of *fanzines* from the mid-1980s as a means of countering the party line.

Programmes have changed. Originally they were exactly what the name suggests, a timetable of events and a list of participants, from the Greek *pró* ('before') and *gramma* ('written'), literally 'written before the event'. Theatres started the fashion in the mid-nineteenth century, football following suit in the 1870s.

Yet even then the classic vendor's cry 'Get your programme, official programme' was uncommon. Early publications, generally single sheets, were simply known as *match-cards* or *team-cards*. *Official Programme* entered general usage only around 1900, partly as a response to the nefarious activities of un-authorised hawkers but also to reflect a more substantial content.

The *Chelsea Chronicle*, launched in 1905, was all but a magazine. So too the *Albion News* and *Villa News and Record*, hot sellers in Birmingham between the wars.

These were the precursors of today's glossy and uniform *matchday magazines*, consciously renamed by clubs since the early eighties to 'justify' charging up to £3 for what once cost a halfpenny. But try listening for someone to say 'I'm just going to get a matchday magazine.' You'll wait a long time. Football followers rarely embrace change for change's sake.

But programme language itself has never been revolutionary. Clubs adhered to a formulaic content for years on end. Most programmes of yesteryear remained flimsy in both fabric and content.

There was always a 'Today's Visitors' feature saying something which 99 per cent of supporters disagreed with: 'We extend a hearty and cordial welcome to our old friends Leeds United this afternoon.' No we don't. Everything about them leaves us shaking with all-consuming rage. It should say: 'Yet again we can expect an afternoon of whingeing and despicable behaviour as the Leeds we all know and despise inflict their odious presence on us yet again.' But it never has and never will.

'The Man in the Middle' imbued referees with lovably human characteristics which made them sound like favourite uncles. How can you hurl genuine abuse at someone who 'sings in his local church choir' and 'in his spare time grows prize leeks'? Forty years ago detail of the referee's 'other' life was commonplace in an age when it was safe to give it without his wife, 'who counts crochet and reading thrillers amongst her hobbies when not looking after their three young daughters at home in Tarporley', receiving death threats if he turned down a half-decent penalty appeal. Today's 'match officials' wisely guard their privacy more closely.

'Pen Pictures' gave stereotyped but curiously charming resumés of the opposition. There was usually a 'gritty little Scot', many a 'club stalwart' who had 'made the left-back position his own', and always a 'local youth' who had 'recently broken through from the reserve ranks and has taken his chance well'. Irish players were from 'the Emerald Isle', Scotland was either 'North of the Border' or 'the Land of the Thistle'. Most Welshmen had 'left the green valleys for pastures new' even if they were born on a grime-covered council estate somewhere completely flat.

Anyone under five foot nine and marginally overweight was 'stocky'. Tall forwards were either 'rangy' or a 'beanpole striker' and players under five foot six were 'diminutive', never small. No one was a 'veteran' until they'd passed their fortieth birthday, when they automatically became a 'loyal club servant'. Goalkeepers were often 'the character of the side'.

Where would the programme editors of old have been without clichés and euphemisms? Probably in the 'twilight of their career', 'confined largely to the reserves', 'contemplating the looming spectre of relegation', 'struggling to make an impact at senior level' or 'harbouring an ambition to run a guest house on the coast in retirement'.

Today's matchday offerings differ. Most are written by professional journalists. Colour photography abounds. Sixty-four pages is standard. But 'better' is a moot point.

I have at hand a 2002–03 copy of *The Ram*, which earned Derby County 'programme industry awards' for 'outstanding quality'. Starting with 'The Boss Writes', subtitled 'Gaffer Gregory', it moves smarmily on through 'Teamtalk', 'Sidelines', 'Past Masters', 'Classic Clash', 'Grassroots', 'Old Moore's Anorak' and 'Stats All Folks', finishing with 'Pride Park Emergency Procedures'. This advises fans that 'in the event of an emergency at Pride Park Stadium you will hear a police message providing information and directions to spectators'. As I write there has been a state of emergency for some time but little in the way of information or direction. Only John Gregory has been shown the exit door.

I choose Derby only because they are my club. It could have been any. Sterility and uniformity rule, the fan regarded as a passive receiver who will buy every last word emitting from the club's tame mouthpiece. Older programmes, by comparison, not only had character, but were transparent enough not to imply reader gullibility.

That's not to say modern programmes don't produce items of linguistic interest. Thanks to managers' programme notes, they do.

Gaffers of old (a sixteenth-century contraction of 'Godfather') played it safe: 'Good afternoon everyone. Back to the League after the grim slog of cup tie soccer' was a trifle gloomy but unlikely to create either mirth or outrage among the good citizens of Rochdale in 1963. This left supporters free to peruse the adverts (once the bulk of the programme) in a calm and receptive state of mind, able to respond to the unsubtle commands accordingly: 'Ask at the tea-bar for a famous Leach's pie'; 'Place

all your electrical work in the safe hands of G. L. Adamson Ltd.';
'Always Insist on Jubilee Piccalilli, the pickle that scores every
time home and away'. Oh, for such simple times.

Many of today's more sophisticated breed of manager try to
play safe in a different way by having the column written for them.
This is a world in which every defeat is 'unfortunate', things will
always 'turn around given sufficient time' and 'despite our
difficulties there is much to be positive about and I know I can rely
on you to keep faith with the club as you always have done'.

It doesn't work. Widespread supporter apoplexy ensues.
This is irresponsible management. There's a definite danger
that fans in a state of high agitation might insist on the wrong
type of pickle or place at least some of their electrical work in
unsafe hands. Managers' programme notes ought to be subject
to Health and Safety regulations.

Bosses (Dutch *baas* = 'master') who regard themselves as
intellectuals understand this weighty responsibility and take sole
charge of their own output. Yet therein lies a graver danger still.
Any man who openly handles his own column must expect flak.

Former Charlton Athletic manager Lennie Lawrence achieved
notoriety for his off-the-wall contributions, but Colin Murphy,
twice Lincoln City manager in the seventies and eighties, went
one better by receiving a Golden Bull Award from the Plain
English Campaign for his 'Murph's Message'. Here's 'Murph' on
breaking down an opposition defence:

> Of the keys on the ring at the moment, we should be
> selecting more correctly to unlock opposing mechanisms.
> However, there is not a lock that cannot be unlocked so we
> shall continue to endeavour to unlock the lock, but in
> doing so we must not get locked out.

Most fans felt Murphy should have been locked up for such
dogged pursuit of metaphor, but his ramblings acquired cult
status. Here's why Lincoln failed to gain promotion:

> I happen to believe no one can work miracles and it strikes
> me that even applies to people like Holmes and Watson,

the Marx Brothers, Bilko, Inspector Clouseau or Winston Churchill. All these had immeasurable qualities, but I don't know whether any of them had the attributes to be able to win promotion for Lincoln City FC with all the injuries and suspensions we have had.

Foolishly bypassing an obvious route into the world of comedy writing, Murphy later accepted positions in Saudi Arabia and the Far East, where confusion duly reigned.

Although Murphy's use of language was an exceptional example of column-talk, he wasn't alone. This is Crystal Palace's manager Alan Smith explaining their lowly position in the 1994–95 season:

Seven games we've lost 1–0, another seven we've drawn 0–0. If we'd drawn the 1–0 games we lost, we'd have another seven points. If the seven goalless draws had been 1–0 to us we would have 21 points more and be third in the Premiership.

Despite the appealing logic Palace were relegated, and the Carol Vorderman of football left the club.

There's a simple message to be gleaned from all this. Football programmes, created by Victorian entrepreneurs largely to impart information, have lost their way. The *Guardian*'s Frank Keating perceptively described today's fodder as 'brick-heavy pop-star catchpennies, sheen without substance'. All we really want is the teams, fixtures, League positions, and a few words of gentle welcome.

I wouldn't pay £14,400 for a Victorian original. Nor can my moral budgeting process any longer justify the outlay for today's equivalent. Many fans share that unease. Isn't a five-figure sum for a piece of football ephemera, no matter how evocative, just as obscene as a player being paid £90,000 a week? And why pay £3 for a propaganda lecture?

The true value of programmes lies elsewhere. It's beyond money. They are mirrors to the games past. If you want to know the real history of football, to learn about the relationship of the club with the fans and community, the place of the game in society, to chart its progress and ills and understand the people who have inhabited it, pick up a programme. It's one medium of football talk that reveals more than it ever intended.

24

Goal, Shoot! and Sweet FA
– The Voice of Footie Mags

'Self-consciousness, lack of confidence, nervousness,
worry, weak-will, unsociability, lack of enterprise,
stammering, blushing, forgetfulness, sleeplessness,
inferiority complex and general negative impulses,
eradicated forever. Reconstruct within yourself a
powerful and more assertive subconscious mind:
Send 2 shillings now.'

Soccer Star advertisement targeting
the typical football supporter, 1957

It's 1873 and 1st Surrey Rifles have just lost 3–1 at home to
Maidenhead in a thrilling cup tie. Curiously aroused by this
epic contest, a visionary publisher decides that the burgeoning
popularity of the association game merits a modest monthly
periodical. He is about to invent the football magazine.

Pre-dating its legendary 1960s namesake by almost a century,
he called it *Goal*, 'The Chronicle of Football'. It lasted just twelve
months, but a new genre had been born, and with it an evolving
style of language reflective of ongoing changes in the game.

More titles followed. The British Library lists 300 since 1873,
launched with unfailingly optimistic fanfares but often folding
without even the dignity of a 'Last Ever Issue' cover flash.

Some have entered football's vernacular as pseudo-
adjectives. 'Manchester United's new green and yellow halved
shirts were straight from the *Topical Times* era' – they were

233

traditional and redolent of the inter-war period; 'With his elaborately-coiffeured hair, long sideburns and moustache, the Albion centre-back might have stepped straight from the pages of an early issue of *Shoot!*' – he was a Jason King lookalike sporting the flamboyant style of the early seventies; 'Robbie Savage's approach to interviews is more *FourFourTwo* than *Charles Buchan's Football Monthly*' – he is frank and laddish, and perfectly comfortable talking about illicit bowel evacuation for an article entitled 'Is Robbie on the Dumping Ground?'.

Magazines mirror changes in football and society, particularly shifts in player–fan relationships. Women and children were taboo subjects in such publications before the Second World War. Sex didn't exist. In fact pre-war footballers didn't have genitals.

They did have kind mothers who still did their washing and fed them porridge to build them up. They all learnt football in the street with a tennis ball – if they were lucky. Many could only afford a bundle of rags tied with string. If you were wearing the rags it had to be paper. If the string was holding up your dad's trousers on his 25-hour shift down the mine, the ball was a tin can rescued from the nearest midden.

Naturally footballers didn't drink, although smoking was fine; it promoted healthy lungs. Most players travelled to matches on the same public transport as the fans. Cromer, Filey and Cliftonville were the hottest holiday spots.

Not that fans weren't hungry for gossip. Before television, watching players live was the only option, so titbits which brought the stars even partly to life were greedily sought. But because the fans knew so little they were prepared to feed off scraps. The diet was meagre and bland.

In 1937 *Topical Times*' 'Intimate Details of Your Favourites' 'revealed' that 'Arsenal's Wilf Copping is a native of Barnsley. Young and single, he enjoys messing about with wireless.' Also that 'Gateshead's Stan Hornsby is a milkman on the move at four in the morning. Busy lad!' They used quaint language: 'Burnley and Everton are pally', 'Tommy Lawton was tickled to see himself on film'. Everybody was a *chap* or *fellow*, forwards were *plucky*, youngsters *game*, defenders *doughty*, scouts went *spotting*, fans were *perplexed*, referees *ticked off* players for *insubordination*, and in the 'Heard on the Terraces' column a wag from the crowd always shouted something that wasn't funny, but 'how we all laughed': 'Hi, ref, you can't give him offside, he's not blooming playing.'

This jackets-for-goalposts style typified a tough but happy monochrome world where everyone had a cheery smile, boys in school uniform were passed over the heads of the crowd to the front of the terracing and England beat 'Johnny Foreigner' every time. It was even possible for *Boy's Own Paper*, perma-frozen in Victorian England, to run a story describing 'a field of gay footballers' in which boys 'ejaculated with glee' whenever a goal was scored. It couldn't last. Both language and football were changing.

According to this fairytale version of the game, the rest of the world only started playing in the 1950s. Vague rumours hinted that something called the World Cup began in 1930, but England had declined to compete because the Football Association said teams like Brazil and Argentina were rubbish. No one questioned their wisdom.

For years we refused to join FIFA. When we did we promptly lost 1–0 to the USA in the 1950 World Cup, where super-fit men with tanned legs and short shorts were constantly pursued by stunningly attractive women. While Brazil's 'dressing room' oozed testosterone, England's 'changing room' still reeked of Elliman's Proprietary Embrocation, which the more progressive of our players had just got around to calling *wintergreen* or, if they were exceptionally modern, *athletic rub*. The pungent aroma of *dubbin* was still ever-present.

The footie mags market responded admirably to the new era. *Charles Buchan's Football Monthly*, an icon for fifties and sixties football, appeared in 1951. *World Soccer* began in 1960.

England inside-right Charles Murray Buchan (1891–1960) made his League debut for Sunderland in 1910 before moving to Highbury in 1925 and then into journalism. He literally brought colour to football by giving punters dazzling polychrome covers and internal spreads for the first time. His garish redefinition of the spectrum (the Buchan variety of grass was the greenest of all

time) enabled armchair fans to glimpse reality at last. Which
players were ginger? Who had gorgeous blue eyes? What did
Blackpool's tangerine and Burnley's claret really look like? The
fans loved it. By 1958 Buchan's circulation was 100,000 per issue.

Language had also moved on. 'Spectators' became *fans*, 'fine
games' were *great matches*, and 'ground' gave way to *stadium*.
But the metamorphosis was gradual. Much of the copy
remained stilted. The sanitised *Football Monthly* letters page,
'For the Good of the Game', was where 'Our readers tell their
stories of the good folk who help to make the game go round'.
In 1969, the 'Why is our chairman such an abject tosser?' era
was still some years away:

Dear 'Good of the Game',
   Jim O'Sullivan is a loyal supporter of Cork Hibernians.
In the past few seasons they have always ended near the
foot of the table and attendances were a mere 500. Even so,
Jim attended their matches home and away. Once, when
Cork Hibs were away, Jim missed his train back and as a
result lost his job. But even that did not deter him. This
season Hibs have really found their form and are third in
the League. Needless to say Jim is delighted.
                                     Coleman Cotter

Note 'foot' of the table. 'Bottom' was considered too vulgar.
Juveniles wrote most such letters, intimating that *Football
Monthly* was their magazine, but the advertisement content
confirms otherwise: 'Are You Going Bald?', 'Conquer the
Tobacco Habit In 3 Days' and 'Art Photos From Life – 30
Lingerie Miniatures 3/6d' were hardly targeting twelve-year-olds.

Many *FM* readers were full-grown anoraks living with their
mothers, but the shocking truth is that legions of happily
married men also went to bed with *Charles Buchan* for company
when the wife had her curlers in.

The small ads suggest the 'typical' profile of the fifties and
sixties reader. He was male, inclined to smoke against his better
judgement, but didn't touch drink. He collected stamps, built
model airplanes, covetously desired a body like Charles Atlas,

but above all wanted to 'get on better with girls': 'Pen Friend Wanted. Male or Female'. Who were they kidding? 'Must Be Willing to Offer Arsenal Home and Away in Exchange for Various Friendly Games'. This was obviously a secret code. *World Soccer* was different. For a start, the use of *soccer* in the title suggested that the publishers hoped to attract an international readership as well as a domestic following. The first magazine to offer in-depth coverage of overseas football appealed to more cerebral types who got their kicks from studying the Finnish League tables rather than fantasising about back-door encounters with the fair sex. Ever gone searching for Greek non-league grounds on your holidays? Or bought *Gazzetta dello Sport* despite not speaking a word of Italian? Do you look at the Turkish Cup results to check for shocks? It's you they were after.

World Soccer instantly enriched football language by introducing a 'foreign' element: 'Government Aid Boosts Sudan Soccer' was exotic fare in October 1962. A photo of Abdul Nhassengo of Belenenses was almost as droolworthy as a 'girlie mag'. Strange positional and tactical words began to emerge, such as *libero* (Italian = 'the free one') for a sweeper cum schemer, and *verrouiller* (French = 'to bolt up') and *catenaccio* (colloquial Italian = 'doorbolt', literally 'chained up') for supposedly 'unlockable' defensive systems. Such exoticisms are commonplace today (although the overseas tactical words have never established themselves in the British game), but back in the sixties they were new and alluring. It would be fully thirty years before an influx of overseas players truly 'internationalised' our domestic football language.

Besides importing words, *World Soccer* also spread football English abroad through its vast overseas readership. Its letters suggest that everyone from Masai tribesmen to Faroe Islands fishermen managed to track down copies. This (almost authentic) example from 1986 was typical:

Dear *World Soccer*,
    I am African boy born in Owerri in 1976 and when I see a picture of Arsenal in your magazine I follow them.

Also sometimes Stockport County and Kilmarnock. Will
your kind reader send English and Scotland football
badges and programme and I will give Nigerian plus
foreign stamps. I play much football and hope one day I
also play Arsenal.

Nwankwo Kanu (age 10)

The editorial policy of printing such letters 'uncorrected'
seemed unduly imperialistic, but the message was clear.
Football English was going global.

Two other magazines launched in the late sixties typified the
newly glamorised game. *Goal* (1968) and *Shoot!* (1969) came to
define seventies football, the age of flares, sports cars, kipper
ties, naff football records, the celebrity boutique and a dolly-
bird on each arm. Money changed everything. In the late fifties
the highest permitted wage for an English footballer was £20.
When the maximum wage system was abolished in 1961
Fulham's Johnny Haynes became the first player to hit the
heights of £100 per week. Peanuts by today's standards, but
enough for players to pursue popstar lifestyles.

Goal and *Shoot!* both acquired cult status and are still
regularly name-checked in football discourse. Each satisfied the
growing appetites of young fans coming fresh to the game after
England's 1966 World Cup triumph. As such they represent a
nostalgic golden age for today's more mature supporters.

Shoot!, billed as 'the terrific new football paper for boys',
was simply well-strained pap without the nasty pips, but that's
what eleven-year-olds wanted. Players were *tough-tackling* not
dirty. They visited the training ground to *hone their skills* rather
than meet their agents to screw a better deal from the club.
Shoot! peddled innocence; most of it was sham, but we lapped
it up anyway.

Its features left their mark. Peter Carson of Manchester
wrote to 'Ask the Expert': 'I reckon Francis Lee of Manchester
City has got the hardest shot in English football – am I right?'
The reply from Fleetway House, Farringdon Street, London
EC4, exuded expertise: 'You're certainly correct about Francis
being a powerful kicker Peter, but he probably isn't the biggest

'bomber'– most experts regard Leeds's Peter Lorimer as soccer's No. 1 big-shot'.

'Shoot Us a Line' was the letters page not a drugs advice column. 'Football Funnies' belied its name. 'You Are the Ref' posed classic refereeing conundrums involving unruly canines, over-zealous linesmen and defective crossbars making rotational appearances week by week – and occasionally all at once. Checking the answers upside down was as much excitement as boys got in 1969.

'Focus On . . .' extended *Topical Times*'s 'intimate details' concept to daring new heights. The favourite meal of Nottingham Forest skipper Terry Hennessey was 'steak, creamed potatoes, mushrooms and braised celery'. Coventry's Willie Carr, a stickler for literalism, listed his 'miscellaneous dislikes' as 'cricket and cheese'. Brian Kidd, later Alex Ferguson's estranged right-hand man, expressed a prophetic aversion to 'moaners'. Most players loyally named 'my wife' as their 'best friend' but Alan Mullery's, lonely soul, was 'my dog Simba'. Everybody wanted to meet Raquel Welch or Frank Sinatra. A long-forgotten show called 'None in Particular' was regularly a 'favourite TV programme'.

All pre-1990s mainstream football magazines stubbornly spurned the irreverence which has developed in the last ten years. So much so that when Frank Worthington gave flippant answers for his 'Focus On . . .' slot, genuine letters of complaint were sent to *Shoot!*'s offices by 'disillusioned' readers. For the record, Frank's 'Most Difficult Opponent' was 'the taxman', his 'likes' included 'birdwatching and browsing round hardware shops' and his 'favourite other team' was 'Bolton Market's half-holiday second XI'.

It was customary for boys to graduate from *Shoot!* to *Goal* immediately they started shaving or experienced other alarming bodily changes. But although *Goal* was more manly, it was still hidebound by convention, becoming an archaic repository for terms considered trendy in the seventies and eighties but which are now self-conciously retro. Try slipping these seamlessly into conversation without getting funny looks: *midfield dynamo, arch schemer, utility man, link man, granite-jawed stopper, razor-sharp finisher, roving front-man, want-away striker, the season's curtain-raiser, the man at the helm, step up the title-hunt, the onus is on us, defensive hit-man, big-hearted keeper, one-club man, basement-dwellers, long-throw specialist, ghosts into the box, our share of the breaks, willing workhorse, tip for the top* and *training-ground hints.*

Again something had to change. In August 1994 Haymarket Publishing launched *FourFourTwo*. Issue one devoted eight pages to a Terry Venables interview and six to Barry Fry. Neither revealed 'steak with all the trimmings' to be the high point of their lives. In September 1995 Future Publishing launched the rival and more laddish *Total Football*. Its favourite word was *blag, geezer* a close second. *Porkmeister* (an overweight player) came in third. In April 1997 the BBC muscled in with *Match of the Day Monthly* but slipped alarmingly back into 'Goalese'. Trying to be both laddish and daddish, it was just plain baddish. Consider their column names: 'Jimmy Hill's Chinwag' was weak enough but Angus Loughran's (aka 'Statto') betting advice column plumbed the depths. For 'Angus' Stake House' alone they deserved to fold, and did.

Total Football later followed suit, leaving *FourFourTwo* as the sole survivor of the original 'glossies', a magazine aimed for the first time at an intelligent adult readership, regarding the past with affection but addressing contemporary issues and the game's future in an informed and detailed style. The writers were quite obviously football fans. It hit the mark and is still going. *Topical Times* it's not.

Its strapline is 'The Ultimate Football Magazine', but even as I write new challengers are being launched. Some have already been and gone. Inspired by cult youth magazines such as *Viz*, the 1995 newcomer *Sweet FA* billed itself 'Footie's Foulest Rag. Bringing the Game into Disrepute'. Entirely true to its word, mostly the F-word, it took football language to an all-time low. Its free gifts alone would have thoroughly bemused those innocent youngsters moved to rosy-cheeked wonderment by the simple pleasures of *Topical Times*'s 'panel portraits of the stars' or the 'do-it-yourself league ladders' free with *Shoot!*. The nadir was their 'Giggsy's Balls' postcard 'complete with pubes' and cut-out hole so it could be 'worn to amuse your friends'. 'Football Bimbo – Humpingham United's Biggest Fan', afforded mild amusement. So did 'Brian Glandular – The Feverish Voice of Football' and 'Save da ball Dali the Surrealist Goalkeeper'. But, all credit to football fans for giving *Sweet FA* the boot. Like the Victorian-era *Goal*, its antithesis, it was condemned to the loft of back-issuedom forever.

Such is the life and death of football magazines. But what will be their legacy? In Arabic *kazana* means 'to store up'. It gave their language *makazin* ('store houses') which the French pinched for their shops (*magasin*), and in the sixteenth century we turned it into *magazine* for a munitions store, which a century later came to mean 'a store of information', and by the 1700s 'a periodical publication'.

The derivation is fitting. Far from being throwaway fodder, footie mags are valuable time-line repositories for the game's evolving vernacular. Should our nation's lexicographers ever get round to scanning properly that storehouse of information, many 'new' words and phrases could be added overnight to the next editions of our dictionaries. Words which football-lovers have been using routinely for years.

25

Aye Aye Rhubarb Pie
– You Too Can Speak Fanzine

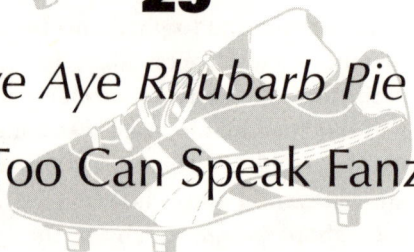

> The only point worth remembering about Port
> Vale's match with Hereford on Monday was the fact
> that the attendance figure, 2,744, was a perfect cube,
> 14 x 14 x 14.
>
> Letter to Stoke-on-Trent's Sentinel newspaper from
'Disillusioned Supporter', 1979

The British Library is a fine institution. Where else in the world
could the urge to see an original copy of Dr Johnson's
Dictionary, Leonard Gribble's thriller *They Kidnapped Stanley
Matthews*, and the children's classic *Topsy and Tim at the
Football Match* be satisfied so quickly? Those are the sort of
urges I've been getting while preparing this book. But for the
British Library, I might have gone through life never knowing
the magnificence of John Toshack's poetry, which masterfully
rhymes 'Barcelona' with 'sauna'.

Yet even the British Library's eclectic listings experienced a
culture shock following their recent acquisition of 15,000 football
fanzines. Their catalogue includes titles which would once have
seemed linguistically impossible. Try this on a po-faced librarian:

I'd like to see the first issue of *Mi Whippet's Dead* please and
the last issue of *Sheep Shaggers' Monthly*. Also the most
recent you have of *Mr Bismarck's Electric Pickelhaube, One
F in Fulham, The Gibbering Clairvoyant* and *Dreaming of an*

Eric Twigg Pukka Pie. And if you've got it the last issue of *The Bonker* before it merged with *The Deranged Ferret*.

If they say 'Will there be anything else sir?' just go for it:

Yes, *Don't Just Stand There, Drink Up Ye Cider, Get Lawrence On* and *Aye Aye Rhubarb Pie*. Oh, and one more. I'd like to look at *Walter Zenga's Right Buttock* if you can put your hands on it.

The influence of fanzine culture on football's language has been dramatic. No medium of the last three decades, not even television, has introduced such a distinctive style.

Fanzine itself is a comparative newcomer, first widely used in America in 1949 to describe 'magazines written for fans, usually of science fiction', a simple contraction of 'fan magazine'. When *fanzine* entered British English in the 1970s, that definition ought to have changed to 'written for and by the fans', because that's what makes British fanzines distinctive. They're not the sanitised pap of club programmes, nor the excitable 'talk it up' style of the tabloids. The newly enfranchised fans have first the photocopier and then the advent of desktop publishing to thank for making their new mouthpieces an economic possibility.

But many voices in the game say it was a bad day for football when the first fanzine sellers plied their Xeroxed wares outside grounds. Most players, managers, board members and referees, indeed all in authority, dislike the fanzines intensely. The reason is simple. These hateful rags dare to criticise, question and mock. Ken Bates is evil. The sausage rolls are cold and taste of fish-glue. Who cares what Beckham likes in his paella? Why are season ticket prices up when we've just gone down? Does the chairman wear a syrup? How many players with beards have scored more than 40 goals a season for Mansfield Town? None! So why don't the directors sanction the signing of more bearded players?

Worse still, they delve into the darkest corners of a club's 'private' business. They uncover things, demand answers, call for heads. Mere supporters aren't supposed to do that. It would be wrong, though, to think that fans haven't always done so. The natives of Birmingham were stirring if not yet revolting as early as 1892. Witness this letter to the *Birmingham Mail* :

> I venture to suggest that the turn has come of the public who bring the grist to the mill. Why not covered accommodation for spectators, dry ground to stand on, and a reduced admission if possible? The profits will stand it. Many a wreath has been purchased by standing on wet ground on Saturday afternoons.

Every football age has its moaners. But, barring the odd carefully edited letter, these things were said in the pub, home or workplace. Now they're in black and white and waved in the faces of club directors. That's the difference.

In fairness to football's 'suits', justification for their anti-fanzine stance comes easy. Much of the genre's output is shameful. Raw production techniques, bad spelling, appalling grammar and apostrophes in place's theyv'e never been s'een before can just about be forgiven, indeed are part of the curious charm of the fanzine format, but overt racism, sexism, sectarianism, homophobia, libellous or groundless personal criticism, and a general disregard of all political correctness are different matters altogether.

That's also why many club-loyal fans find 'the zine scene' just too distasteful. More football followers don't buy fanzines than do. Research at Leicester University revealed average fanzine sales ranged from a sorry 45 to a thumping 11,000 per issue, but the key finding was that 55 per cent sold between 200 and 1,000 copies a time. By comparison, clubs allow for a one in three take-up rate on official programmes. But that minority who do support what has become known as the 'alternative football network' see another side. The better fanzines campaign vigorously against prejudice, displaying genuine humour, acute understanding of issues and above all a love for the game which only fellow fans might truly identify with. Take this from a long-suffering lower division dweller:

I don't really mind the club not winning anything. I can
cope with losing. It's the hope I can't handle. Always
dashed, season after season. Sometimes so near after years
of waiting. You have to have hope otherwise there'd be no
point going, but it gets so painful I sometimes wonder if I
can go on any more. But I always do. Next season's my
36th and it might just be the one. There you are you see.
Hope again. But I know in my heart it won't happen.

It's unlikely that such impassioned and incisively perceptive words would ever emerge from the mouth of a player,
manager or director. And when (it has to be 'when' not 'if')
'it' finally does happen for our hapless fan, will the archetypal
board member really understand why he walks to the centre
circle, secretes a tuft of grass in his pocket, and sobs his heart
out? I think not.

As for justifying their overt 'criticism', the editor of Bradford
City's *City Gent* assures us that all vitriol is born entirely from the
'concern' and 'warmth' fans feel for their clubs. He labelled this
'critical allegiance'. Put simply, 'you only hurt the ones you love'.

This intelligent lobby in the fanzine world isn't surprising
considering the genesis of the genre. The first-ever British
publication to adopt an 'alternative' approach was fabricated in
October 1972 by a group of Cambridge graduates. Disillusioned
by much of what was happening in football, namely increasing
wages, hooliganism, defensive tactics and the dubious antics of
the incumbents of the ruling bodies, they named their innovatory *Private Eye*-style monthly *Foul*, a deliberate parody of
the 'safe' magazines like *Goal* and *Shoot!* which were all the fans
had to choose from at the time.

Importantly they introduced humour – spoof letters, cartoons,
bubble-captioned photos, anything off-the-wall. It was all right
to laugh at football. Nothing and no one was safe. Although
Foul folded four years later due to a libel action and never
labelled itself a fanzine, it put into circulation a new form of
honest, irreverent and often surreal football language which
profoundly influenced the way the game is spoken and written
about today.

The football fanzine explosion didn't immediately follow *Foul*. Music, and specifically punk, got there first. The earliest British publication actually christened a fanzine was launched in 1977. Badly written and poorly produced, *Sniffin' Glue* chronicled the punk explosion, paying homage to bands such as the Sex Pistols, the Clash, the Damned and the Jam. It was a cult success and a catalyst for football's first equivalent. In October 1984 a Bradford City contingent launched *City Gent*. Other early followers were *Terrace Talk* (York City), *Fingerpost* (West Bromwich Albion), *The Web* (Queen's Park), and the first of many title oddities, *Pink 'n' Blue Bushwacker* (Dulwich Hamlet).

They were followed in March 1986 by the most significant event in fanzine history when Chelsea supporter Mike Ticher launched a fanzine aimed at the general supporter rather than those of one club.

Named after a line from a track by the Undertones, *When Saturday Comes* became such a success that it's still going today, now a fully fledged 'magazine' but retaining its original ethos. Eighteen years on from issue one of *WSC*, something like 2,000 separate fanzine titles have been launched, aimed at every conceivable sub-market: *The Football Pink* for the gay community; *The Rusty Staple* for programme buffs; *Game for a LAFF*, the august organ for Librarians as Football Fans; *Under the Wires*, the world's first football/trainspotting cross-over fanzine.

I jest not. These are a paradise for word lovers. Outrageous wordplay, anagrams, unlikely headlines and surreal sentence constructions abound. Many of the titles are conundrums.

Music has influenced a number. The Scottish rival to *WSC* was named *The Absolute Game* after a line by The Skids. The Proclaimers line 'going to Kilmarnock to see Hibernian play' explains every Hibee's favourite fanzine *The Proclaimer*. Gillingham's classically named *Brian Moore's Head Looks Uncannily Like London Planetarium*, in honour of the late commentator who was once a director of the club, was lifted verbatim from a track called 'Dickie Davies' Eyes' by the Birkenhead band Half Man Half Biscuit. Blessedly, the

Gills' drawing-board title didn't prevail. 'A Sixth of a Pint' is too obvious.

Many titles could have been conceived only by fans steeped in the colloquialisms of football. Phrases heard at matches or on away travels are favourites. *Come On Dagenham Use Your Forwards, Bring On a Sub* (Telford United) and *Up the Work Rate* (Irvine Meadow) all suggest painfully enduring moments of exasperation.

Official-baiting also looms large. *No Way Referee* (Bray Wanderers), *Get a Grip Ref* (Scunthorpe United), *Linesman You're Rubbish* (Aberystwyth Town) and *Flippin' Heck Ref, That Was a Foul Surely* (Waterlooville) celebrate berating fodder standard throughout the land.

Some fans have had throwaway remarks cruelly preserved for ever. Whichever hapless Dover Athletic regular slipped up with *Rhodes Boyson, Oo's Ee Play For?* has not been allowed to forget it. Telford United's *The Pies Were Cold*, Hearts' *Still, Mustn't Grumble* and Nuneaton Borough's anguished *What Have I Done to Deserve This* keep him company.

Those fans at least enjoy the dignity of anonymity not extended to better-known personalities who find their names etched into bibliographic permanence for reasons they'd rather not remember. After Gordon Smith missed a gilt-edged chance to win the FA Cup for Brighton against Manchester United in 1983 he quickly moved to Manchester City to forget. But Brighton's less forgiving fans wouldn't allow it. Pinching a famous line of commentary they promptly launched *And Smith Must Score*.

Others are more personal. There was little playful about Scottish football's *We Hate Jimmy Hill*. Nor were *Ellis Out!* (Aston Villa) and *A Load of Cobbolds!* (Ipswich) intended as tributes to the clubs' chairmen. As for *Peter Hicks' Wig* (St Austell) and *Roger Connell's Beard* (Wimbledon), both confirm the fanzines' peculiar fetish for hairpieces, or should I say 'pieces on hair'? Articles titled 'Fishy Mullets of Our Time', generally majoring on Chris Waddle and Glenn Hoddle, are standard. 'Strand By Your Man' pitted Bobby Charlton against Ralph Coates for the 'Golden Comb-over' award. Malcolm

Macdonald, Geoff Blockley, Mike Pejic and Terry Paine were always in the frame for any 'Sideburn King' title, and the less hirsute Terrys, Hennessey and Mancini, reigned supreme in the slaphead stakes for years, until Nottingham Forest signed the Dutch international Johnny Metgod from Real Madrid. Regrettably the current trend for shaven heads has spoilt all the fun. 'Oi, baldy, you're rubbish' is one of football's lost insults.

If there's a serious message here (and there has to be, surely), it's that the fanzines were the first publications to place football in its widest context, looking not just at the game's history or action but at its role as and within popular culture. Articles linking football to film, music, art, literature, politics, travel, drink, sex, drugs, theatre, fruit, philately, window-cleaning and vegetables have all appeared in fanzines.

This is the fans saying, 'Look, we're not merely football obsessives. We're interested in lots of subjects besides, but football's all-pervasive. Nothing in life can escape a football linkage.' In that sense the fanzines invented the craze for football trivia that's now running at unprecedented levels, but it was a craze waiting to happen ever since football's early days. A telling line in Arnold Bennett's *The Card* (1911) has a female character say, 'But I don't see what football has got to do with being mayor,' quickly followed by the knowing riposte, 'Football has got to do with everything.'

Many fanzine titles are a nod to cross-cultural interests. *From Hull to Eternity* (Hull City), *Rebels Without a Clue* (Slough Town), *Dial M for Merthyr* (Merthyr Tydfil), *Blazing Saddlers* (Walsall), *Friday Night Fever* (Tranmere Rovers) and *A Nightmare on Dee Street* (Glentoran) all assume a reader's wider knowledge. Rotherham United, nicknamed 'The Merry Millers', gave a healthy nod towards children's television with *Windy and Dusty*, and non-league Whitley Bay tweaked Otis Redding's song lyrics for *Sitting in the Lounge of the Bay*.

At least one title merits etymological analysis. A 1980s publication covering the Scottish scene was appropriately called *Hard Lines*, a colloquialism for bad luck. According to *Cassell's Dictionary of Slang* this comes from a biblical passage, Psalm 16 verse 6: 'The lines are fallen unto me in pleasant places; yea, I have a goodly heritage'. The 'lines' denote one's lot in life, which can be easy or hard.

The influence of fanzine culture also explains the 'laddish' content of cult television programmes like *Fantasy Football League, They Think It's All Over* and Sky's *Soccer AM,* which all major in irreverence. This influence has also crept into mainstream television and newspaper coverage. It would have been unthinkable for Kenneth Wolstenholme to have made any truly 'personal' remarks about a player's appearance in the 1960s, for example, but today's media types declare open season on anything that moves.

Consider the *Sun's* 'turnip head' campaign against the England manager Graham Taylor in 1992. It started with the headline 'SWEDES 2 TURNIPS 1' after England lost to Sweden. A defeat against Spain added 'onion head' to Taylor's list of sobriquets. To his credit he took it in good part. Talking to the press before a game in Oslo he was rueful: 'I'm beginning to wonder what the bloody national vegetable is in Norway.' Would they have dared to call Alf Ramsey an 'avocado head' or 'Mexican has-bean' when England flopped in the 1970 World Cup? Vitriol is now par for the course.

So have fanzines enriched football's language or sullied it? It's for you to decide. Much may depend on age. Evidence from Port Vale certainly suggests that some older supporters don't quite get it. As a sop to the 'better in the old days' Valeites, the Vale fanzine team invented a former player whose ethos they expounded in *The Memoirs of Seth Bottomley.* The editor swears that he once heard a disgruntled oldster say of a present-day Vale midfielder that 'he couldner owd a candle ter Bottomley'.

Surely that gem alone makes fanzines worthwhile. They have also had notable campaigning successes. The Football Supporters' Association's *Reclaim the Game* has done much under that banner to make supporters heard. Charlton Athletic's *Voice of the Valley* was hugely instrumental in convincing the club to move back to its old ground after a period in exile.

On the down side, even those who embrace fanzine culture fully have suggested that the publications themselves have become formulaic, even unintentionally self-parodic. Indeed several fanzines have already consciously lampooned their own breed by creating 'spoof' issues full of all the standard fare.

I'll go with the approval vote, swayed by a nice line in *The Book of Football* (1906): 'Football is not a game. It is a virus. One which pervades our very existence and to which few men are immune.' That long-dead author was imbued with the fanzine spirit eighty years ahead of his time. He ought to have been launching *Leicester Fosse Be With You.*

That virus has now been isolated, put under the microscope, and had its component parts analysed in the utmost detail. The antidote, as we all know, is a course of 'avoidance'. But, despite the ongoing pain, it's hugely unpalatable and comes in jars labelled 'Saturday Afternoon Shopping' and 'DIY'.

Those who have taken that course have surely missed out. They will never have the pleasure of knowing, courtesy of the fanzine title dreamed up by loyal followers of Cowes Sports, that *99% of Gargoyles Look Like Pete Groves.*

If you speak fluent 'fanzine' you'll already be musing who the other one per cent look like.

Extra Time

26

Give Us a 'B', Give Us an 'O' – Football's Troublesome Words

'I started the shirt-lifting thing and I'm still the best at it.'

Fabrizio Ravanelli, struggling with colloquialisms at Derby, 2002

Football and the blooper are well acquainted. The simplicity of our alphabet ought to make written and verbal expression a pitfall-free affair. It doesn't.

The trouble is, we're lulled into a false sense of security. How can we possibly go wrong with an alphabet of just 26 letters?

Think of the poor Chinese, inscrutably making sense of 50,000 characters. Or the Japanese, who 'only' have 7,000 pictographic symbols and two separate 'clarifying' alphabets each of 48 characters. These 'clarifiers' are added above the symbols, to specify which of a multitude of meanings the characters actually stand for. The word *ka*, for example, has 214 different meanings. The 'clarifier' tells you which. Not being sure who got the last touch for Shimizu S-Pulse's 89th-minute winner against Kashima Antlers is the least of a Japanese pressman's worries.

But English has its traps too, far more devious ones. Although we make just 40 specific sounds in English, we have more than 200 ways of spelling them. The 'sh' sound of English itself can be rendered fourteen ways: '*Ambitious* Alan *Sugar* had a *shameful passion* for *special champagne* and *ocean* liners' contains seven. Spelling, like Spurs' former chairman, is unpredictable and frequently difficult.

Take Ayr, without its suffix 'United' British football's shortest club name. Including proper nouns, the English word with the most sound-alike spellings is *air*, with a remarkable 38 variants. I have never seen Heir United, Eire United, Eyre United or E'er United, but I have seen Ayre United and Aire United. And frequently Ayrsome Park instead of Ayresome Park for the former home of Middlesbrough.

David Crystal's *The English Language* makes it all sound so simple by telling us that there are 'only' 400 or so irregular spellings in English and that a 'mere' three per cent of our words are spelt in a truly unpredictable way. But 'only' and 'mere' are dangerous labels. We confidently write that a club have 'played *twenty-four* games, won *fourteen*, lost *four* and lie *fourth* in the table', but those comforting 'rules' for spelling number *four* words go sadly awry when a side hits the *forty* points mark. Chaucer spelt it *fourty* in the fourteenth century, but by the eighteenth it had mysteriously lost its 'u'. No one knows why. Consider also the well-known phrase, 'go *forth* to *Forfar*, the *foremost* centre for *semaphor*'. Make no mistake, whatever the *English Made Easy* books say, our wonderful language is a quiet assassin. That's why Everton's official 1998–99 yearbook described Duncan Ferguson as 'a floored genius'.

Club names ought to be safe territory but aren't. Inconsistencies historically introduced into place-name spellings make life difficult. Peter*borough*, Scar*borough*, and Farn*borough* all embraced the most common corruption of the Old English *burg*, meaning 'town' or 'fortress', while *Bury* and Salis*bury* altered it sufficiently to be readily remembered.

Not so Middles*brough*, whose long-lost 'o' has seen them misspelt Middles*borough* ever since, even in some of the best places. *The Book of Football* (1906), a lavish tome intended for the libraries of educated Edwardian gents, stands guilty of the first really public 'bloomer' in football history. Page 203 is boldly headed 'The Rise of the Middlesborough Football Club', and the piece repeats the error eighteen times for good measure. For truly spectacular effect, the writer was the club's own assistant secretary, George F Allison, who later managed

Arsenal. Doubtless he put his hand up to the error, but only to claim a printer's flag.

The club hasn't eased the confusion, slipping an 'o' back into their official nickname 'Boro', so that even the more erudite have been lured into the trap. 'Middlesbrough' is the only football-related word in Bill Bryson's *Troublesome Words*, which delightedly reports that in 1985 *the Financial Times* ran a special feature on the town headlined 'MIDDLESBOROUGH'. Bryson further gleefully cites their misspelling of *Teesside*. They decided it should be 'Teeside', even though Middlesbrough is definitely beside the River Tees, not the Tee. Poignantly, those who finally master 'Middlesbrough' are apt to lapse into 'Peterbrough' in sympathy. You really can't win.

Others of the troublesome breed are *Mil*wall, East *Fyfe*, Grim*bsb*y Town, Sten*hous*muir and Living*stone*, all of which are errors I've seen recently in books that should know better. Some clubs look peculiar even when they're right. Stranraer, for example, which is allowed its eccentricity because it's from the Gaelic *sron reamhar*, 'a broad headland'.

A rare letter combination makes one defunct club an alphabet celebrity. How many words contain 'ieo' in succession? When financial problems caused Airdrieonians to withdraw from the Scottish League at the end of the 2001–02 season, a consortium of logophiles ought really to have come to their rescue. Airdrie United, the new club now representing the town, may claim an 'ieu' run, but that doesn't count.

Tottenham Hotspur are regularly misnamed Tottenham Hot*spurs*, their 'Spurs' nickname again not helping. The Argentinian Ossie Ardiles resolved conflict by inventing another version altogether. Imagining himself a master of English he famously rhymed the club with Nottingham, later making capital from his gaffe by singing on the club's 1981 Cup Final record 'Ossie's Dream', which included his solo line 'in the cup for Tott*ing*ham'. Hamilton Academical also suffer from rogue 's' trouble, often appearing as Academica*ls* despite officially dropping the 's' in 1965. Even more common than Tottenham and Hamilton trouble is the inclination to name Crewe after Egypt's chief port or the 'great' King of Macedon who founded it, but neither 'Crewe Alexand*ria*' nor 'Crewe Alexand*er*' have yet replaced 'Crewe Alexandra' in the official records. Play safe and go for 'Crewe Alex'.

That's an accepted abbreviation, unlike another which is just plain wrong. Contrary to popular belief, the repeated use of 'Notts Forest', erroneously making them short for Nottinghamshire Forest, isn't a product of modern-day sloppiness. Victorian newspapers were equally guilty, which so rankled James Catton, the writer of the club's entry in *The Rise of the Leaguers* (1897), that he began it with a glorious rant against 'one of the common errors of the football world, nothing but a popular corruption'. It made no difference. Probably just to annoy Catton, they still appeared as 'Notts. Forest' in the official 1898 Cup Final programme. If you must truncate, stick to 'Nottm Forest'.

Today's Catton types prefer to espouse the cause of Hartlepool United, long the subject of petty argument. Those wrongly calling them Hartlepools United are wont to scurry off to the attic for an old programme to 'prove' it. It was correct once: the club went plural in 1908 after a merger of two Hartlepool clubs made them literally 'Hartlepools United'. But in 1968 they changed to plain Hartlepool, the name of the town itself, and finally to Hartlepool United in 1977, which they remain today.

Changes in name are another potential source of confusion. Lots of older fans still call Swansea City by their former name Swansea Town, even though they upgraded in 1970. More worrying still are the apostrophe-obsessives who engage in earnest internet debate about Queen's Park and Queen's Park Rangers, arguably the only two apostrophised first-class clubs in Scotland and England. I say arguably because there is some doubt about the true punctuation of QPR. On the club's official letterhead the name has appeared both 'with' and 'without' over the years; so too in the football 'bible' *Rothmans*, normally a reliable arbiter in such matters. But 1890s Ordnance Survey maps show 'Queen's Park' near where they were established, and the British Library catalogue, which includes entries for the club from as early as 1899, adheres doggedly to the apostrophe. Meanwhile there are even amateur advocates for 'Queens' Park'. Such anorakism ought to surprise me, but doesn't. In a world where there's a non-league fan who takes photographs of the corner flags at all the grounds he visits, there's probably someone out there who supports Brighton & Hove Albion and Rushden & Diamonds purely on account of an ampersand fetish. All very worrying.

The safest way to avoid being strung up by the sticklers ought to be to avoid writing anything at all, but sticking purely to spoken English can be more hazardous still. The ITV commentator John Helm would never have written football's most famous *spoonerism*, yet in 1991 he cheerfully told millions of viewers that 'Viv Anderson has just pissed a fatness test.' *Metaphasis* is the technical term for the famous word-mangling named after the Reverend William Spooner, the eccentric warden of New College, Oxford from 1903 to 1924. David Coleman was obviously a fan, having once passed over to 'our boxing Carpenter, Harry Commentator'.

Closely related to the spoonerism is the *malapropism*, named after the character Mrs Malaprop in Sheridan's *The Rivals*, via the French *mal à propos*, 'ill for the purpose'. A *faux pas*, French for 'false step', is similar, as is the verbal *gaffe*, from the French for 'blunder', as if giving them French names lets us off the hook. Football folk are good at these. David O'Leary spent the entire 2002 World Cup referring to 'the Belgiums', while his co-pundit Mark Lawrenson was adamant the referee hadn't booked someone because 'he didn't want to set a *president*'. World leaders encased in concrete? Not an unappealing prospect.

At least they're close enough to be understandable, but what colourful visions could possibly have assailed the mind of Scotland coach Andy Roxburgh in 1991? Asked about the threat of the Romanian superstar, Gheorghe Hagi, in the forthcoming European Championship qualifier, he said: 'He's a brilliant player, but we're no' getting all *psychedelic* about him.' Psyched-up? Psychotic? Who knows?

Sometimes the words come out fine but historical context does the damage. It's Roxburgh again, Scotland having lost 1–0 to Romania, naturally to a goal from Hagi. This time he forgets that British fighting forces have sometimes been roundly slaughtered and don't fire guns from horseback: 'We need to go into our next match with all guns blazing – like the charge of the

Light Brigade.' Despite the inappropriate analogy, Scotland overcame the might of San Marino to qualify.

Not all such slips are accidental. Skilled journalists evoke *imagery* by deliberately using 'wrong' words. Ivan Ponting's description of Arsenal's carrot-topped Perry Groves as 'a vivid high-velocity vegetable' was complete nonsense but so right. So too the *Independent*'s description of Airdrie's Broomfield Park as 'a cauldron of apathy'. But clever word choice doesn't always work. Rugby man Cliff Morgan should have stuck to the oval ball when he announced that 'sadly, the immortal Jackie Milburn died today'. And the commentator who contrived the worst pun ever may wish he hadn't bothered: 'This match was like an Australian archery range . . . strewn with errors.'

Even the mere passage of time can inflict damning injury. Our Prime Minister once made great capital from fondly recalling 'sitting at the Gallowgate end at Newcastle's St James' Park, watching Jackie Milburn play'. But simple chronology suggests a strong case of compound spin. Jackie Milburn last played a League game at Newcastle in 1956. The birth certificate of Anthony Charles Lynton Blair is dated 1953. Maybe he has a prolific memory. But hang on, the Gallowgate end was terracing back then!

Many genuine mistakes are forgivable. Who can really blame Manchester United's shirt printers for sending Ole Gunnar Solskjaer out against Newcastle United in November 2002 with 'SOLJKSAER' on his back? On the other hand, Costa Rica's Mauricio Wright graced the 2002 World Cup with 'WRIGTH' emblazoned on his shirt. David Crystal once wrote that 'there is no linguistic impropriety more likely to irritate people than a mis-spelling of their name'. In that case, the genuine Bill Shankley, Dave McKay and Nobby Styles, three of the most regular victims of such shameful mistreatment, even in quality publications, must have been the angriest men in football. Dennis Bergkamp was regularly doubly abused as 'Denis Birdkampf' when he first arrived at Arsenal. Bolton's Jussi Jaaskelainen and Youri Djorkaeff could be forgiven for being suicidal.

Rather more pardonable are dialectal blunders, really speech traps rather than 'errors' per se. These are often the result of differences in regional accents, to which football fans are more widely exposed than most other groups in society. In fact the game is probably responsible, via the large away followings enjoyed by many clubs, for more mass inter-regional communication than any other activity. Away supporters quickly learn that even people who share a common tongue 'dunner orlwez spake loik wot way duz'. That's Wolverhampton. Ish. In time, we begin to doubt what's right and wrong. I always believed Bury were 'Berry' until I first visited Gigg Lane and heard the locals urging 'make haste Burry, letsavver gaul'. At Everton they told me to 'get back to Durby'. And why, when I say NEWcastle with first-syllable emphasis, do the Geordies insist on NewCASTLE? TRANmere and TranMERE is another. Are you a COWDEN-beath person or an advocate of CowdenBEATH? And should the *Shrew* of Shrewsbury rhyme with *throw* or *through*?

Occasionally, so-called errors of pronunciation have been perpetuated so doggedly that they're no longer questioned. Have you ever puzzled why we refer to 'Celtic' music, language and folklore with a hard *k* sound, but Celtic Football Club with a soft *s*? Radio 5 recently revealed we should have been saying it the K-way all along. The club were founded in 1887 by the Catholic priest Brother Walfrid, and christened to reflect both Irish and Scottish roots. The name proved so harsh to supporters' ears that, much to the founder's chagrin, the *k* sound evolved to an *s*. Celtic historians assert that Brother Walfrid insisted on pronouncing the club 'Keltic' until his dying day.

The BBC takes such matters sufficiently seriously to employ dedicated *orthoepists* (pronunciation experts) to make the correct decisions, and John Motson is said to be a devotee. Motty always says 'Berry' not 'Burry', but is it really fair to suggest the natives are wrong?

There are definite echoes of medievalism in such a diversity of pronunciation. One legacy of the proliferation of dialects during the period of Norman rule was that, by the fifteenth century, people in one part of England couldn't always understand those in another part. It's worth recalling the famous tale told by William Caxton, the first person to print a book in English, and as such a facilitator of standardisation in both spelling and meaning. In the preface to his *Eneydos* in 1490, he describes how a group of London sailors asking for *eggys* at a farm in Kent just fifty miles away, were unable to make themselves understood. The farmer's wife answered that she could 'speke no Frenshe'. In Kent, eggs were *eyren*.

That may sound a quaint yarn of a bygone age, but even in the twenty-first century a journey to an away game can provoke puzzlement because we call things by different names. Having once asked for a 'cheese *cob*' in Sunderland, a request met by a blank look, I know this from personal experience. In the East Midlands, a *cob* is what typically encases a beefburger or other savoury filling, but the same thing elsewhere can be a *bun, bap, roll, barm-cake, batch, stottie* or *tea-cake*. My 'tea-cake' has currants and sultanas in it. A 'barm-cake' is a daft person. A 'roll' houses a hot-dog. A 'bun' is an individual cake probably with icing and a cherry on top. Yours, maybe not.

With this in mind, it's difficult not to feel sorry for the band of men dubbed 'football's foreign legion', who have to get to grips not just with the English game but with English itself. Their efforts fall into the genre which has been informally labelled *mistaken English*. Stories of new recruits being 'looked after' by teammates are legion, usually involving being told to ask the canteen ladies for 'dog's bollocks on toast' or some other such unsavoury savoury. Sometimes they don't even need help. Giving his first press interview on arrival at Chelsea in November 2002, the Spanish midfielder Enrique de Lucas really did tell the gathered throng that 'away from football I very much like cocking'.

Not that foreigners can't give reciprocal 'help'. An English fan in Japan for the 2002 World Cup asked a T-shirt vendor to print something suitable on it in Japanese, something like 'I love Japan' or 'England for the World Cup'. The result was admirable. Everywhere he went, the locals smiled. Some more overtly than others. The slogan translated as 'Gay Submissive Englishman Seeks Muscular Japanese Boy'.

Considering the inherent difficulty of learning English, particularly its numerous colloquial phrases, most overseas players in the British game have done remarkably well to get to grips with it. Put yourself in the place of a new recruit with just enough English to find his way around with the aid of a dictionary. These are his manager's instructions on the eve of his debut:

> Get your head down tonight, son. No drinking. Make sure to get plenty of fluids down you. Then go out tomorrow and get tight. I want you right inside their striker's shorts. Up his backside. If you get tired, it's OK to drop off. But make sure you stay awake. And don't drop your head. We keep them up at this club. And our tails. And remember, if you feel any stiffness just lie down and I'll bring you off.

Can we really blame our foreign brethren for occasional bouts of confusion?

Most of us simply accept these illogicalities. But not children. What young boy hasn't asked his father, 'Why are we going in the stands when you said we'd got seats?' Patient dads explain that it's short for *grandstand*, originally the 'grandest stand' on a racecourse; it's the structure itself that 'stands', not the people in it. Most don't bother. The standard response is 'Shut up and drink your pop.'

There are a string of these *misnomers*. Why does the ticket say 'Enter at Gate 34' when there isn't a gate? Every ground did have such a rudimentary point of access before the Victorians introduced 'patent rush-preventative *turnstiles*' to stop unruly fans 'storming the gates' and getting in for free. Now its only survival is in *gate*, which by association means both the size of the crowd and the takings. And curiously *turnstiles* has taken on a much wider figurative meaning – in a phrase such as 'Player power is increasingly attracting criticism from the turnstiles', it means 'supportership' in general. And why do we talk about teams *running up cricket scores* when no one ever wins 347–0? Presumably they must be England cricket scores. Why is the weakest team in the club called the *A-Team* when that expression usually means the best? Time was when a club's lowliest 'anonymous' eleven was simply described by the press as 'a team', say 'Liverpool Reserves v Everton (a team)'. By a process of metamorphosis, lower case 'a', the indefinite article, became capital 'A', the letter. And who dubbed the 1953 Blackpool v Bolton Cup

Final 'the *Matthews Final*' after Stan Mortensen scored a hat-trick for Blackpool in their sensational 4–3 win? The *Guardian* had a nice take on that one. When Mortensen died in 1991, they commented 'they'll probably call it the Matthews funeral'.

What all this nonsense proves is that although the English language can be sublimely precise, it's equally capable of luring the unwary into error. Should you wish to minimise (avoidance is simply impossible) your own footie-error count, I can only suggest four basic guidelines.

If you're hitting a 'live' keyboard, take it steady and think it through. When Hendon lost at Hayes, the BBC teleprinter operator who posted the hellish result 'HADES 3 HENDON 0' was obviously rushing. Similarly, whoever typed the TV commentary transcript for the deaf during England's 2002 World Cup campaign was listening but not thinking. When Ashley Cole was substituted, they put up on screen: 'He's expended so much energy he deserves arrest'.

Secondly, remember that English, unlike Arabic, is written and read from left to right. Derby County once had the marvellous idea of sending their twelve players out for the kick-in each carrying a giant placard with a letter on it to convey a seasonal message to the fans. A nice thought, but whoever carried the first letter turned right instead of left out of the tunnel. The choreography was otherwise perfect as the players wheeled around to each side of the ground to wish us all 'RAEY WEN YPPAH'.

Thirdly, if like me you are ever unwise enough to write about bloopers, prepare for the certainty of committing some absolute purlers yourself. For all I know, some typesetter with a grudge might well have changed all my carefully checked Middlesbroughs to Middlesboroughs.

And lastly, if all else fails, do what Cloughie once advocated and 'say nowt'. Although even this isn't foolproof. Ron Atkinson (who has his own language called *Ronglish*), tried desperately when managing Aston Villa to adhere to Clough's dictum, but just couldn't bring himself to heed it literally. Commenting to the press on his rumoured interest in Dean Saunders, he still managed to get himself into *Private Eye*'s 'Colemanballs' column: 'I don't want to say anything – not even "no comment".'

27

Every Trick in the Book – Wordplay

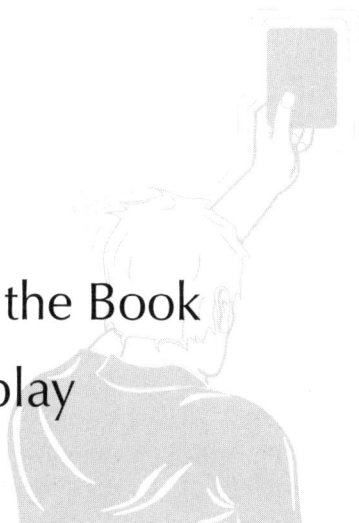

FAT CHEQUES, NOT FAT CZECHS

Derby County fan's banner,
aimed at chairman Robert Maxwell, 1991

Only the mischievous set out deliberately to score verbal own goals, but many attempt the opposite, word trickery. According to a Gallup poll, crosswords and other word puzzles are indulged in by most of the population. *Countdown*, a television show relying on the heady excitement of anagrams for its most heart-stopping moments, is cult viewing for millions. Even children, with sophisticated computer games at their fingertips, delight in verbal silliness. You'll make a friend for life if you ask a seven-year-old to say 'One smart fellow, he felt smart' six times very quickly.

Tony Augarde rationalised this phenomenon in his *Oxford Guide To Word Games*: 'The 26 letters of the alphabet can be combined in 403,290,000,000,000,000,000,000,000 different ways. Surely only the dullest of folk would restrict their usage to what is merely functional.'

Since football fans are not generally the dullest of folk, it's natural they should indulge. Kicking a ball around is fun; so is kicking words around. Do both together and you've got a specialist genre.

The first serious attempt at football punnery was a riddle from 1580 posed by Humphrey Gifford:

What am I that, wanting both handes feete and head,
Of all them that see me being deemed for dead,
Of breath I have great store, and move too and fro,
Now up, and now downe, now hye, and now low?
Alas what hard fortune doth mee befall:
That guiltless am spited of great and of small.
They strike me and push mee, South, West, North and East:
Yet doe I not harme to most, neither least.
When as my breath fayling, I can doe no more,
They then give me over, and never before.

Despite the archaic tone, you'll probably have anticipated
Gifford's answer: 'A footeball made of a bladder'.

Nor was the eighteenth-century version massively more
taxing. 'A football' was again the cunning answer to 'What flies
high, lights low, wears shoes and has none?' Weak, perhaps, but
it confirmed that football and wordplay were legitimate
bedfellows, although even in the nineteenth century real
intimacy remained elusive. Consider this 'joke' from *Punch*:

Q: What's the best football fixture for the fifth of
   November?
A: A match against Guy's.

Junior readers were scarcely better served. In 1910, *Boy's Own
Paper* gave a hint of more surreal times to come by 'challenging'
its readers to 'think up an entire team of players named John',
but the heights had yet to be hit.

Now we've hit them, we're still at pretty low altitude, but
that's the appeal. Even today's 'intelligent readership'
magazines like *When Saturday Comes* and *FourFourTwo*
recognise 'the groan factor' as a key ingredient of wordplay. It's
pointless printing a reader's 'All-Time Fish XI' if it's perfect.
Steve Guppy, Geoff Pike and Peter Haddock are in on merit but
it's the fringe players who add controversy. Mark Fish is iffy.
Does the rogue 's' disqualify Geoff Salmons? Can intimate
acquaintance with the piscatorial world justify the inclusion of
Sammy Salt and Liam 'Chippy' Brady? Should John Scales be

eligible as cover? I've even seen Jimmy Floyd Stickleback on the subs' bench. Patrik Berger, Malcolm Macdonald, Frank Leboeuf and Paulo Wanchope generally make the 'Select Meats XI' on similarly spurious grounds.

So am I really suggesting that intelligent grown men indulge themselves in such banalities? I am, and they do. Most football magazines, fanzines and websites give space to wordplay. Sober-sided accountants wonder if 'anyone can better my "Kitchen Implements XI"'. A female internet correspondent writes: 'As far as I know, the only first-class football club (that disqualifies "Corinthians") mentioned in the Bible is Queen of the South (Luke 11:31), which is actually a reference to the Queen of Sheba. Are there any others?' A Derby fan sees the light: 'I've just discovered why Ravanelli always gives me gut-ache. In Italian his name means "little radishes".' Just when you think it can't get any dafter, it does: 'Someone told me the former Sheffield Wednesday player Imre Varadi had a younger brother called Ollie. Are they having me on?' 'If Newcastle United's goalkeeper opened a French restaurant, would it be "Chez Given"?' The *Guardian*, especially, is a forum for lively debate on just such weighty matters.

The subterranean world of wordplay fulfils the need to dig ever deeper into football's psyche. Why else would anyone have plundered the reference books to compile 'Fantasy Five-a-sides' like the fiery line-up of Moore, Strong, Curry, Makin, Windass or the highly promising Mutch, Moore, Joy, Withe, Trebilcock. The line on decency has to be drawn somewhere, probably at Le Saux, Hassall, Little, Brown, Dick. There's also a 'Six-a-side' version. The best I've come across is Fuller, Beer, Tankard, Makin, Standing, Hardman. That these things need working at is part of the game. This enjoyable nonsense generally starts at school with the word game known as 'Hangman'. Odds on, I wasn't the only smug boy to string up all opposition with 'Bournemouth and Boscombe Athletic', their full name until 1971. The motto is, 'If it's too easy, it's not worth doing'.

Cue the anagram, as old as language itself. Greek examples exist from the third century BC, and the Romans were also adepts. There's an undeniable cleverness in transforming *Quid est veritas?* ('What is truth?') into *Est vir qui adest* ('It is this man here').

But that noble art is under threat. Computer programs now do instantly what was once achieved only by cerebral stealth. The fun's gone out of it. Even so, most anagram generators miss the point that they should make a degree of sense. One website lists at least 5,000 (I stopped counting) of 'Manchester United', which sounds impressive until you scan the results. The first is 'A dec eh en tit ms urn', the thousandth is 'A cede he min strunt'. And so it goes on. Most are complete gibberish.

Not that 'appropriate' versions don't exist. Fans of Manchester United are either 'Entertained Chums' or 'The Mancie Red Nuts' depending on your allegiance. And at least one wouldn't make it past the *Countdown* censor. To United haters, they've always 'Remained the Cunts'.

Less controversially, England's 'World Cup Team' has often proved as lightweight as 'Talcum Powder'. 'Kilmarnock' lack flair because they 'Kick Normal'. Do a fired-up 'Leicester City' on a snowbound pitch play like 'Electric Yetis'?

Sometimes it gets nasty. Southampton fans love it that Portsmouth's 'Fratton Park' backwards is 'Krap Nottarf'. Likewise Evertonians aren't too unhappy that 'Idle fan' and 'Anfield' are inextricably linked. They're passable, but those who connect 'Tiny rich cow' with the boardroom set-up at 'Norwich City' just aren't being fair. Some anagrams are arguably pointless. 'Bristol City' becomes 'Stoic trilby'. So what? Bob Stokoe and his 'pork-pie' hat played no part in their history. Others are simply off the mark. Has 'Port Vale' ever been a 'Love trap'? Admirers of 'Alf Ramsey' certainly weren't a 'False Army'. And Sunderland at their abject worst have always played marginally better than 'Larded Nuns'.

'Football' itself doesn't lend itself well. Unfortunately, the Welsh for *darkroom* isn't '*foto-llab*'. 'Float lob' pleases the purists, and 'Loot flab' suits the boardroom fat-cats, but critics of the players' unseemly habits ultimately score best with 'flob a lot'.

The players are harshly treated. The wonderfully titled book *Guano Stains Grandma* (aka *Astounding Anagrams*) pulls no punches, apparently knowing things that haven't been made public. Teddy Sheringham ('He'd shag dirty men'), Geoff Hurst ('Hog stuffer') and Dennis Bergkamp ('Spank big red men') emerge particularly badly. And only Rodney Marsh knows if he really has 'Horny dreams'.

Others have their characters neatly exposed. Dennis Wise ('Snide swine') and Darren Anderton ('Darn! Rear tendon') are perfect. Graeme Souness personifies 'A gruesomeness'. 'Go get beers' for George Best seems fair enough. Others are merely cruel. Peter Beardsley was hardly a Greek god, but even the *Sunday Sport* wouldn't use the headline 'Player Beds Tree'. Occasionally, hidden forces are obviously at work. The hand of God surely blessed us with 'O dear, I'm a gonad' for Diego Maradona.

If you're serious about anagrams, you may have spurned the computer to advance to *fanagrams*, which incorporate cryptic clues for added difficulty. A team name provides the letters, followed by a clue leading to the answer. 'Manchester United' with the clue 'Cestrian fellow released from bondage' gives 'Chester man untied'. The answer to 'Port Vale – Cold animal doctor' is 'Polar vet'. They're the easy ones. If you manage to solve 'Bolton Wanderers – Robert Maxwell and the captain of the *Titanic*' within the next five minutes, you should be setting the questions.

Either that, or graduating to the hard addictive stuff. At least 2,000 years ago the Greeks were getting high on words or sentences which read the same backwards as forwards. Others since tempted to dabble with *palindromes* seldom fully recover. In *Mother Tongue*, confirmed addict Bill Bryson suggests that the palindrome is the most demanding form of wordplay in the English language. You might well sneer 'He goddam mad dog, eh?', but he's probably right. If you suffer from *aibohphobia* (fear of palindromes) you should skip a few pages while the rest of us go in search of a 'gateman's nametag'.

Probably the best known palindrome is 'A man, a plan, a canal, Panama!', which tells an entire story in just seven words. That's the essence of a good palindrome, and why they're so difficult to construct. Napoleon's impotence in exile was neatly summed up by 'Able was I, ere I saw Elba', but it takes a major rewrite of linguistic history to suggest that the first conversation was palindromic: 'Madam, I'm Adam,' met by the curt response, 'Eve.'

So how does football fare? The *Guardian* recently generated fevered debate on the subject by posing the question 'Are there any palindromic first-class footballers?' It seemed not. The correspondent who claimed that the Canadian League's York Region Shooters had a player called Mike Kim was spot on, but obviously clutching at straws. Although less so than the sad case who pointed out that 'Ugo Ehiogu would have been palindromic if he'd been called Ugo Ihiogu'. For that matter, so would Ruud Van Nistelrooy if he'd been christened Robert Trebor. A miss is as good as a mile. All seemed lost until seventeen-year-old Leon Noel made his youth team debut for Liverpool. Let's hope he makes the grade.

The debate soon widened. Did the rebellious Derek 'Doog' Dougan have a bad influence on young players at Wolves in the sixties? There are certainly those who claim 'Good was I ere I saw Doog'. How did Bobby Charlton explain the influence of his mother Cissie on his career? 'Ma is as selfless as I am'. Someone even emailed to say that 'I love football and drink' in Bulgarian is 'Az obicam mac i boza'.

This rapidly escalated to a quest to discover the longest football palindrome that made sense, a debate that still rages. Best to date is the series of faxes sent by Eric Cantona to the Manchester United doctor during a dispute about his fitness. The club wanted Cantona to lose weight by fasting. He preferred his own special fish diet: 'Doc, note I dissent. A fast never prevents a fatness. I diet on cod'. The club agreed, provided the fish was supplied under laboratory controlled conditions. Cantona acquiesced: 'Doc. Ref. football. Lab to offer cod.' Despite this, ill-feeling prevailed, culminating in a dispute over folk remedies for the treatment of Cantona's skin problems. His parting shot before leaving United was: 'Straw? No, too stupid a fad. I put soot on warts.' So do better!

And your five minutes is now up. The fanagram answer is 'Notable drowners'.

Only marginally less taxing are posers relying on powers of recall. Remembering all 92 English League clubs sounds straightforward, but most people really begin struggling after about eighty.

Nor is it entirely straightforward naming the five League and Conference clubs with an 'x' in their names. As I write, these are Oxford United, Wrexham, Crewe Alexandra, Halifax Town and Exeter City. Odds are, you struggled with at least one.

These conundrums rely on the brain's susceptibility to blind spots. For example, 'Which is the only club in the English and Scottish Leagues not to have a single letter from the word "football" in its name?' It's astonishing how many people blunder in with Bury or Celtic. Full marks if you recognised *Dundee* as a unique footie word.

Read the following sentence once only and very quickly, then say the number of times the letter 'f' appears: 'Football fixtures are the result of years of scientific study combined with the experience of years.' According to psychologists, you should be a high-ranking member of Mensa if you correctly said six. Most people say four or five at most, but many opt for three. Average brains translate the 'ofs' into 'ovs'.

Other testers rely on the ear to be deceived by words that sound the same but mean different things. 'Which member of the royal family played football for England?' was a playground favourite for years. Joe Royle, naturally. Similarly, 'Sunderland did it in 1979. Villa did it in 1981. Who did it in 1980?' The answer is Brooking. Alan Sunderland, Ricardo Villa and Trevor Brooking scored the winning goal in those FA Cup Finals.

A number of players have suffered at the hands of fans, usually in lewd fashion, because of the same effect. Commentators have taken the opposite stance, fudging the issue by contrived pronunciation wherever possible. When Chelsea played Frem Copenhagen in 1958, exposure wasn't widespread enough for the Copenhagen keeper, Bent Koch, to attract too much notice, but by the time Stefan Kuntz turned out for Germany in Euro '96 it was open season. Since then, Fukal, Nikersov, Chiqui Arce and Totti have all had their moments on British television. Note that our propensity for 'Carry On' humour of the toilet variety is well to the fore. Celtic were so aware of this that they changed a player's name to avoid the *double entendre*. In 1999 their fans honoured their new Brazilian signing by sporting 'Rafael' on their shirts rather than 'Scheidt'. Sometimes it works the other way. When John Toshack took charge of Besiktas in Istanbul he was never quite sure how to take the fans' chants. In Turkish his name means 'testicles'. Nor is it wise to be too quick-witted on the wordplay front. In 1991, Bristol Rovers sacked their tannoy announcer Keith Valle when he announced the arrival of Bristol City's substitute: 'Here comes Junior Bent. I bet he is.'

It's a small step from the dual meaning to the *holorime*, a poem of two related lines in which each line is pronounced the same, but uses different words. The French are adept at these, but English examples are rare. The only serious attempt I know of is a vintage 1988 effort by the humorist Miles Kington entitled 'A Lowlands Holiday Ends in Enjoyable Inactivity', but even that resorted to French for its climax:

> In Ayrshire hill areas, a cruise, eh, lass?
> Inertia, hilarious, accrues, hélas.

In fairness, it's a difficult art, and the definitive football holorime has yet to be written. There's certainly potential in 'United' and 'you knighted', or 'six-one' and 'sick swan', but I've got deadlines to meet. Untold fame awaits the composer of one longer than my own pathetic quickie, 'Diary Record of an Allergic Reaction to a Sickening Defeat':

> Redditch One, City Nil (Dyer, o.g.)
> Red itch, wan, sit in ill, dire, oh gee!

Lest the internet should soon be awash with them, I'll take the blame. The same happened with the haiku (a seventeen-syllable Japanese poem) a number of years ago. There's now a website dedicated entirely to football examples.

Similar to, but more visual than the holorime, is the *rebus*, a riddle where words and symbols are arranged to give a cryptic meaning. For years they were a lost art, but made a comeback as *Dingbats*. GO AL is 'open goal', GO   AL is 'wide open goal'. FwLiErXe is 'Leeds United'. ME is 'half-time'. LEEH is 'back-heel'. 4amDOOR6amDOOR is 'early doors'. One of the more satisfying elements of such puzzles is that they're apt to stump even the cleverest wordsmiths if they know nothing about football. A quiz wizard of my acquaintance once agonised for days over 'What's the missing letter in the following sequence? – P W D _ F A.' Every mathematical trick possible had left him joyless. His face was an absolute picture when I explained, in barely a second, why it was L.

Although most wordplay is for fun, it's played a part in the more permanent lexicon of football itself. Enduring player nicknames are often the result of subtle, if usually rude, word trickery, which might well leave future football historians baffled. How could Manchester United's Remi Moses possibly have acquired the name 'Dogshit'? Because he 'got everywhere'. Even the earliest known player nickname, that of the 1880s England forward W N 'Nuts' Cobbold, relied on a pun for its effect, although the explanation given by C B Fry is almost certainly a fudge: 'I believe his friends gave him the name because he was of the very best Kentish cob quality, all kernel and extremely hard to crack.' So it wasn't because his surname resembled 'cobblers', which, like 'nuts', was Victorian slang for 'balls'? If he was playing today he'd be known as 'Bollocks'. Or maybe he just liked nuts. Arsenal's 'Chippy' Brady got his name because he loved chips, not because of his ability to loft the ball delicately into the net over an advancing goalkeeper.

Blessedly there have been more cerebral punsters than the players. One of the most widely known words in the world is a football one born from wordplay. When Peter Adolph from Tunbridge Wells registered the name of his table football invention in 1948 he tried to call it 'The Hobby', but was refused permission because it was too all-embracing. Being a keen ornithologist, Adolph decided on a neat subterfuge by calling the game after the Latin name for the hobby falcon, which is *Falco subbuteo*. He launched *Subbuteo* in 1949, and over half a century later it competes with *Coca-Cola*, *Adidas* and other heavyweights for the title of most-recognised brand name worldwide. The game also gave other words and phrases to the English language. 'Just flick to kick', its sales slogan, is still used to suggest that something difficult can be achieved effortlessly, and it's likely that 'moving the goalposts' also evolved from Subbuteo, where the 'accidentally on purpose' subterfuge has been widely employed since the game began.

Another term entering English via football prompted a devious poser: 'Which word was invented solely as a result of the 1908 Cup Final at the Crystal Palace?' You could guess for ever without getting the answer. Having seen his team lose 3–1 to Wolves, Newcastle United fan Gladstone Adams travelled home in a motorised charabanc through an unseasonal snow storm which continually hampered the driver's view. But for Adams's subsequent invention, it might have been many years before *windscreen wipers* made it into the dictionary .

While Adams was obviously a bright spark, lesser lights have unwittingly entered the wordplay frame by careless use of English. Constructing phrases which can have two meanings is officially *amphibology*, although they've recently been coined *literalisms* by the broadcaster Denis Norden, the kind of man who fully expects to see a queue of bald Chinamen outside any establishment advertising an 'Oriental Rug Sale'. If he murdered someone, he'd scan Yellow Pages for a 'Same Day Framing Service'. Doubtless he'd admire the sign which once graced the snack bar at Stoke's old Victoria Ground: 'Try Our Home-Made Pies. You'll Never Get Better'. Equally ambiguous was the turnstile sign at Leeds United which read 'Blind Disabled Press'. *Inattention to syntax* is the grammatical name for such lapses.

Newspapers sometimes perpetrate these deliberately to boost sales: 'FOOTBALL VIOLENCE. JUDGE HITS OUT' from the *Nottingham Post* might have been accidental, but 'ROBBO PUT OUT TO PASTURE' from the *Middlesbrough Evening Gazette* at a time when Bryan Robson managed Boro certainly wasn't. The story was a retirement tribute to 'Robbo', the nineteen-year-old police horse. When Derby County signed Giorgi Kinkladze, local placards announced: 'RAMS NEW

SIGNING. FULL KINKY STORY' and a corruption scandal at Swindon Town in 1990 enabled *Today* to run the delicious headline, 'I'LL SPILL BEANS ON SWINDON'. One from the Scottish *Sun* grabbed the wordplay of the season award in 2000 after Inverness Caledonian Thistle beat mighty Celtic away in the Cup: 'SUPER CALEY GO BALLISTIC, CELTIC ARE ATROCIOUS'. Another real eye-catcher, concerning Crystal Palace's Gerry Queen, appeared as a *Guardian* headline in 1970: 'QUEEN IN BRAWL AT PALACE'. And even the fans play this game. When Fulham supporters chanted 'Dicks out! Dicks out!' in 1991 prudes may have blanched, but there was no cause for alarm. Fulham's struggling manager was Alan Dicks.

Considering such ingenuity, it's surprising that at least one well-established wordplay genre appears to have passed football by. According to Rex Collings in *A Crash of Rhinoceroses*, there is no collective noun for a group of footballers. Yet pornographers (a *smut*), dermatologists (a *rash*), astronauts (a *galaxy*), accountants (a *column*) and countless others are collectively honoured. Collings himself coined 'a collapse of cricketers' after England's antics in Australia in 1990, but footballers, except when they're a *team*, *squad* or *eleven*, are merely footballers. The fifteenth-century term for a group of jugglers was a *never-thriving*. Might today's wealthier ball-jugglers be a *thriving*? Or what about an *adoration* or a *gobbet*? As for football managers, look no further than a *rant*.

Other newer disciplines have also yet to make a football impact. *Mondegreens*, misheard lines in popular songs, are currently flavour of the month, devotees willingly admitting 'the ants are my friends' from Bob Dylan's 'Blowin' in the Wind', and 'the girl with colitis goes by' from 'Lucy in the Sky with Diamonds'. 'I believe in milko' and 'me ears are alight' have also been well aired, but I've yet to meet anyone who thought England's 1970 World Cup song about an international hairdressing competition: 'Back-comb, they'll be washing and waiting . . .' Although I once heard a corporate guest sing a full-throated 'Three lions on a shirt, *jewels remain* still gleaming', instead of 'Jules Rimet still gleaming'.

Obviously he'd never heard of the FIFA president who gave his name to the original World Cup.

It's clear that football and wordplay have a future. If nothing else, the new languages of text messaging and the internet will see to that. For the textually active there just isn't time to explain in 'old English' how 'Giggs crossed for Van Nistelrooy to open the scoring with a header and Keane got dismissed by a poor referee'. 'RG X 4 VNR HDR 1-0. RK S/0. POLL WNKR' now does the job.

As for the internet, it's a massively useful tool, but scant editorial control leaves the English language wide open to wild abuse. A recent trawl revealed several startling 'facts': 'Marco Polo introduced football to Europe when he saw it in the Orient and brought it back to Italy'; 'Roy Keane is a better player than his *brother* Robbie'; 'Exeter City are "The Grecians" because one of their first captains was a Greek'. If you despair of the thousands of inaccuracies being perpetrated daily via the latest wordplay technology, there's always light relief to be had from playing the brand new game of 'Word Association Football'. The rules are easy. Select a search engine and type in an unlikely football phrase. Wait for the hits. Choose another phrase. The lowest number of hits above zero wins. In a recent visit to the Google Stadium I managed the following results: 'Making a football blancmange' 248 'Looking inside Graham Taylor's ears' 7; 'Eating rancid goat's cheese at Turf Moor' 8 'Smelling Stanley Matthews' socks' 9. Tightest game of all was 'Collecting Delft pottery with Sol Campbell' 2 'Nailing beefburgers to pictures of Alan Gilzean' 1.

Who says technology will kill wordplay? *Punch* and *Boy's Own Paper* it's not. But that's progress.

28

Any Moment Now
– The Final Whistle

'Even if George Orwell's Big Brother is ruling us in the future, people will still be talking about football.'

Neil Franklin, Stoke City and England, 1956

There comes a time in every game, whether you're playing or watching, when you know that what's done is done. That 'any moment now' instant when the referee has the whistle in his mouth, glances fleetingly at his watch, checks his mincing run to a ludicrously abrupt halt, and brings one more game to a close. Books are no different. Time for post-match analysis.

Had I taken notice of a kindly friend during the research stages, there wouldn't have been anything to analyse. 'How can you possibly write a whole book on the language of football?' wasn't the best pep-talk I've ever had, but that it came from an 'only a game' advocate was enough to push me on.

What soon came through strongly was that football's written and verbal communication systems are inseparable from its physicality, part of the essence of football itself. In the event, so much material presented itself that some worthy candidates failed to make the squad. I only briefly touched on the language of the press, managers and referees. Football film, drama, poetry, art and prose, not at all; likewise songs and chants (as I began writing this chapter, West Bromwich Albion's 'Boing Boing Baggies' had just become Football Song of the Year 2003). The wit and wisdom of banners

('Joey Ate the Frogs' Legs, Made the Swiss Roll, Now He's Munching Gladbach') also remained under wraps. So too the language of numbers. Will the once ubiquitous 'Come in number six, your time is up' ever make a comeback? Who was the first to say '2-4-6-8 who do we appreciate'? And how will dull old number '23' cope with the superstar status thrust upon it by Real Madrid in the Beckham-crazed summer of 2003? Will 'lucky 7' survive the crisis? Such crucial questions remain unanswered.

Having gone the distance I'm left not so much with new impressions, as with a much firmer conviction of existing ones. It became apparent that football is still a dirty word for substantial sectors of society. The billions who actually like the game remain part of a closed society, sniffily disregarded by those who 'know better'. To pilapediphobes, 'football talk' is still the uncouth dialect of the common masses.

Such attitudes have afflicted so many men of learning throughout centuries of football's history, that an incomplete picture of its past has emerged. That in turn distorts our view of its modern form, which remains far too one-dimensional. Generations of historians, archaeologists, lexicographers, professors of linguistics, and students of art, literature and poetry, have all doggedly pursued their pet subjects, but at an elevated level, one at which the wearing of breathing apparatus for the exclusion of the dreaded football virus is obligatory. Hence missed opportunities and a real paradox of the game. Billions of words have been written and spoken about it by its workaday devotees, yet so much remains undiscovered. Amid all the froth, the precise nature of football's ancient origins remains a mystery. Even the Victorian era, so assiduously chronicled by scribes not too long dead, isn't often given a second glance by today's enthusiasts. But what tales that age has to tell.

Not that progress isn't being made. New breeds of pro-football writers and academics, who see much deeper than the Premiership veneer, have begun to probe beneath the game's surface. 'History revisited' is a fast-expanding genre in football publishing. So too the 'supporter unburdened'. Nick Hornby's

Fever Pitch, the most perceptive 'rationale of fandom' yet written, made even those who thought they knew football inside out think afresh about why it really matters.

Yet still the definitive answer remains elusive. In a world full of horrors, there are many things that 'really' matter. So why can something as 'trivial' as football move us in the way it does? Isn't it shameful that it moves us at all? The French legend Michel Platini once cited that very elusiveness as part of football's charm: 'It is loved because it has no definitive truth.' He's right. Something that can't quite be grasped is always attractive, at least to those with enquiring minds.

As for the shameful pursuit of 'triviality', even in 1950 that was being nicely addressed by Dr Percy Young in *The Art of Spectatorship*:

> Football, whether for performers or spectators, renews childhood. Instinctively we return to what we were. We become serious about trivialities. It is a great thing to be able to take seriously what is unimportant. When we can do this, we can begin to take seriously what is important.

Young was a footie philosopher before it became fashionable. Too few people have read his books. Another Percyism was that 'to feel poetically about football is one way to a proper appreciation of life, for we see in it the beauty of what is familiar'. Again he's tantalisingly close. That familiarity is born of age-old exposure. What really ties the British to football is that it's so deeply ingrained in our past.

Time and again that 'antiquity' really struck me. The game is much more ancient than we are commonly led to believe. Consider this from a continental professor: 'The first time I came to England, I said to myself: "Without a doubt, football was created here!"' Arsène Wenger may well be more right than he intended.

The 'gulf' between old and modern is also narrower than we perceive. Too much in football today is presented starkly as black and white, or past and present, so that even the word itself has become pigeonholed. To many, 'football' simply means the Premiership, the Champions League, the European Championships, the World Cup, and the ritual torture of 'penalties'. Yet they're the tiniest apex, historically and physically, of a huge pyramid.

Arguably, they're the oddities. What lies below the gilded capstone is the real football, still close to its roots. In my last year at Gayton Avenue Junior School in 1966–67, I played every lunchtime in a contest dubbed 'The Big Match', a 20 or so a side game played entirely without offside, corner kicks, throw-ins, goal kicks, fouls and officials. There were no pitch markings, the ball was a tennis ball, and (although I hate to say it), we did use jumpers for goalposts. Grazed knees and other accidents were frequent. Occasionally a group of squealing gingham-frocked females strayed inadvertently into the action. A Staffordshire terrier once made off with the ball. Yet amid all this apparent chaos, there was a strict sense of order. The cumulative score, religiously recorded daily in an exercise book by one Les Kirkland, finished something like 1,342–1,296. Which game was that? Association or medieval? Such primeval contests are still played daily.

There's the perversity of being a 'lover of football'. It has different meanings to different men. More than once in this book, I've trapped myself into referring to the '*true* football *lover*'. But both words are meaningless. The man following his side home and away every game probably sees himself as 'a true fan', yet might appreciate nothing of the game's cultural history. Likewise the hooligan who 'protects the honour of the club' through routine violence, yet tarnishes the game's image so badly in the process.

And not everyone is turned on by 'big football'. Many fans cherish the non-league game, where it's still possible to transcend time by standing close enough to the action to hear the tackles and smell the liniment. The sausages for the hot-dogs were delivered that morning by the local butcher. The right-back is your postman. The chairman says 'Hello' if he passes you in the street. Countless devotees at that level genuinely despise the Premiership ethos. And many Premiership fans scoff at the anoraks of the lower reaches.

Somewhere in between there are those balanced souls who appreciate both ends of the spectrum, recognising the strengths and weaknesses in each. That probably comes close to the 'true football lover' I had in mind, but it's a difficult label to pin down. Probably the best test is that 'real fans' seldom profess to 'love football'. The way they behave says it for them, demonstrating a deep 'feeling' towards the game rather than a fanciful 'love' of it.

Do you turn to the back page of a newspaper first? Have you ever taken a diversion to drive past an empty ground? Looked back from a train window to see the outcome of a corner in some anonymous trackside contest? Do you recognise old players in the supermarket, and do you tell someone later? Have you ever strained that extra inch just for the merest touch of a ball flying into the crowd? Hugged someone of your own sex? Would you deliberately slow down walking past a kids' game in the street, hoping for a wayward pass to come your way? Ever mended a burst ball with a bicycle repair kit or a hot iron, watched a training session, got to a game early to see the teams arrive, or paid £2.50 for a paper abroad just to get the results? And has football featured in your dreams? Or moved you to tears? If you can say 'yes' to at least a couple of those, there's a chance you're the sort of football lover I'm talking about.

Not for a moment do I expect *Football Talk* to revolutionise your view of the game. But you might recall I embarked on it in the spirit of the artist Arturo Rand, he of the upside-down canvases. So if you've been able to see football from a different perspective, my aim is complete.

As for my own perception of the game, I can't possibly articulate that in a few words. I have likes and dislikes. Football regularly enraptures me, but elements of it increasingly infuriate me. I suppose the answer lies embedded in the book. That makes me little different from anyone else. Few men have been able to pin down why on balance they're passionately pro-football rather than anti, although many down the years have tried.

In 1581 the Elizabethan educationist Richard Mulcaster, the first man to recommend a 'trayning maister', was moved by the game's healthful properties, claiming among other things that it was 'good for the bowells'.

Others have been more lyrical. Pelé famously labelled football 'the beautiful game', and other pithy epithets have attempted to sum up its appeal concisely: 'the rude and manly game', 'the people's game', 'the only game', 'the absolute game', 'the ultimate game', 'the world game', 'the global game' and simply 'the best game in the world'. None of them really says enough.

In 1999, 418 years after Mulcaster, Alex Ferguson adopted the 'less is more' approach to football appreciation. Interviewed moments after Manchester United's last-gasp victory over Bayern Munich in the European Cup Final, his reply was succinct: 'Football. Bloody hell.' Time divides them. Football unites them. They speak a common tongue.

Men of the future will continue to do likewise. Both the game and its language will evolve, but must surely survive. The words of those who have said for centuries that 'football has no future' continue to ring hollow. Take Robert Maxwell in 1990, who stated: 'Football in Britain could not be in a sorrier state. Sport is dying. The future lies in culture, spirituality and religion.' But doesn't religion lie at the heart of most world conflict? And unless I'm seriously mistaken, sport is still very much alive but Captain Bob isn't. One is fundamental to the lives of billions; the other just as dispensable, a mere drop in the ocean. Only the truly cataclysmic will stop football dead in its tracks.

As it moves forward, future historians and linguists will look back at its 'ancient past' that is our present, and muse sagely at the words of today's deep-thinking philosophers, so full of wit and profound perception. Men like Peter Reid, who'll be lauded as the Confucius of his age: 'In football we all know that you stand still if you go backwards.'

Football won't stand still. In truth the game as we know it is barely out of infancy. As the 2004 European Championships play to a global audience, association football will be just 141 years old, the Football League a mere 116, the World Cup 74. And the new kid on the block which is the Premiership, founded in 1992, has yet to embark on its adolescence.

So the same whistle that now signals full time for *Football Talk*, merely sets the ball rolling on the game's continuing progress. Far from being all over, it's only just kicking off.